Going on a Meditation Retreat

This book provides a straightforward, accessible guide to going on a silent meditation retreat.

Written by experienced retreat facilitators, this book presents a mix of Buddhist wisdom, insights from modern psychology and mindfulness research and personal accounts from meditators who have attended retreats with them in the last 30 years. The chapters provide advice on preparing for the retreat, such as booking and what to pack, and offer practical day-to-day guidance about how to sit whilst being kind to knee, back or other physical issues. There is detailed information about how to work compassionately with the difficult thoughts or emotions and other challenges participants typically encounter on this kind of more intensive meditation programme, as well as how to cultivate joy, gratitude, compassion and balance. The focus is on in-person retreats, but this book also offers some guidance for teaching and participating in online home retreats, a new development which has emerged from the COVID-19 pandemic and lockdowns.

This book is an invaluable resource for anyone considering going on a silent meditation retreat to step out of the often frantic and overwhelming round of day-to-day activity and find space for reflection. It will also be of use to mindfulness teachers or trainees who are required to go on retreat for qualification purposes and to current or trainee retreat facilitators.

Frits Koster lived as a Buddhist monk in Asia for six years. He is a qualified MBSR, MBCL and IMP teacher and teaches mindfulness and compassion internationally. He is the co-author of various books (Silkworm Books and Routledge).

Jetty Heynekamp is a qualified physiotherapist who has been practising insight meditation since 1982. She is a certified mindfulness teacher and leads meditation retreats and communication workshops.

Victoria Norton is a certified mindfulness teacher whose professional background is in teaching and communications management.

Going on a Meditation Retreat

Embracing Silence to Cultivate Mindfulness and Compassion

Frits Koster, Jetty Heynekamp and Victoria Norton

LONDON AND NEW YORK

Designed cover image: Getty Images

First published in English 2025
by Routledge
4 Park Square, Milton Park, Abingdon, Oxon, OX14 4RN

and by Routledge
605 Third Avenue, New York, NY 10158

Routledge is an imprint of the Taylor & Francis Group, an informa business

© 2025 Frits Koster, Jetty Heynekamp and Victoria Norton

The right of Frits Koster, Jetty Heynekamp and Victoria Norton to be identified as authors of this work has been asserted in accordance with sections 77 and 78 of the Copyright, Designs and Patents Act 1988.

All rights reserved. No part of this book may be reprinted or reproduced or utilised in any form or by any electronic, mechanical, or other means, now known or hereafter invented, including photocopying and recording, or in any information storage or retrieval system, without permission in writing from the publishers.

Trademark notice: Product or corporate names may be trademarks or registered trademarks, and are used only for identification and explanation without intent to infringe.

Published in Dutch as 'Op retraite' by Asoka 2021

British Library Cataloguing-in-Publication Data
A catalogue record for this book is available from the British Library

Library of Congress Cataloging-in-Publication Data
Names: Koster, Frits, author. | Heynekamp, Jetty, 1957– author. | Norton, Victoria, 1960– author.
Title: Going on a meditation retreat: embracing silence to cultivate mindfulness and compassion / Frits Koster, Jetty Heynekamp and Victoria Norton.
Description: Abingdon, Oxon; New York, NY: Routledge, 2025. | Includes bibliographical references and index. |
Identifiers: LCCN 2024048935 (print) | LCCN 2024048936 (ebook) | ISBN 9781032856230 (hardback) | ISBN 9781032856209 (paperback) | ISBN 9781003519072 (ebook)
Subjects: LCSH: Mediation—Buddhism. | Spiritual retreats—Buddhism.
Classification: LCC BQ5620 .K677 2025 (print) | LCC BQ5620 (ebook) | DDC 294.3/4435—dc23/eng/20250110
LC record available at https://lccn.loc.gov/2024048935
LC ebook record available at https://lccn.loc.gov/2024048936

ISBN: 978-1-032-85623-0 (hbk)
ISBN: 978-1-032-85620-9 (pbk)
ISBN: 978-1-003-51907-2 (ebk)

DOI: 10.4324/9781003519072

Typeset in Times New Roman
by codeMantra

Access the Support Material: www.routledge.com/9781032856209

Contents

Foreword   *xiii*
MARIE MANNSCHATZ
Foreword   *xv*
JIUN HOGEN ROSHI
Acknowledgements   *xvi*

How this book came about   xviii
Frits' story xviii
Jetty's story xix
Victoria's story xix
Dilemmas in writing xx
A word of caution xx
The intention of this book xxi

Introduction – Why go on retreat   1
Seeking rest in a busy life 1
Being with grief 1
Entanglement in unhelpful patterns 2
In search of existential insight 3
Going on retreat as an escape 3
Looking for inner space and freedom 3
Kindness and mindfulness 4
Preparations 4

1 Going into silence: Day 1 – Basic advice for kindness and mindfulness   6
Being allowed to be 'unsociable' 7
The basic structure – The meditation programme 9
Kindness to yourself – The body 10
Courtesy to others 10

*The theme of this retreat – Ten beautifying virtues
  or 'perfections' 11
A leap of faith 12
Kindness 13
Pitfalls in kindness meditation 15
Kindness in the retreat 15
Kindness in the practice of mindfulness 16
Walking meditation 19
Bowing meditation as a complementary practice 21
Awareness of daily activities 23
Kindness meditation – Yourself and loved ones 25*

2 **Wisely and compassionately relating to reactivity:
  Day 2 – Inquiry meetings with the teacher and patience**   27
  *Learning to be at ease with unease 27
  Mindful movement and posture advice 28
  Lying down 30
  The breath as a basis 30
  Struggling with the breath 31
  Mindfulness is being on good terms with everything 32
  Benefits of walking meditation 32
  The value of regular inquiry meetings with a teacher 33
  Discovering pitfalls and blind spots in the practice 34
  Checking motivation and commitment 35
  Supporting meditative insight 35
  Supporting processes of healing 35
  The understanding of common humanity 36
  Meditatively relating to physical discomfort 36
  The content of an inquiry meeting 36
  Check your attitude 37
  Reporting on one's own experiences 37
  Reporting about the sitting meditation 38
  Reporting on walking meditation and daily activities 38
  Specific life themes and suggestions for further practice 39
  Befriending discomfort 39
  Mindful inquiry with the teacher on Day 2 39
  Evening introduction – Reactivity and patience 40
  Story – The dung heap 40
  Vertical and horizontal practice 42
  Washing long-worn socks 43*

Fatigue 44
Meditative journaling 44
Revealing is healing 46
*Kindness meditation – Yourself, a benefactor
   and loved ones 46*

**3 Being aware in a relaxed way: Day 3 – Mindfulness
   and generosity**   48
Mindfulness of physical sensations 48
Focused and receptive mindfulness 49
Yin and yang compassion in sitting with discomfort 50
Be careful of 'No pain, no gain' 51
*Walking meditation – A relaxed attitude and standing
   meditation 51*
Inquiry meetings – Searching for an inner balance 52
Different views in Dhamma-land 54
Caring for the body 56
Evening talk – Relating to thoughts and generosity 56
Three characteristics of thoughts 57
Thoughts and relationality 58
*Viewing thoughts as small flows of energy
   and information 60*
The power of generosity 60
Generosity in every moment of awareness 62
Meditating with a hidden agenda 63
Kindness meditation – Self and loved ones 65

**4 Becoming at ease with impermanence: Day 4 – Inner patterns
   and wisdom**   66
Noticing the inner weather report 67
Wisdom and the law of mortality 67
Unwinding with choiceless awareness 69
Walking meditation – More advanced instructions 69
Inquiry meetings – Inner patterns 70
Playing Bingo 70
Inner patterns 71
Playfulness in relating to an inner pattern 72
Evening talk – The RAIN model and uncontrollability 73
Aspects of wisdom 74
The wisdom of the information technology specialist 75

Disappointment as a friend 76
Wisdom in uncontrollability 77
Working with dilemmas 78
Kindness meditation – Micro-moments of positivity resonance 79

5 The art of living: Relaxed commitment: Day 5 – Mindfulness in daily activities and compassionate breathing (*tonglen*)   81

Commitment as a virtue 82
Finding the right level of effort 82
A low level of energy 83
Struggling with sleepiness 83
Working with sleepiness wisely and compassionately 84
Relaxed commitment 85
Walking meditation – New instructions and curiosity 86
Awe of the senses 87
Mindfulness on the toilet 88
Inquiry meetings – Tonglen 90
Resilience 92
Evening talk – Who am I? 93
Who owns the clouds? 93
The five constituents of human existence 94
Kindness meditation – A difficult person 96

6 The power of simplification: Day 6 – Moments of intention and cultivating integrity and gratitude   99

Simplification in the practice 99
Different forms of concentration 100
Three systems of motivation 101
Nurturing the soothing system with mindfulness 102
A programme without a programme 103
Five spiritual faculties 103
Walking meditation – Catching the intention 107
From impulsive to meditative 108
Evening talk – Pleasant experiences and integrity 109
Pleasurable experiences 110
Under the spell of the pleasurable 110
Being honest and truthful in the practice 111

Nothing special 112
Am I still allowed to enjoy myself? 113
Kindness meditation – Gratitude 113

7 **Recognising the feeling tone: Day 7 – Steadiness and equanimity in the practice**   115
Going to the end of the retreat with determination 115
Three feeling tones and their conditioning effects 116
The tracks of a tiger 117
The rollercoaster of our moods 118
Strengthening spiritual abilities 118
Walking meditation – May you walk in beauty 119
Inquiry meetings – Looking back and to the future 119
Evening talk – Four expressions of kindness 119
The fertile soil of kindness 120
Eleven benefits of kindness 121
Explanation 121
The rainbow of compassion 122
Scientific research on (self-)compassion 122
The difference between acceptance and acknowledgement 122
The fresh water of sympathetic joy 123
The cool shadow of equanimity 123
The four friends of life in cohesion 124
Equanimity in joy and sorrow 124
Equanimity in mindfulness 125
Kindness meditation – The last evening 127

8 **Fruits of the practice: Day 8 – Ethics and returning to daily life**   130
Fruits of the practice 130
The neuroscientific perspective 130
The Buddhist perspective 132
Inner freedom 132
Different stages of existential understanding 133
Enlightenment with a big E 133
Enlightenment with a small e 134
Olympic meditators 136
Back to daily life 137
Practising ethics in relation to others 138
The courage of forgiveness 139

Practice at home 140
Dilemmas and problems 141
Don't try persuading people to practise meditation 142
Interpersonal mindfulness 143
Kindness meditation – All beings 143

9 A few last words of advice: Choosing a suitable retreat   145
How do you find a suitable retreat? 145
Silent or not? 145
A checklist for choosing a retreat 146
The venue 147
Sharing rooms 147
Things to consider when sharing a room 148
What NOT to take on retreat 148
Day long and shorter retreats 148
Work period 149
Paying for the retreat 150
Receipts and confirmation 150
Food allergies and intolerances 150
Meditation-related adverse effects 151
Safeguarding 151
Sleep 152
What to take on retreat 152

10 Taking part in an online retreat: Dos and don'ts   154
Some practical suggestions 154
A daily schedule for an online retreat 155

Bibliography   *156*
Audio and video downloads   *160*
Index   *161*

Foreword
Marie Mannschatz

Dear reader, take a moment to exhale completely. Your breath is the gift of life, that you will investigate deeply, if you decide to reward yourself with a silent meditation retreat!

Nowadays there seems to be hardly any space for solitary inner exploration. We present our lives in one-minute stories on Instagram. We rush through the days until we feel overwhelmed and hurry on vacation, where we choose adventure or sensual wellness or social entertainment. But why go on retreat?

Well, in the course of human existence, there have always been a few who felt the mysterious urge to withdraw from the hustle and bustle of daily life and seek peace in deep silence. I have no clue how my life would have evolved without my early encounter with meditation practice. Even as a child I felt drawn to spend each day regular times in silence. I learnt the first steps of meditation from books and discovered immediately that I needed a teacher. But the question was, where to go, which teacher, which meditation technique to choose?

This book provides answers! It is an easily readable compendium that takes us through the course of a silent meditation retreat day by day. It addresses all you need to know in order to slow down and create a good retreat experience for yourself. At the beginning of silent meditation days, we meet a bunch of unfamiliar and even unpleasant experiences. How can we find a patient and mindful attitude that allows us to accept the tiredness and fatigue that wells up in the first retreat days? How can we talk to the teacher about the resistance we feel, the "fleeing-the-mat-syndrome" and our personal struggles with posture and thoughts? Each retreat is packed with unforeseeable ups and downs. One day we assume to gain enlightenment very soon, an hour later it seems absolutely ridiculous to spend even another day in silence. A teacher knows how to steer the course and helps to encourage stamina. We gradually realise that we are not alone with our constant dilemmas and conflicts – on the contrary, we begin to understand how much of our inner pain and suffering we share with all human beings. We give up fighting against and learn to develop a kind accepting attitude with everything we encounter in our retreat practice. To me it seems on retreat we finally take the time to clean out the often neglected cellar in ourselves. Sometimes it smells bad, we have to sort out lots of rubbish and in the end we feel relieved and liberated. We depart with much less luggage and refreshed hearts.

Whether you want to train as a mindfulness teacher or you are a keen beginner, looking for growth adventures in the inner world, this guide addresses how to prepare or begin yourself and understand the dos and don'ts of silent retreats. The authors share their own experiences as facilitators as well as meditators. They introduce you to a variety of meditation techniques in every possible posture. Eating meditation and various guided meditations are included, and you continually discover ways to relax and be kind with yourself. They teach you to listen to your heart and guard your sense-doors. The voices of their own retreat participants enhance this valuable advice, embedded in a subtle sense of humour.

Each retreat is different, but we can always be sure that a deep sense of appreciation and wonder will grow naturally during these times of silent investigation. Liberating insights will reward us for our effortless efforts. We learn to change perspectives, which helps to understand ourselves and our fellow human beings in astounding new ways. After all, we can relax, be who we are and savour our precious human existence with a smile in our heart.

Marie Mannschatz, born in 1950, has been working as a psychotherapist in private practice for more than 20 years. At the beginning of the nineties, she was trained by Jack Kornfield as a meditation and retreat teacher. She lives in Germany and has published Vollkommen unvollkommen (O.W. Barth Verlag, 2019) and several other books in the German language. See www.mariemannschatz.de.

Foreword
Jiun Hogen Roshi

Over 20 years ago, Frits first guided a *vipassanā* retreat in our Zen Centre. Since then, Frits and Jetty have led several long retreats every year and have become like family to us.

We have grown closer and we have inspired each other in the Buddhist practices. For example, we 'zennies' have seen how important the walking meditation is in the mindfulness retreats. Whereas in our Zen practice we initially only did shorter walking meditations (Japanese: kinhin) in the group, we saw with Frits and Jetty how the long individual walking meditation is a very valuable and enriching part of a retreat. This stimulated us to build one mile of paths in our large landscape garden for the walking meditation outside. Not only the participants of Frits and Jetty's retreats but also 'our' participants make grateful use of this now.

On the other hand – as is described in this book – the meditation in activity, as we know it in the Zen tradition, has led Frits and Jetty to include something we value in their own retreat programme. Every morning after breakfast there is working meditation, which in Zen retreats is called *nitten soji*, or daily cleaning, practising mindfulness in washing the dishes or vacuum cleaning.

Going on a Meditation Retreat is unique because it describes in such detail what is done and not done in a retreat, what you can encounter and experience. At the same time, the teachings of the Buddha are presented throughout the book in a very unique way – complemented by the experiences of Frits and Jetty themselves and those of participants, the teachings are explained with concepts and expressions of our time, clear, challenging and with a smile. In short, a *Dharma-mani*: a jewel of the Dharma.

It becomes clear that going on a mindfulness and compassion retreat is much more than only retreating and unwinding.

The richness of this book is due to Frits and Jetty's own many years of practice and the constant loving effort with which they have guided retreats for many years. I would read this book before a retreat, perhaps during a retreat if allowed by the facilitators and after a retreat. With a deep bow of respect and gratitude.

Jiun Hogen Roshi is Zen master of Zen Centre de Noorder Poort in Wapserveen, the Netherlands. She is also the spiritual director of the International Zen Institute. See www.zeninstitute.org.

Acknowledgements

Gratitude is not only the greatest of virtues, but the parent of all others.[1]
– Marcus Tullius Cicero, Roman statesman, philosopher
and writer (106–43 BC)

Research shows that gratitude is very important for well-being[2]. In Buddhist psychology gratitude and appreciation are mentioned as important expressions of *muditā* or sympathetic joy. We realise that as meditators and authors, we are only small links in a practice that is centuries old. First of all, we wish to express our gratitude with regard to the historical Buddha, Gotama Buddha, who more than 2,500 years ago let go of his comfortable life as a prince and focused his life entirely on finding and sharing deeper wisdom. We also feel gratitude towards the many teachers we have had. We would especially like to mention Achahn Asabha, with whom I (Frits) meditated for much of the time in Thailand. Also Sayādaw U Kundalabhivamsa, Sayādaw U Lakkhana, Sayādaw U Tejaniya and Sayadaw U Pandita from Myanmar should be mentioned here, as can Achahn Somsak, our current teacher in Thailand. We have also had teachers from whom we have learned that it is not always good to follow someone blindly and we should only trust where we sense that there is sound wisdom. As the Buddha himself once articulated in the Kālāma-Sutta in the Anguttara-Nikāya:

'Now, Kalamas, don't go by reports, by legends, by traditions, by scripture, by logical conjecture, by inference, by analogies, by agreement through pondering views, by probability, or by the thought, 'This contemplative is our teacher'. When you know for yourselves that, 'These qualities are skillful; these qualities are blameless; these qualities are praised by the wise; these qualities, when adopted & carried out, lead to welfare & to happiness' – then you should enter and remain in them'.[3]

This has been a valuable learning experience for both of us; we are grateful for these life lessons. Then there are many teachers we met later, who have shared a wealth of wisdom and knowledge with us. Among others, we think of Joseph Goldstein, Jack Kornfield, Sharon Salzberg and Tara Brach. We are also very grateful for teachers who have turned to a more secular form of mindfulness and compassion practice, such as Jon Kabat-Zinn, Mark Williams, Paul Gilbert and Rick Hanson. We would especially like to mention Erik van den Brink as co-founder of the Mindfulness-Based Compassionate Living programme,[4] Zohair Elabd as the founder of the Deepening Mindfulness & Mindful Communication or DMMC training[5] and Joyce Cordus as co-founder of the Mindfulness-Based Training in Forgiveness.[6]

The German philosopher Arthur Schopenhauer (1788–1860) once defined reading as 'equivalent to thinking with someone else's head instead of with one's own'. Reading broadens the mind and brings an insightful meta-perspective. We are therefore delighted to have worked with Gerolf T'Hooft, who established publishing house Asoka and published our original book in Dutch language titled *Op retraite* in 2021. We are also very grateful to Grace McDonnell, Joanne Forshaw, Manon Berset, Gayathree Sekar and other staff at the Routledge Taylor & Francis Group for this English language publication Either that or "this publication in the English language".

We are very grateful to Victoria Norton, who has helped us in editing and expanding this book and who was willing to join us as a third author. Thanks to Jiun Hogen Roshi and Marie Mannschatz for their generous forewords and to Martine Batchelor, Susan Gillis Chapman, Paul Gilbert, Rick Hanson, Bridgette O'Neill, Joost van den Heuvel Rijnders, Linda Lehrhaupt, Bart van Melik and Anne Speckens for their supportive endorsements. In addition, we are very grateful to Rachel Holstead for her generosity in sharing her beautiful poetry.

We have come to greatly appreciate our own life struggles, like mud from which all kinds of lotuses have come to bloom. After all, without this mud, we would never have started to practise meditation. Thanks to our dear colleagues who teach meditation, friends and dear ones who have supported us in writing. Finally, much gratitude to the many participants, who have had the confidence and courage to join our retreats, and in practising together have inspired, mirrored and taught us. We are very grateful for all the beautiful, moving, funny and at times lucid evaluations they have sent us throughout all these years. Through their generosity, this book has actually been written by many and not just by a few retreat teachers. May reading this book support you in your practice and in *Going on a Meditation Retreat*.

Frits Koster, Jetty Heynekamp and Victoria Norton, January 2025

How this book came about

The real voyage of discovery consists not in seeking new landscapes, but in having new eyes.[7]
— Marcel Proust, French novelist and essayist (1871–1922)

For many years now, we have been planning to write a book on meditation retreats. We have also been asked regularly by participants, but we have always put it off. Why? To answer this question, it might be helpful to introduce ourselves.

Frits' story

At the age of 21, I had an identity crisis and this led me to come into contact with the Thai Buddhist meditation teacher Mettavihari in 1979. He taught the practice of *vipassanā* or insight meditation, a practice in which the development of mindfulness or awareness is central. I found it quite challenging, and although I encountered a lot of agitation and tension, I also noticed that a deeper interest had been touched. I soon started attending meditation retreats – in those early years, they were often offered in the form of ten days of intensive practice. My motivation was so strong that instead of studying psychology I went to Southeast Asia in 1982 and spent more than five years as a Buddhist monk meditating and studying in various monasteries and meditation centres in Thailand, Burma (now Myanmar) and Sri Lanka. In those years I participated in many longer retreats and eventually I was asked to translate during inquiry meetings from Thai teachers with Western retreat participants; gradually I had the freedom to start guiding myself.

I continued the practice in the Netherlands, taking part in a four to six week retreat every year, usually in Thailand or Myanmar. In addition, with the permission of several Asian teachers, I have been leading retreats of 3–30 days in length since 1994. When Jetty came into my life in 2003, we started to lead retreats of five to eight days together in the Netherlands, Belgium and in recent years also regularly in other European countries. For me, following and guiding a retreat is something I experience as very valuable; something indispensable in my life. In my experience, every retreat brings new revelations, which can be pleasant, unpleasant or neutral. But after a retreat, I always notice the fruits of this form of practice.

Jetty's story

When I was 18, I left home to study physiotherapy. I was also looking for more inner meaning and practised all kinds of yoga, including meditation. When I was 25, I came into contact with *vipassanā* meditation and the concept of mindfulness and I noticed that this was what I had been looking for. I went to Sri Lanka a few times for a longer retreat of six weeks but decided not to become a nun there because I did not feel at home with the position of women and nuns in Sri Lanka. I chose to follow my meditation path in the Netherlands. I married and had two children. When I was bringing up my children, the experience I had gained with mindfulness proved to have great value, enabling me to recognise my own patterns 'in real time', so I could avoid passing them on to the next generation. The marriage came to an end, yet we were able to separate in relative peace and co-parent as long as the children were at school until they left home to go and study. Here, too, mindfulness and kindness were a great support to me.

In 2003 Frits and I got to know each other and from 2004 we started to lead retreats together. At first, I was only a retreat manager, but because of my background as a physiotherapist, I occasionally gave sitting advice when I saw people struggling with physical difficulties/complaints. People found this very helpful and passed it on to each other. So I got more and more requests for sitting advice. That's why I started giving sitting advice to everyone at the beginning of a retreat, with the offer of personal sitting advice for anyone with special issues. This has proven to be a very valuable part of going on retreat for many participants.

It also became more and more customary to give additional mindful movement exercises during a retreat, partly due to the influence of the eight-week Mindfulness-Based Stress Reduction (MBSR) training which was emerging at the time. That's why I myself, just like Frits, started training as a mindfulness teacher and I offered this training for a number of years. Although I never did a yoga teacher training course, leading exercises in mindful movement was something that came naturally to me because of my medical background. As a result, I have developed a number of exercise sequences that are especially suitable for retreats. It gives me a lot of satisfaction and a lot of inner joy to co-lead a retreat with Frits. He takes care of the mental well-being of the participants whilst I look after their physical well-being. During these retreats I often meditate with the group, so there is an ongoing personal practice throughout the year. We also go on a longer retreat together every year, during which new developments show up and old patterns are further dissolved.

Victoria's story

Unlike Frits and Jetty I came to mindfulness not via Buddhism but by a secular route. A friend gave me the book *Full Catastrophe Living* by Jon Kabat-Zinn (2013, first edition 1990) at a time when I was experiencing a lot of stress and it inspired me to learn mindfulness meditation and ultimately to go on retreat. I have been attending silent retreats for many years now. Once I told my sister-in-law, a busy teacher and mum of two young boys at the time, that I was preparing to be in silence for a week. She wistfully said 'it sounds wonderful, I could really do with some peace and quiet like that'. Unfortunately, just being with your own mind without external distractions is not quite as simple as it sounds. I have been teaching the secular eight-week courses in mindfulness and compassion, MBSR and MBCL, for over a decade now. One of my aims is to equip my participants with some of the basic skills they will need to profit from a silent retreat: sitting, being in silence and working with difficulty. At the end of the eight weeks, I provide them with some information about the different kinds of retreats and how to find the one that is right for them. If you haven't been on a retreat yet, this book will hopefully inspire and set you on a path to drinking deeply from the well of silence and ultimately to cultivating the peace and spaciousness that will enrich your life.

Dilemmas in writing

Why have we taken the step of writing this book now? Firstly, from a sense of incompleteness in understanding the Buddhist teachings – the Dhamma.[8] We have both been practising insight meditation for more than 40 years and have noticed all kinds of beneficial effects in our lives, all of which have to do with a greater inner flexibility in dealing with life's many vicissitudes.

I (Frits) also thought it would be quite exciting to devote a book to retreats. My previous books have all been much more of an introductory nature, in theory and in practice. The book you are reading now, however, is a sequel and I doubted for a long time whether I would be able to do this. But the encouragement of many participants and colleagues has been very supportive and I was delighted that Jetty was willing to be a co-author, focussing more on the important physical aspects of being on retreat.

Another dilemma we encountered was whether it would be possible to write a book for those already familiar with going on retreat, as well as readers who are familiar with the practice of mindfulness but who have never been on a retreat. Would it be possible to convey the taste of a mango through a book to someone who has never tasted one? It gave us peace of mind to accept it may never be possible, but that a book might inspire and encourage people to go on retreat themselves, in whatever meditative tradition.

It was very moving to look through the evaluation forms we have used since 2003 for participants of retreats we have led together and we have quoted a selection of the most striking evaluations throughout the book.

A word of caution

We would like to include a warning in this preface. As is clear from the above, it is very common to be confronted with challenges when we go on retreat. This requires a good deal of courage as well as sufficient inner strength. For example, if you have just had an operation or your mental health is unstable in any way, it is good to reflect beforehand: do you have enough inner space and stability to face what may come up? There are some contraindications. It is not wise to go on a retreat if you are in the middle of a depressive episode or if you have severe anxiety symptoms or emotional swings that can easily throw you off balance. It is also advisable not to go on a retreat if you are currently experiencing psychosis or if you are susceptible to it. Using a retreat as detoxication for alcohol or drug addiction is also not advisable. Finally, there may be social circumstances, such as being in the middle of a move or an acrimonious divorce, which may make going on a retreat too intensive. That is why we always ask participants to discuss their participation with their therapist (e.g. psychiatrist or psychologist) first, if they are in treatment or therapy. We also point out that it is never a good idea to change medication without consulting a doctor. If there are any doubts about whether it is wise to participate in a retreat, please contact the retreat teacher(s), this includes questions about physical limitations or other specific constraints that might make going on retreat difficult. After all, the practice of mindfulness can also reveal old and therefore more difficult blockages, traumas or pain, as discussed in David Treleaven's book *Trauma-Sensitive Mindfulness* (2018), among others. Indeed, we ourselves have experienced these kind of issues first-hand. Contacting the retreat teacher will also give you an opportunity to explore beforehand whether it feels safe enough for you to begin the adventure. In our opinion, it is important to know that – if you cannot or do not want to do certain exercises – you are in no way obliged to do them.

If you have no meditation experience at all, we often recommend that you first attend a meditation weekend or course, or an eight-week mindfulness training (e.g. MBSR or Mindfulness-Based Cognitive Therapy [MBCT]). Then you will gain some experience and understanding of how the practice of mindfulness works.

The intention of this book

Going on a Meditation Retreat is not meant as a manual. Every retreat teacher has his or her own style and offers a different structure and emphasis. However, despite this, we think it is valuable to describe how we offer a silent retreat in more detail. We have noticed that our lives have gained much more depth which we attribute to regularly going on retreat and 'finding ourselves (again)'. This spiritual dimension is, in our opinion, aptly expressed by the 16th-century French philosopher Michel de Montaigne: 'The greatest thing in the world is to know how to belong to oneself'.

Going on retreat, however, is quite an art; it requires courage and willingness. Stephen Batchelor (2020) therefore speaks of the 'art of retreat'. So we hope this book will serve as a compass if you have never been on retreat, and as a way of enhancing insight if you have. We have decided to write in the you-form and at times in the we-form; after all, retreat experiences are personal and at the same time universal.

In 2020 and 2021, due to the Covid-19 issue, we were asked to participate in group activities as little as possible and only travel when really necessary, which meant we had a mandatory sabbatical. Despite all the trouble caused by the coronavirus pandemic, this suddenly created the space to write this book.

As extra support we have been able to place some audio exercises and a video recording with posture advice on the server of the publisher. A list of these files can be found on p. 160 and are indicated in the text by a download icon with a corresponding number: for example: ⬇

We hope this book may contribute to a greater interest in the value of going on retreat and may contribute to 'retreat competence' and to a deepening of wisdom and compassion.

Frits Koster, Jetty Heynekamp and Victoria Norton, January 2025

Notes

1 *The Orations of Marcus Tullius Cicero*, published by George Bell and Sons, London, Covent Garden 1891. Translated by Charles Duke Yonge (1812–1891).
2 See for example Wong, Y.J., Owen, J., Gabana, N.T., Brown, J.W., McInnis, S., Toth, P., & Gilman, L. (2016). Does gratitude writing improve the mental health of psychotherapy clients? Evidence from a randomized controlled trial. *Psychotherapy Research*, *28* (2), 192–202.
3 Translated from Pali by Thanissaro bhikkhu, see https://accesstoinsight.org/tipitaka/an/an03/an03.065.than.html.
4 See www.mbcl-international.net
5 See www.schoolofmindfulcommunication.com.
6 See www.traininginforgiveness.com.
7 La Prisonniere" published by Chatto and Windus London, translated by C. K. Scott Moncrieff (1889–1930). Available from Project Gutenberg Australia.
8 In older Theravāda Buddhism, the word Dhamma is usually used to denote the Buddha's teachings. In later Mahāyāna Buddhism, the Sanskrit term Dharma is more common. Since we ourselves have 'grown up' more in the Theravāda tradition, in this book we will mostly use the word Dhamma.

Introduction – Why go on retreat

The journey of a thousand miles begins with one step.[1]
— Lao Tzu, ancient Chinese philosopher

For many centuries and all over the world, people have been going on retreats. They withdraw for a time from ordinary worries and are motivated by all kinds of factors. These fall into the following categories.

Seeking rest in a busy life

Sometimes we are looking for inner peace. The busy-ness of modern culture can make us feel quite exhausted. We have become alienated from the simplicity of just being. A retreat offers an opportunity to pause and take a breath in the midst of a hectic life. A retreatant once put it in a blog as follows: 'You don't have to go to faraway places to recharge and rest'. Or as Longchenpa, a 14th-century Tibetan master, once poetically expressed it: 'Let go and be happy in your natural state. Leave your complicated life and everyday confusion to itself. And from rest – not doing – behold the free nature of your mind'.

Being with grief

Another motivation we often hear from people is that they are very busy and totally overwhelmed. This can be partly due to external factors, such as doing volunteer work or being a caregiver, or internal factors, such as a tendency towards perfectionism or a strong sense of responsibility.

It may also be that a participant has had a profound loss but has not had the time and space to reflect on this. And often this leads to inadequate grieving, such as working extremely hard to avoid feeling the grief. A retreat then has the function of creating space for delayed grieving processes.

Entanglement in unhelpful patterns

Another motivation is the occasional entanglement in latent drives that interfere with life and inner balance. For example, we may struggle with unfulfilled longings or get stuck in complaining behaviour or in conflicts. Or we may encounter occasional periods of gloom, fear, loneliness or compulsion. Some suffer more than others, but we all have such tendencies, which can start to torment us especially when we get caught up in the busy-ness and lose contact with the present. In this context, Buddhist psychology refers to ten *kilesas* or 'defilements'. These are ten tendencies or limiting habits that easily cause distress: clinging desire and attachment, hatred and resentment, confusion or misunderstanding, pride, unhelpful beliefs and ideas that harm ourselves and/or others, sceptical doubt, fatigue, restlessness and finally, shamelessness and recklessness.

All of these drives have a limiting effect, which may be either visible or bubbling below the surface. Attachment can make us become obsessive to a greater or lesser degree. Feelings of hatred or resentment can smoulder and can destroy a good relationship or friendship in no time. We might make foolish judgements from a lack of understanding. Unhelpful beliefs and ideas drive us to fanaticism and other compulsive behaviour. Sceptical doubt prevents us from taking new steps, or we think we cannot change and sink into hopeless apathy. Fatigue can cause us to get nowhere or react in an unskilful way to others. Restlessness makes us dither ineffectively or run around without any wisdom and creativity. Finally, shamelessness and recklessness cause us to engage in ethical transgressions, which automatically causes us to get hurt ourselves or hurt others.

> Participant: *I have come to realise that I always want to be somewhere other than where I am. It seems to be an ever-present form of restlessness and an unquenchable longing. But for what? I have accepted the restlessness and stopped fighting it. I felt that this was a good step.*

If we get absorbed in our everyday life for a longer period of time, these mental viruses start to proliferate and we can become physically and/or mentally ill. Fortunately, we live in a society where most people can take a day off or go on holiday. We can have a rest, but after that, the stress often starts up all over again.

In this respect, we have found that going on a retreat can often have a much deeper beneficial effect on our functioning than the average holiday. Often, when we go on holiday, we get involved in all sorts of activity and develop less attention or awareness than during a retreat. And it is precisely the quality of awareness or mindfulness – *sati* in Pali[2] – that has a protective effect in our lives. In a way mindfulness is like an inner guide, showing us wiser ways of dealing with the capricious, vulnerable nature of existence.

In search of existential insight

Sometimes people are not actually experiencing specific suffering but are seeking deeper wisdom in the chaos of ordinary life. Their motivation then has a more existential character. Great religious leaders, such as Jesus Christ, the Prophet Muhammad and the Buddha, have provided us with examples. Jesus Christ withdrew into the desert for 40 days and came to a deeper sense of God, Muhammad experienced his revelations at times when he was on his own, in order to be closer to God. Buddha left the palace and his princely life in search of deeper wisdom. It used to be very common for people to make a pilgrimage or live in a monastery for a time.

This motivation is often accompanied by a deeper curiosity about the workings of the mind. After all, observing mental, physical, sensory and emotional processes from moment to moment with attentiveness also offers a 'study of phenomena': a phenomenology. What happens, for example, when I smell a fragrance or hear a sound? How does a thought arise? And what happens to it when I perceive it as a thought? How does a physical sensation arise? How do I relate to such experiences? Are there experiences that usually cannot be noticed? You could also call a retreat a more intensive way of looking at life, studying it with fresh eyes.

Going on retreat as an escape

Sometimes people go on retreat as an escape from the struggles of daily life. I (Frits) think that I definitely belonged to this category. My first meditation teacher suggested I join a retreat during my very first meditation weekend in Groningen in 1979. He said 'It's nice, it's in the forest' and that it would make me 'more peaceful'. That seemed like a good idea. The oasis of peace turned out to be a cold, former Catholic convent with long corridors and very small boarding rooms with an open ceiling, so that you could hear all the noises. And 'the forest' turned out to be just a few trees outside my window, but we were told on the first day that we were not allowed to go outside at all anyway. In addition, the 'more peaceful' turned out to be very disappointing as I met a lot of agitation in myself. I had always escaped that unrest by doing all kinds of things. I had tried travelling drinking and smoking cannabis to try and escape from the restlessness in myself and unconsciously I had sought a similar escape in meditation. My meditation teacher wisely responded to this by indicating that insight meditation works like a mirror and that I could therefore gain more insight into how my mind functioned. He explained that meeting all kinds of pain, unrest and suffering in ourselves is a very common starting point and that inner peace would come naturally by patiently acknowledging everything that came up. So what started out as an escape actually turned into a coming home to all that unrest and unprocessed frustration in myself.

Looking for inner space and freedom

One participant might come to a retreat because of fatigue. A second might participate as a way of coming to terms with grief. A third wants to learn to deal with recurring gloom or chronic pain. A fourth wants peace, a fifth just wants a little more awareness in his or her life. All these motivations are directly or indirectly related to a basic reality: we experience life as unsatisfactory and are looking for inner space and freedom.

We have noticed that in recent years a new motivation for participating in a retreat has emerged, namely as a component in training courses for MBSR/MBCT trainers or to be recognised as a teacher by a professional association. When we then ask about the motivation for going on a retreat, we sometimes first get a response such as 'I'm participating because I have to do this as part of a mindfulness teacher training'. However, if we explore more deeply, we usually get more personal motivations and also the need to learn how to support others in this. After all, no one is obliged to follow a mindfulness teacher training, there are always deeper motivations that can be uncovered when we explore more deeply. In all cases, going on retreat offers a wonderful opportunity to achieve greater self-insight and deeper inner freedom.

Kindness and mindfulness

Various different types of retreats are offered, see our remarks about choosing a retreat at the end of this book. In this book, we focus on a silent retreat in which kindness and mindfulness are central. Mindfulness is the ability to notice what is happening in the present moment, without immediately having to proceed to judgement or rational analysis of what is observed. It is being aware of an experience while it is happening. Training in mindfulness meditation has an important place in the Buddhist worldview. In recent times it has also become established in secular settings and has been used very successfully to help people live more skilfully with chronic pain and stress, fatigue and depression, among other things.

Kindness is the ability to be kind and compassionate to ourselves, to others and to what we experience. The practice of kindness and mindfulness sets in motion all kinds of awareness and healing processes, which help us to develop insight, better energy management and inner freedom.

Preparations

First of all, it is important to choose a suitable retreat, in terms of location, form, guidance and dates. As many people nowadays live very full lives, several retreat facilitators recommend reserving a time slot and signing up for a retreat a year in advance. We ourselves are often busy planning dates and making appointments several weeks beforehand, so that we can avoid being rushed prior to a retreat. It is advisable to make it clear at home and at work that you will not be available for a number of days, or will be difficult to reach, and to complete or (temporarily) pass on work to others.

The very last week before the retreat starts can often be quite intensive, we notice how many responsibilities we have in our lives: partner, family, friends, colleagues, own company, bookkeeping, websites and many other things. We know from our experience as facilitators that we are definitely not the only ones with this kind of 'pre retreat stress'; most participants recognise this. Preparing well in advance has the advantage that you can actually go on the retreat in a calmer state of mind and with a more carefree heart.

Notes

1. Page 32 of *Sayings of Lao Tzu* translated by Lionel Giles. In the public domain and freely available for download from Global Grey eBooks.
2. Pali is the language in which the scriptures of Theravāda Buddhism are written. We usually translate the word *sati* in this book as awareness or as mindfulness. We are then not talking about the eight-week course Mindfulness-Based Stress Reduction (MBSR) or Mindfulness-Based Cognitive Therapy (MBCT) but about the inner capacity to be aware in a non-judgemental way of what is occurring in the present moment as a human experience within or to us.

Chapter 1

Going into silence
Day 1 – Basic advice for kindness and mindfulness

On Day 1 we turn our attention to the way we often guide retreats. We cover do's and don'ts in meditating in silence and give basic advice for the practice of kindness and insight meditation. We introduce kindness as the first of ten virtues or 'perfections' that can support us in the practice of meditation and in daily life in general.

Give yourself the gift of attention.
Catch the whirlwind rush
and gently, calmly, set it aside.

Sit still and watch its flurries
echo inside you...
    – Rachel Holstead (first verses from Gift)[1]

On the first day we always pay attention to the practical house rules and also the rules for living together during the retreat. This provides a clear structure and secure atmosphere in which as a participant you can begin to feel at ease in being together in silence without too much uncertainty. Being with yourself and with others in silence for a week can be very new. There is no chatting to other meditators, even though the temptation can sometimes be strong, and at the beginning, it can feel uncomfortable not to talk.

> ### The laughing fit
>
> *On my very first retreat, I (Frits) had a completely uncontrollable fit of laughter on the first evening because of a comical incident. We had all eaten our first meal in silence and with attention. After the meal, someone passed the tables in silence with a jug of tea and a jug of coffee. Some people – including myself – gratefully accepted this silent invitation to a last cup of*

> *coffee. My neighbour, however, did not react at all, he did not look up and seemed to be deeply concentrated on chewing and tasting his food. After the coffee round, the organiser put the jugs aside and the meditation teacher – Mettavihari – wanted to say something. At that moment, my neighbour got up very slowly and, to my surprise, walked to the coffee pot and took it, whereas a minute ago the organiser had been standing right in front of him. Another meditator and I then lost our minds and started laughing. Our teacher first tried to just tell us something and ignored us, but it turned out to be so distracting for the others that he sent us out into the hallway, almost as if for punishment. This caused us to laugh even more and we ended up spending more than a quarter of an hour in the corridor, doubled over with laughter. It was probably just release of tension, but it was also very liberating.*

Being allowed to be 'unsociable'

There are very valuable retreats today in which mindful communication is a central theme that is explored and practised. In this book, however, we will be focusing on silent retreats, as an old and proven form of practice. Here our advice is on the one hand not to be sociable and thus not to have to take care of other participants but on the other hand not to be unsociable by pretending that the other participants do not exist.

Participant: *The benefit of silence ... in silence there can be a greater sense of being part of a greater whole.*

Rather, we invite the middle way in the form of a kind silent attitude. This means not having to talk to each other and, as a practical support for this, not having to make eye contact with each other either. This makes it easier to maintain the silence; we do not have to keep asking ourselves what others think or what we ourselves think about everything we see around us. The eyes are downcast, with the gaze is a few metres ahead resting on the ground, in an unfocused manner, with a soft gaze. This simplifies the influx of stimuli which has been found to give enormous peace.

Of course, there is no need to be dogmatic about this. For example, if someone would like to have something at the dinner table but just can't reach it, there is no need for complex sign language, but it can be very wise to make this need clear with a few words. In general, keeping the eyes downcast does not have to feel like a restriction, but is more of a general reminder to simplify the sensory input; if you do look up once in a while, then seeing or looking can simply be observed. And of course, in that case, a silent smile can be very helpful.

> Participant: *During this first retreat, I met a nun on the little square near the church of the monastery where the retreat took place. She said, 'You're not allowed to talk, are you? Tell me ... how is that?' It was very funny.*

On the first and also the last day, we often invite participants to communicate mindfully in pairs and get to know another retreat participant and share something about themselves and about their motivation for taking part. We will also tell you about the possibility of regular inquiry meetings with the meditation teacher(s) during the retreat, either individually, in a small group or both. This will be covered later in this book.

Being in silence of course also means not calling, texting, using communication apps or using other (digital) means of communication. Often participants do not realise this at the beginning and make an appointment with people at home to call after a few days. We have often seen that such a seemingly innocent contact can have a surprisingly large impact on the accumulated awareness and often cause a great deal of worry or agitation, just like a quiet pond into which we throw a stone. So, it is wise to make it clear to your loved ones that you will not be seeking contact during the retreat and will be putting your mobile phone on flight mode. Of course, there can be exceptions and sometimes urgent matters that require a phone call. In that case we ask you to let us know so that we can explore where and when this would fit into the programme. Apart from this, your family can always contact us in case of an emergency, because we always give our phone number in a confirmation email that we send to all participants well over a week in advance.

We also invite you to simplify things in other ways, for example by not reading – or only reading one or two pages per day in a book about the practice – and also not writing or only very briefly (some keywords) and then with awareness.

At the beginning, living together in silence is often quite uncomfortable, whereas at the end of a retreat participants usually report having found the silence very restful – a relief from a hectic life. That is why traditionally we talk about 'Noble Silence'. Everyday communication takes much more energy than we usually realise. In silence we experience what in Buddhist psychology is called *kāya viveka*: an oasis of peace through physical isolation.

> Participant: *I did not know that it would be so easy to be silent for a week and to look less at each other (I only became aware of the latter on the first day of*

the retreat and frankly it frightened me, I thought 'It will be awful'). Of course it helps a lot that everybody is behaving the same way, but still... I have to do it myself. I experience how much space it gave me just to be with myself. I see that it is true that a lot of energy goes into verbal and non-verbal communication. Even without that, of course, I saw all sorts of things and became aware – fortunately with kindness – of all sorts of judgements, about myself and about others.

The basic structure – The meditation programme

During the introduction on Day 1, we also talk about the retreat programme, which we put up in various places in the retreat centre. The programme helps to create peace and clarity and to support the group in practising together in harmony. We have noticed over the years that a classical traditional meditation programme, which often runs from 4 am to 9 pm with (only) two meals and with periods of 60 minutes for walking and sitting meditation, can be very demanding for people, who are not accustomed to sitting in a meditation posture for a long time. This is why we have adapted our programme, which is somewhat more gentle. It also seems that meditators usually need time to find their balance and are often very tired at the beginning of a retreat. Therefore depending of course on where the retreat takes place, we often use a programme like this:

6.00 am: waking up
6.30 am: sitting meditation
7.00 am: mindful movement exercises
7.45 am: breakfast
8.30 am: informal meditation[2] and/or working meditation
9.15 am: walking meditation
9.30 am: sitting meditation (with guidance)
10.15 am: walking meditation (with guidance in the beginning and tea/coffee)
11.15 am: sitting meditation
12.00 pm: walking meditation
12.30 pm: sitting meditation
1.00 pm: hot meal
1.45 pm: informal meditation
3.00 pm: walking meditation
3.45 pm: sitting meditation
4.30 pm: walking meditation
5.15 pm: sitting meditation (and sometimes a short guided body scan)
5.45 pm: evening meal
6.30 pm: informal meditation
7.15 pm: walking meditation

7.45 pm: evening talk
8.30 pm: walking meditation
9:00 pm: sitting meditation (with kindness meditation)
9.30 pm: informal meditation and rest.

We make it clear that this programme is not intended to be coercive. It is intended as a helpful structure; however, sometimes deviating from the programme can be very wise. Different retreat teachers have different emphases. We usually invite participants to practice with the intention of arriving punctually for the sitting meditation; however, you are also welcome to join if the door to the meditation hall is already closed. The meditators who are already inside can then simply be aware of hearing sound and other phenomena that can be experienced with it; the latecomer can sit in silence with awareness. As one of our teachers sometimes used to say: when you are mindful you are not too late but exactly in time. Talking about this in the group often helps to dissipate any tension.

Kindness to yourself – The body

On Day 1 we pay extensive attention to the attitude towards yourself during the retreat. For example, we pay a lot of attention to physical limitations you may encounter as a participant and invite you to explore these in an open way, what is helpful for the practice and what is not. We make an inventory of specific physical vulnerabilities in the group and invite everyone to explore how the sitting and walking meditation can be made accessible. For some participants, it is, for example, necessary to lie down regularly instead of sitting down or to take regular rests. For others, sitting still for a longer period of time or walking more slowly may not be wise. In general, we invite you to be kind, to respect your limits and not to harm yourself and to tune in wisely to possibilities and limitations. We usually also announce that Jetty, who is a qualified and experienced but now retired physiotherapist who has a lot of meditation experience herself, will lead a morning session of mindful movement and on the first morning will also give specific recommendations for sitting, walking and lying meditation. We also tell everyone that Jetty prepares a daily schedule for participants who wish to sign up for an individual consultation about physical posture while meditating.

> Participant: *I immediately applied the tip for sitting with a relaxed back as a result. And if I did feel a twinge, a small correction was enough. Thank you!*

Courtesy to others

Finally, we also pay attention to 'practical ethics' during the retreat. In the confirmation email that we send everyone before the retreat starts, we already touch on five suggestions which are commonly used in Buddhist meditation centres and which facilitate the meditation practice and living in community.

- Respect for everything that lives.
- Not to take what does not belong to you.
- Not to speak untruth but to speak with integrity.
- Not to engage in sexual activity.
- Not to use alcohol and drugs.

In the retreat itself, we express these ethical guidelines according to the so-called Golden Rule of Confucius, a universal rule of life that excels in simplicity and depth: 'Do not treat others as you would not want to be treated yourself'. And vice versa, this rule can also be formulated in a positive way: 'Treat others as you would like to be treated yourself'. In this way, we introduce one of the ten valuable qualities or values that we will be introducing later on in this book: wise and compassionate ethics, which might possibly also be called courtesy in silence.

The theme of this retreat – Ten beautifying virtues or 'perfections'

We often weave themes from Buddhist psychology into the guidance we give during a retreat. After all, Buddhism has all kinds of lists that can very well be used as helpful stepping stones or reminders to accentuate or clarify something about the meditation process. One of these lists expresses ten wholesome qualities or virtues which are called the ten *pāramī*. The word *pāramī* is usually translated as 'perfection of mind' or as 'perfection', Joseph Goldstein also addresses these ten helpful qualities as 'ten aspects of integrity'.[3]

It refers to the life of the Buddha. According to tradition, the Indian prince Siddhartha did not become a Buddha or 'Fully Awakened One' in just one lifetime. In the Theravada tradition, the most original Buddhist tradition still found in Southeast Asia today, Gotama Buddha the historical Buddha of almost 2,600 years ago, was not the first Buddha either. It is said that once in so many centuries a Buddha or fully Awakened One lives and appears at a time when the teachings of Buddhism, the Dhamma, have fallen into oblivion. Therefore, six or seven Buddhas are named in the Theravada tradition who lived before Gotama Buddha who we now think of as the Buddha.[4] Buddhas who will live in a distant future are also named.

The predecessor of the individual we know as the Buddha was called Dīpankara. A young man named Sumedha had heard of this special teacher. It was in the rainy season and when Dīpankara entered his village, Sumedha sat down on the side of the road to see this special Buddha. However, due to the rain, the road was quite muddy and full of puddles. As Dīpankara approached, the young man was struck by the peaceful radiance of the approaching man and became filled with deep confidence. He then made a vow that he too would one day become a Buddha and dedicate his life to the prosperity of all living beings. He then knelt down on the ground and unknotted his hair to lay it on the mud so that Dīpankara Buddha could place his feet on dry ground.

Making this profound vow, Sumedha then started to train his mind to Buddhahood. According to Buddhist teachings, there were many lives between life as Sumedha and life as Prince Siddhartha. Especially the Jataka or birth stories of the Buddha tell of many lives, in which the Buddha-to-be trained himself as a human, animal or invisible being in the ten perfections and was therefore called a *bodhisatta*: a being that aims at deeper wisdom and compassion.[5] The ten *pāramī* or perfections are as follows:

- Generosity.
- Ethics and discipline.
- Renunciation, simplification.
- Wisdom.
- Patience, forbearance.
- Effort, dedication.
- Determination, steadfastness.
- Truth or reality.
- Kindness, benevolence.
- Equanimity.

In this book we will relate to these beneficial qualities one by one and how we can bring them to fruition on retreat and in daily life. We will not use the classical enumeration as above, but we introduce them as is appropriate to the needs of the participants.

A leap of faith

The beginning of a retreat is usually quite exciting, especially if it is your first retreat. I (Frits) remember my first retreat being so exciting that I went out and bought ten chocolate bars an hour beforehand, one for each day, these bars were gone within four days by the way, and before the start of almost every retreat, I follow I almost always notice a type of nervousness in me. Going on a retreat certainly requires courage. It is much easier to just go on with the life you are used to. And it seems very easy to just be mindful and study your own body and mind without the usual distractions for a week, but it is definitely not always that easy. We never know in advance what we will encounter and whether we will be able to face ourselves in an open and gentle way. Especially if it is the first time we are going to a new retreat location or if we choose a different facilitator, this is additionally exciting. Will it be okay? Will the teacher understand me? How will I feel at ease with people I don't know at all?

Every retreat is a leap of faith, a journey of adventure in which we can discover all sorts of special, pleasant and unpleasant things about ourselves. Because of the courage this requires, the Buddha used the word *dullabha*, which can be translated as 'rare'.

Kindness

We notice that it usually brings us more space and relaxation to start a retreat with a guided exercise in kindness meditation – after the general introduction described above. Daniel Siegel (2010), clinical professor of psychiatry at the UCLA School of Medicine, stated 'science confirms that kindness and compassion are to the brain what the breath is to life'. See audio 1 for a guided exercise in kindness meditation in relation to yourself.

Exercise: Kindness meditation – Yourself

Make sure you are sitting at ease, relaxed and upright, on your bench or meditation cushion. If you like you can also put a cushion under your knees, so you can sit comfortably. If you are affected by any specific physical disability or injuries, you can always sit on a chair or lie on your back. If during a sitting period you find that sitting still really becomes a big struggle feel welcome to adopt the following policy: take care of yourself wisely and kindly.

You can define meditation as the art of connecting. This starts in a very direct way in connecting with awareness to what is happening in the present moment. For example, you can be aware of the mood you are in, and whatever that is, it is okay. You can be aware of hearing sounds or listening to the voice that is guiding this exercise; it may be good to realise that the guiding voice has the intention to offer a structure. This can be helpful, at times when this is not helpful there is all the freedom to take another course.

There will also be times when you will notice that you have become engrossed in a thought, or that you are experiencing a physical sensation. At such times you can notice the thinking or the feeling as such, without having to regard anything as a disturbance. And if nothing clear occurs, you can always connect with the breathing movements, as they can be felt and sensed in the abdomen or in the chest.

In daily life, we often put a lot of time and energy into looking after the welfare of others. This is deeply rooted for example in the Christian culture, where the advice of Jesus Christ 'Love your neighbour as yourself' has for many become 'Take good care of others but taking care of yourself is selfish'. From this subtle distortion of the original advice we easily force ourselves to become overly strict and judgemental towards ourselves and this can encourage the development of all kinds of physical and mental complaints. Meditation has something inherently peaceful about it, namely making peace with the moment and with how we are at the moment. Therefore you can wish yourself something kind and start the retreat with the practice of kindness. You can start wishing yourself something kind, as if you were repeatedly sending yourself a kind greeting card, as if it is your birthday. In Buddhism, this is the beginning of a very extensive form of meditation, also called mettā bhavanā or loving-kindness meditation.

And so, as a beginning, you can wish yourself something kind. After all, we take ourselves everywhere and life can become so much lighter if we are on good terms with ourselves. Therefore, do not hesitate to make a wish for yourself. A spontaneous wish, for example for courage, patience or trust. Or you can use one of the four wishes, which are often used in the Buddhist tradition. Four wishes in which very basic human needs are expressed: 'May I feel safe', 'I wish myself the best possible health', 'I wish myself happiness or joy in life' or 'May I experience inner peace and ease of life'.

It is not always easy to be human, so feel free to wish yourself something supportive or helpful. Use words that mean something to you. One or a few wishes, in the form of a sentence or just one or two key words from a sentence, with the rhythm of the breath or independently from it.

And what effect does this have on you? Cultivate an awareness in which all experiences can be included. If it is difficult, for example because you feel tired, sad or worried, sometimes a paradoxical wish can also be very helpful. For example a wish like 'May I be sad or worried', or 'I grant myself this tiredness'. It helps in just tuning into what is happening and to what can be helpful. Nurturing a friendly intention, in this case towards yourself, as a vulnerable human being. You can continue with a kind wish towards yourself or sit with mindfulness, as long as you wish. It might be nice to end with the poem Care by the Irish poet Rachel Holstead.

> In those moments
> when you want to care for all the world,
> Remember that in you
> is also the whole of the world.
> And you can only begin here
> – caring for this skin,
> These bones, this heart.
>
> Delve deep into caring,
> and every cell becomes a temple
> in which to honour the world.

The power of a paradoxical wish

I (Frits) know that in the beginning I hated the practice of kindness meditation. As a 21-year-old, I didn't think that mild-mannered meditation was cool at all, and I just couldn't bring myself to 'brainwash myself with a soft phrase that I had to keep repeating like a parrot'. At the same time, I became aware of an enormous inner harshness and gradually began to uncover a very low self-esteem within myself. By doing the loving-kindness meditation regularly I noticed that the resistance to it slowly but surely began to soften.

As an extra strategy in case of great resistance, I started to change the kindness wish into 'May I at some stage be free of resistance' or 'May I accept myself in time'. I then discovered the power of a playful paradoxical approach when I once felt very weak and tired and spontaneously wished myself: 'May I feel as weak/limp as a dishcloth' ... 'May I be as tired as a long-used mop'. In this way I noticed that a whole lot of tension and hardening in myself could gradually thaw.

Pitfalls in kindness meditation

We can fall into a trap when we practise with the idea that we should immediately get a very deep feeling of peace and connectedness. Sometimes this happens and we can be very moved or realise there is a deep feeling of happiness. However, it is good to know that this will not always happen, nor does it necessarily have to happen, but that the effect of this practice may be okay just as it is experienced in the moment. This already contains a type of kindness, namely the kindness in acknowledging what is happening. It can be reassuring that there is something beneficial in the friendly intention towards yourself. A wish does not have to be realised immediately, it can be expressed with an attitude of 'If it ever happens, that would be great. And if it doesn't happen then never mind, this is also fine'. The moment we wish ourselves or others something kind, we activate a kind, benevolent state of mind. And this healing attitude grows with every moment that we wish ourselves something kind. You can think of it as a patient work in progress.

Kindness in the retreat

In the practice of *vipassanā* or insight meditation, the quality of kindness is implicitly present in the acknowledging, accepting attitude we cultivate in the face of our experience. This absence of aversion – *adosa* in Pali – itself is considered very valuable in Buddhist psychology. However, we can also cultivate it explicitly in loving-kindness meditation; it is then called *mettā* and manifests as one of the ten perfections.[6] Both expressions of kindness are valuable, so after this introductory meditation, we invite you as a participant to make space for an explicit kindness meditation every now and then during the retreat. This can be at the beginning or at the end of a sitting period, or when you feel stuck or sometimes during the walking meditation. Use it whenever it is needed and adapt it to the moment.

> Participant: *The insights and experiences are still very much alive. What allowing compassion can bring about. Very valuable and another step further in my development.*

Kindness in the practice of mindfulness

In a subsequent guided meditation, after a brief practice of kindness meditation, we invite you to put the kind wish to rest and continue with mindfulness. And where kindness was explicitly being developed before, this can continue in acknowledging whatever is happening at this moment and indeed moment by moment. After all, during the retreat you may encounter all sorts of things in yourself. For example, you may experience joy and peace but you may also encounter fatigue, agitation, physical discomfort, resistance or thoughts with a disturbing content. In the practice of insight meditation, we can continue letting kindness grow in the receptive warm attitude in relation to our experience in the now. Below is an example of a guided meditation, which brings out the basic principles of mindfulness when sitting or lying down. See audio 2 for a guided exercise with basic advice for sitting meditation.

Exercise: Developing mindfulness – Sitting meditation

We are going to continue with the practice of mindfulness or vipassanā meditation, in order to gain more insight into what we experience from moment to moment as human beings. For a large part of our lives we function on automatic pilot, without paying attention to what we do or experience. In a sense we have become more or less estranged from the simplicity of now. Vipassanā or insight meditation helps us to come home to the present and make inner contact with what is happening from moment to moment. And the beauty of mindfulness is that it automatically brings with it all kinds of healing and valuable skills, such as a fundamental kindness to ourselves as outlined before. There is no need to try to be anything other than what you are. All experiences are perfectly valid. Sometimes you experience pain, tension, doubts along the lines of 'What on earth have I got myself into', restlessness, impatience, a chaos of thoughts, and at other moments you experience calmness, ease or joy. Whatever you are feeling right now and whatever you are experiencing: it is okay. You do not have to change anything, just allow yourself to be as you are.

You do not have to solve anything either. If, for example, specific life questions come up about how to proceed with your relationship or work, we would advise you not to try to find an answer to them. You may just be aware of the dilemma as a dilemma, without an agenda. And if sometimes a solution to a life question presents itself, then you may notice this as a 'seeing' or 'understanding' but you do not need to force answers. The only thing to do is to be aware of what is happening from moment to moment in body and mind, nothing more.7

However, to support developing awareness when faced with the multiplicity of experiences, it is advisable to use an anchor for your attention. Here we follow the suggestions for vipassanā or insight meditation of a well-known and respected Buddhist monk, meditation teacher and scholar from Myanmar: Mahāsi Sayādaw (†1982). In the sitting or lying meditation, he recommends being aware of the breathing movements, as they manifest themselves clearly somewhere in the body. In the abdominal area, the chest or elsewhere. Be aware that the abdomen or chest is naturally expanding or rising a little when you breathe in and it is contracting, descending or falling when you breathe out, just like a balloon that expands and returns to its original state when the pressure on it is released. You can be aware of these movements.

It is fine to be aware of these processes in a relaxed way, without feeling the need to influence them. If you find that this supports your practice, then you can explore naming or labeling the breathing movements lightly within yourself as a valuable tool. The rising and falling of the abdomen can then be named internally, for example, as 'rising', 'falling', 'rising', 'falling'. Be aware and name in your mind the rising and falling of the abdomen as these processes occur naturally ... Thus, while you are aware of the rising and falling of the abdomen, you name or kindly register these movements simultaneously and in accordance with the experience.

Naming or noticing what is perceived can be a valuable support but it need only be a very light touch, a soft whisper in the background while something comes up. So it is not the most important thing, but merely an optional extra. The most important thing is and remains being aware of what is happening.

After a while, all kinds of other experiences can demand your attention. It can then be helpful to realise that terms such as 'disturbance', 'blockage' or 'distraction' do not really fit insight meditation. In this sense, mindfulness is not so much meant as a means of control but more as a way of integrating what arises. You can experience all kinds of things when you sit or lie down in this way and then always integrate *this as a new object of awareness, which is just as valuable as the rising and falling of the abdomen.*

Physical feelings, for example, may come up. In that case, you can be aware of them and name them as you recognise them and as long as they are on the foreground; for example, as 'itching', 'itching', 'itching', as 'feeling', 'feeling', or as 'warmth', 'heat'.

All exercises are unforced and fall under the heading of 'take care of yourself'. For example, if there is a persistent pain that is becoming so prevalent that you can no longer quietly contemplate it, first name the inner reactivity, for example the resistance or anxiety that has arisen. If, however, the practice becomes an intractable struggle, it is good to understand that you do not have to obsessively force yourself to remain sitting still. In that case, you can quietly change your posture, but also consider the change of posture as part of the meditation. Instead of just sitting down or lying down, you can notice the intention to move and slowly change your posture with awareness. You then refrain from the posture but you don't refrain from the most important thing in the practice, which is awareness.

The same is true if you notice that you hear sounds, see images with your eyes closed, notice thoughts come into your mind or recognise a specific emotion in yourself. Sometimes thoughts or sounds stop immediately when they are recognised. Then you do not need to do anything with them, they are gone already. You can then be aware of the next thing that presents itself. If, however, the experience is still clearly present at the moment of recognition, then you may notice it or register it, as 'hearing', 'seeing', 'thinking', 'feeling', 'judging', 'sadness', 'joy', 'emotion', as long as the phenomenon arises and stays in the foreground by itself.

During the meditation exercise you do not need to concern yourself with the content of your experiences. For example, you do not need to identify exactly what you are hearing, why you think or experience a certain state of mind, or where, when and with whom a remembered event took place. It is enough simply to acknowledge this during meditation as 'hearing', 'remembering', or 'thinking'. On the other hand, there is no need to try to get rid of experiences or to 'name them away'. It is enough simply to perceive and register sounds, thoughts, feelings and the like as phenomena as long as they are clearly present, without having to go into the topic or try to stop them.

To summarise the above: you are always looking at and naming or noticing what is happening in body and mind. Without having to judge or explain why you are experiencing something, you are aware of what is clearly occurring at the moment, as long as it is clearly occurring. Naming or registering can be seen as a valuable and supportive tool to strengthen a kind but also objective, non-clinging mindfulness. Being aware of what is happening in the moment, however, always remains the most important thing.

> *If the object of observation falls away or dissolves of its own accord, and if nothing else clearly presents itself to you at that moment, then you can always return in this meditation technique to knowing and lightly naming or registering the rising and falling of the abdomen as the basic object.*

Participant: *That you only need to be observant and that you don't need to push away, change, judge, explain. Everything is allowed to be there. That saves a lot of energy.*

Walking meditation

Like sitting meditation, walking meditation is an important part of a *vipassanā* retreat. If you visit a garden shop or garden centre you will see lots of Buddha statues in a sitting position, which easily evokes the idea that meditation is mainly sitting meditation. In fact, this is a misconception. Insight meditation can be practised very well when we stand, lie down, walk somewhere or perform general daily tasks like eating, drinking, washing the dishes or going to the toilet. In our opinion, this makes insight meditation very accessible for daily life practice.

Another important part of a retreat, therefore, is the practice of walking meditation; below is some basic advice, as we often guide participants at the beginning of a retreat.

> **Exercise: Suggestions for walking meditation**
>
> *Find a place where you can go for a walk or where you have about three to ten metres of space to walk back and forth. This can be a place in the meditation hall but you can also practice walking meditation elsewhere, inside or outside. Stand at ease. The feet slightly spread and a slight bend in the knees, so they are not locked or overstretched. Keep the body relaxed and upright. Many meditation teachers, ourselves included, generally advise holding the arms in such a way that the hands grip each other behind the back. This posture gives the feeling of strolling. But you do not have to do this all the time; you can also let the arms hang down along the body or keep them crossed in front of the chest for a while – as you wish. It is also advisable to keep your head upright. To make it easier to keep your balance when standing and in order not to bump into anything while walking, you can keep your eyes open. Also to avoid being unnecessarily preoccupied with your surroundings and*

with others, it is best to keep your eyes slightly downcast, i.e. loosely allowing your eyes to rest on the ground about five to ten meters in front of you, without having to be visually focused on anything in particular. There is no need to look at your feet or straight ahead or around you. In this way you can create a good environment for awareness.

You can be aware of the standing posture of the body and at the same time name or notice this internally as 'standing', 'standing', 'standing', being aware that there is a standing position of the body. Sometimes the contact of the feet with the ground may be noticeable, sometimes there may be a little stiffness in the calves or in the back, which is caused by the slight muscle tension in standing. Or there may be awareness of the whole body standing in this posture and noting this very generally as 'standing', 'standing', 'standing'. You know there is a standing posture.

You can then notice the intention to walk and start the walking meditation. There are several ways to explore this. For example, if you feel tired or experience a cramp, then mindfully making a stroll may be the most appropriate. You can then mindfully put on your coat and shoes and start walking in a relaxed way, without having to rush. You can be aware of the walking movements of your feet or legs, the gentle swinging of your arms, the feeling of the outside air on your face, or the whole body walking. Sometimes at a faster pace, sometimes slower, whatever is helpful. Then there is no need to look for sensory stimuli, but you can be aware with a relaxed and receptive presence. At moments when there is seeing, hearing, smelling, thinking or feeling then this can be acknowledged.

You can fill a whole or a part of a walking period walking mindfully in a relaxed manner. If there is the inner space for it then you can choose to slow down to walking step by step. For most people, it is then helpful to take smaller steps, preferably in a relaxed way. And then to be aware of the movement of the feet.

You can be aware of how the foot rises from the ground into the air, moves through the air and is placed back on the ground. Slowing down can facilitate more precision in being aware, but preferably not so slowly that you start to wobble.

There is no need to make a great effort or to get obsessive about observing movements. It is sufficient to be aware of the movement of the foot in a light and relaxed way. While you are aware of this movement, you name or notice it at the same time as 'left step', 'right step' or as 'left', 'right', in a way that does not require much effort but facilitates connection with the present moment. To be aware of the movements of the feet in such a way can be considered as a gentle anchor during walking meditation, comparable to the function of the rising and falling of the abdomen during sitting meditation. So, in principle, during walking or strolling meditation, you do not need to pay explicit attention to the rising and falling of the abdomen; it is sufficient to be aware of the movements of the feet or to be aware of the walking or strolling body.

> *If other experiences occur briefly, for example no longer than one or a few micro-moments, you can acknowledge this and simply continue walking. If, however, something else comes up clearly and remains prominent for a longer period of time, then you may want to stand still and acknowledge this as it occurs. You do not need to consider other experiences as a disturbance or distraction, but you can simply integrate it as a new meditation object, just as valuable as the movements of the feet. For example, you may see something with your eyes being in a downcast position, hear a sound or notice a thought, recognise a bodily sensation, a smell or an emotion. On such moments you may merely be aware of this experience or have this accompanied by a subtle inner noting, as for example 'hearing', 'seeing', 'smelling', 'thinking' or 'feeling'. You can do this as long as the experience is clear or until you decide to resume walking – you do not have to stand still all the time.*
>
> *When you have come to the end of your path, bring your feet together again. For a few moments you can again be aware of the standing position and mentally note this as 'standing', 'standing', 'standing'. Then you notice the intention to turn and with your left or right foot you can turn about sixty degrees and register this as 'turning'. Then you join with the other foot and you can note this inwardly as 'closing'. In this way you turn three times sixty degrees and close the movement each time with the other foot. After again noticing the standing and the intention to walk, you continue with the walking meditation.*

For the first day of a retreat, we advise you not to move on to more detailed exercises with the walking meditation, even though you may be familiar with them. In this way, you give yourself time to develop the awareness slowly. You can compare this with driving a car or taking driving lessons. There are four or five gears in a car. When you start driving, it is unwise to put the car immediately into third or fourth gear. It would cost a lot of energy, and it is also bad for the engine and the gearbox. You do not have to force anything, just give space to the walking meditation in a relaxed way. The following days new suggestions will be added daily, these will also be described in this book.

Bowing meditation as a complementary practice

In a retreat walking and sitting meditation are considered as the most basic exercises for developing mindfulness. In addition, however, you may also practise 'bowing meditation' as many meditators experience physical stiffness during a retreat with only walking and sitting meditation. The following exercise may then be a welcome change and ensure greater physical suppleness.

Exercise: Bowing meditation

After the walking or sitting meditation, sit with your knees on the meditation mat. You can sit in the direction of the retreat teacher or a Buddha statue, or sit towards the centre of the circle if everyone is sitting in a circle. Ultimately, any direction you wish to bend is fine, as this is more about mindful movement than 'bending towards something or someone'. Your buttocks rests on your heels; your feet rest with the top of the foot flat on the ground or your feet stand with the toes curled up on the ground. This last suggestion has the physical advantage that a number of nerve junctions are stimulated or activated in this way. However, it is not compulsory. If, for example, your age or physical discomfort or limitation makes it impossible to sit in this position with curled toes, you can keep the top of the foot flat on the ground, it need not become an exercise in masochism. The back is straight in a relaxed way. Now let the palms of the hands touch each other; traditionally this is done as a respectful salute. Hold the thumbs against the chest at heart level and you can be aware of sitting in this posture, naming this as 'sitting', or as 'knowing'. Knowing that you are sitting like this.

You then can notice the inner decision to move and slowly raise the arms and hands. You name or note this inner movement as 'moving', 'moving', 'moving' or as 'lifting', 'lifting', 'lifting'. You notice the touching of the thumbs against the forehead as 'touching'. You are then aware of this body posture and notice it again as such.

Then you bend forward your upper body slowly towards the ground and mentally note this as 'bending', 'bending', 'bending'. The contact of the hands, the elbows and the forehead with the ground is again noted as 'touching', and you may acknowledge the relaxing of the abdomen and the body sitting/being in this posture.

Finally, the upper body is slowly moved upwards again, noticing it as 'rising up'. You bring the palms of the hands together again, noticing the contact of the palms with each other and the touching of the thumbs against the chest as 'touching', and so you return to the starting position.

If other experiences come up during this exercise, note them and then resume the bowing exercise, similar to practising walking meditation. You can do this series of movements and postures, for example, three times or more often at the end of walking or at the end of sitting, as required.

Some meditators like to put something of value clarification into the practice as well. For example, my first meditation teacher regularly advised me to name the three basic postures in this exercise successively as 'purity', 'compassion' and 'wisdom', but you can also let other life values express themselves here: for example, 'openness', 'patience' and 'kindness'. There is no need to philosophise about the meaning of the words you use. And if you still do this sometimes, then you can, of course, note this as 'philosophising'.[8]

The bowing exercise appears to have a beneficial effect physically and to work for many as a healthy form of exercise therapy or stretching. In addition, the exercise can generate inspiration and is also simply a mindful movement exercise. You can also do it in a modified way sitting on a chair. However, it is worth noting that this is a complementary exercise; you do not have to do it if you feel uneasy about this exercise or if you simply cannot do it physically. You can also just practice walking and sitting meditation alternately.

Exercise: Reclining meditation

Vipassanā meditation can also be practised lying down. For this you can lie on your back in a comfortable way, if necessary putting a cushion under the head. Allowing the arms to rest alongside the body or letting the hands rest on the belly area. Reclining meditation can also be practised lying on the right side, you may then wish to put a cushion under your head so it is supported and your spine remains straight. You can bend the arm underneath and let your head rest on it. The right side is preferable to the left side when lying down after a meal. By lying on the right side, the digestion is facilitated and we put less pressure on the heart area. And of course, in case of physical limitations, a variation can always be sought whereby you can lie still for a longer period. For the rest, the same advice applies as for sitting meditation.

Awareness of daily activities

Some meditators only consider the periods of sitting meditation as important and they can then sit very motionless and disciplined. The rest of the time they let things go a bit and during the walking meditation they go and get cups of tea or sit down to rest from the sitting meditation. This is allowed of course, but the question is whether this brings much depth meditatively speaking. It is like spending an hour every now and then building a dyke to protect your house against rising water. During the sitting meditation, a beautiful dyke is created, but if you neglect continuing the practice in periods of walking meditation the water can easily come in again and you keep mopping up the water, so to speak.

Other meditators are more astute and they make sure that the walking meditation is done with outer and inner discipline. The dyke then does not crumble during the walking meditation and is even strengthened. However, they let the awareness slip during the daily activities, so that all the strength that has been built up is lost again.

That is why we are very glad that in many meditation centres there is a request for a daily practice of cleaning or working meditation. We consider this as a very valuable part of the practice. We therefore ask the participants to perform a specific task every day, for example vacuuming, working in the garden, cleaning the toilets or doing the dishes, as a meditative exercise. It turns out to be very insightful to specifically do this task for a week with the intention of being mindful.

> Participant: *What I found amazing was to notice how important the most ordinary tasks become. Cracking nuts and watering plants every day. This will stay with me all my life and I hope to be able to enjoy and be just as mindful of the tasks at home. And of course, it is also good if it feels neutral or unpleasant.*

In a retreat it is very valuable to train ourselves to be mindful of what we usually experience as routine actions. In order to be more aware of these ordinary daily activities, many retreat teachers recommend relaxing and slowing down in a playful way. The benefit of this can be compared to a discus or javelin thrower who will often practise slow movements during training. Then it is much easier to see and notice exactly how the body movements proceed – where unnecessary energy is lost, whether the discus or javelin is released at the right moment, and so on.

This example may show the value of slowing down. It usually reveals hidden information and can reveal previously unnoticed patterns, excessive effort and so on. Unwinding and slowing down, however, do not have to be forced and can be practised with a kind unforced atmosphere. Some participants experience this as very valuable while for others it can bring a sense of constraint. Here again, the invitation is to be playful with suggestions that are offered during a retreat.

As an example, during one of the first days we usually start a meal with an invitation to eating meditation, as an extension of the raisin exercise in the MBSR that is well-known to many.

Exercise: Eating meditation

You can sit at the table, at ease and with awareness. If you feel like it, you can first of all silently offer a kind wish to yourself and your fellow diners and all those who have helped to prepare this meal. You can be aware of moments of seeing, looking, hearing, smelling, feeling or thinking, or be aware of the sitting, breathing body. Then you may notice the intention or decision to eat and slowly and mindfully pick up the spoon and scoop up, for example, a piece of food with it. Then you may be noticing the decision to lift the spoon and being aware of the lifting of the spoon. Then the opening of the mouth, putting the food in the mouth, taking the spoon or fork out again. You can then be aware of the closing of the mouth, the touch of the food with the tongue and with the inside of the mouth. Then (the intention to) chew

> and during chewing the moments of tasting and through to swallowing and feeling the food descend through the throat.
>
> And if during eating you notice that other experiences occur, these can simply be acknowledged, as 'hearing', 'judging', 'enjoying', thus eating can take on a new dimension.

Many meditators say they have never been so clearly aware of what they are really experiencing when they eat, although of course, we do this very often. And it doesn't mean that we should always eat this way, we ourselves also sometimes like to sit in front of the television eating pasta. But it certainly appears to be healthy and restful to eat with presence of mind and this can be developed further in a playful way.

> Participant: *During the coffee/tea break I enjoyed a biscuit as usual. Mindfully I put my teeth into it, chewed quietly, let the smell and the flavours penetrate me. The ingredients forced themselves on my attention, unfortunately I tasted mainly flour and sugar. The other days, I mindfully drank a cup of tea without a biscuit. It was a lightning-quick way to start living healthier. Well ... I mean eating.*

Kindness meditation – Yourself and loved ones

We always end the retreat days in the evening with a short guided kindness meditation. Here we invite everyone first of all to allow some space for a kind wish for yourself, as described on page ... – giving and receiving in one person. Subsequently, the kindness can also be connected to one or more loved ones, for example, parents, a partner, children or grandchildren, a good friend. The poem *Be gentle* by the Irish poet Rachel Holstead below might be a good way to end Day 1.

Be gentle

Be gentle with yourself these days.
Sometime the currents beneath
bring tangles to our hearts.

And we don't notice
and glide smoothly on
but wonder why we are
tired or angry, or fractious.

Sit yourself down,
with your wise grandmother,
and let yourself
be a small child again in her arms,
and let what comes, come.

And when the small child
has done her crying,
set her gently on her feet again
and send her softly back out into the world.

And sit as only grandmothers can
calm and grounded
Wise with twinkling eyes
amidst the ups and downs
of this crazy world.

Notes

1. The poems or parts of the poems have been placed with the permission of Rachel Holstead. See www.rachelholstead.net/these-are-not-my-words/.
2. Informal meditation includes walking, sitting, lying down, doing the bowing meditation, yoga, walking, taking a shower or a nap – with attention and in silence.
3. See *Creating a Life of Integrity* (2020) by Gail Andersen Stark.
4. For a suitable book on the life of the Buddha see *The Historical Buddha* (2003) by Hans Wolfgang Schumann.
5. In early Buddhism, a bodhisattva is someone who strives for higher wisdom and a state of perfection or enlightenment, out of compassion for humanity. To achieve this, a bodhisattva works (for many lifetimes) to perfect the ten perfections of mind. In Mahāyāna Buddhism, this concept has been broadened and includes anyone who practices with the intention of a bodhisattva.
6. See *Lovingkindness* (1995) and *A Heart as Wide as the World* (1999) by Sharon Salzberg and *Love 2.0* (2013) by Barbara Fredrickson for more information about the practice of kindness meditation and its effects.
7. We usually translate the verb related to mindfulness in this book as 'to be aware', 'to notice' or 'to acknowledge'. We noticed that the word 'observe' can sometimes be understood as a colder, clinical gaze and therefore easily induces an inner remoteness.
8. For more detailed descriptions of sitting, walking, lying and bowing meditation see *Liberating Insight* (2004) by Frits Koster.

Chapter 2

Wisely and compassionately relating to reactivity

Day 2 – Inquiry meetings with the teacher and patience

On Day 2, we focus on practical posture advice for the sitting meditation. We emphasise the value of kindness towards self and of mindfulness of the breath. We address the value of walking and strolling meditation and explore aspects of regular inquiry meetings either individually or in little groups with the teacher(s) and reactivity in the practice. We introduce patience as a second helpful virtue.

Patience is the best remedy for every trouble.[1]
– Titus Maccius Plautus, Roman playwright (254–184 BC)

Learning to be at ease with unease

Often the beginning of a retreat is about adjusting and adapting to the whole setting of being on retreat. Being in silence with others is quite strange if you are not familiar with it. You notice the urge to say something and then realise that you should be silent. Perhaps at such moments, it is possible to name the desire to talk as such. The advice not to look around is also strange at first and may seem a bit zombie-like. Then there is the food that may not be familiar to you as well as sleeping in a new place. Some meditators come from a busy city and then hear 'the murmur of silence' for the first night. In addition there is the meditation programme where you are completely detached from your television, your computer, work, friends, maybe a partner or family.

Being mindful from moment to moment and having to immediately hear and express sensory stimuli, thoughts and feelings instead of just being immersed in everyday experiences is perhaps the most uncomfortable. You may take your time and 'land' quietly in the silence and in this mode of 'non-doing'. The second day is often marked by tiredness. Life, with all its vicissitudes and unpredictability, usually takes a lot of energy; it is quite an art to live wisely.

There may be external sources of stress. For example, if you work in business you will usually be focussed on targets, whereby you have fulfil key performance indicators such as winning a minimum number of customers or orders every year or every month. And if you don't hit your targets once in a while, it can cause a lot of pressure. Working in health care you may experience fatigue because colleagues have been off sick or due to low staffing levels. You may have had to deal with many deadlines, or being self-employed you will always have the hassle of administration and having to comply with all kinds of tax and other regulations. Then there are the potentially unforeseen problems we may experience in the family or with our health, or unpredictable uncertainties such as regulations surrounding a disease like Corona.

On top of all this, there may be an inner pattern that easily causes stress, such as a strong tendency towards perfectionism when speed is needed or a huge sense of responsibility. Such outer and inner sources of stress result in most meditators simply being very tired at the beginning of a retreat.

Mindful movement and posture advice

Usually, I (Jetty) lead a daily 'mindful movement' session, where we do all kinds of movement exercises together. This is hardly ever done in a more traditional *vipassanā* retreat. However, we noticed that for many this can be very beneficial and a source of relaxation and insight. We usually do this in the morning before breakfast in the meditation room. It is optional though, those who prefer to do their own series of movement exercises, such as yoga, mindful running or tai chi, can do this somewhere else: in their own room, elsewhere in the centre or outside.

> Participant: *I used to meditate on a chair. Now – after the good advice from Jetty – I sit on two cushions and can sit very still. Lovely!*

On Day 2, I usually start in the morning with basic advice on physical posture while sitting. After all, if we sit still for much of the day this can cause all sorts of problems. The suggestions I give are for preventing unnecessary suffering and injury by offering adjustments. We have noticed that many meditators develop all kinds of complaints as a result of practising sitting meditation intensively for several days in a row. These kinds of problems can also develop in top sportsmen and women, also think of the repetitive strain injuries so common in people who have to do a lot of computer work. I explore the following postures: sitting on a meditation cushion, sitting on a meditation bench and sitting on a chair. See video 1 for a short video with posture recommendations.

Sitting on a cushion

Many people have the idea at the beginning that sitting on a cushion should be perfect, with a fully stretched back, on a high cushion. This is fine, but unfortunately, it is not true that the higher the cushion, the better the posture. For many, a high cushion puts more pressure on the knees and can also put more strain on the lower back. A cushion that is not too high can therefore be very wise. Do not sit completely on top of the cushion, but rather on the front half of it, so that the pelvis and the back can adjust more easily.

With regard to the position of the legs: sitting in a full lotus or in a half lotus is perhaps feasible for some, for most it is not, or at most for one or two minutes. Placing both feet in front of each other is easier to maintain for a longer time, but for most, it requires some adjustments, such as one or more supports under the knees. For all options, sitting on a meditation mat is recommended. Some may tend to sit on a very thin sitting mat as is often used for yoga. This can be fine on soft carpets and for the more supple among us. However, if you are on retreat and find that this is very hard, it may be wise and compassionate to use a thicker and more comfortable mat or to bring one from home.

The back can be kept relaxed and straight, the hands can be placed on both knees or in the lap, whichever is comfortable. Many participants welcome the suggestion of placing a cushion in the lap and resting the hands on it. This gives the hands and arms some counter-pressure and there is therefore less pull on the shoulders, this can also make relaxed sitting upright easier. The head is relaxed and upright, with the crown pointing up towards the ceiling, the eyes closed or half-opened with gentle contemplation.

Sitting on a meditation bench

Most meditation benches have a high and a low side. The intention is that you sit on the bench with the low side forward, on your knees with your lower legs under it. To put less pressure on the tops of the feet, you can let your toes rest just over the edge of the meditation mat. The hands may rest on the thighs, but you can also choose to place a high and narrow cushion between both legs and let the hands rest on it, or put the short sides of a shawl or longer cloth under the buttocks and let the hands rest in the hammock thus created, like a sling or pouch for both hands. The latter can also be used when sitting on a cushion.

Sitting on a chair

The Flemish mindfulness teacher Edel Maex once said: 'It seems that the wisdom level in a group increases, as more people allow themselves to sit on a chair'. For some people, sitting in a chair is very wise, for example, if they have varicose veins or hip or knee problems. Another possibility is to alternate as needed: sometimes sitting on a chair and other times sitting on a cushion or bench. When sitting on a chair, the back can be kept away from the chair or against the backrest, whatever is desirable and conducive to a relaxed presence. It may be helpful to place a cushion under the feet if the feet cannot be placed flat on the floor.

Lying down

For participants with specific complaints – such as back pain, fatigue or other limitations that make sitting very difficult – lying down (regularly) can also be very wise. A small cushion under the head and/or a cushion under both knees can be very compassionate. The following applies to all postures: take good care of yourself. A little discomfort can be a valuable object of observation, as will be shown in the next chapter. The practice, however, need not become an exercise in torturing yourself. A mindful change of attitude can sometimes be wise and compassionate.

We have found that the extensive exploration of different sitting and lying positions proves very supportive. In addition to these general instructions, we are always available for individual advice, as described in the previous chapter. After this sitting advice, we usually guide lying, sitting and standing movement exercises, where it is less about *what* you do as a participant and more about *how* you do it, namely with relaxed presence.

> Participant: *I had an insight during posture instruction – after three days of pain I asked for some advice – and learned that I needed to change a tiny bit. I then suddenly realised: 'OK, being gentle is really becoming gentle towards that spot in my back'. Whereas before I was always trying hard to adjust my posture with a strict and determined attitude.*

The breath as a basis

Stick with the stillness
and find calm in your breath...
   – Rachel Holstead, from *Gift*

When we guide the sitting meditation, we usually start with the invitation to make contact with awareness and from there, as needed, to give space to a friendly wish for oneself. After some time, the emphasis then shifts back to developing awareness, as the ability to be aware of an experience while it is being experienced, without having to judge what is happening. If judging happens, then to notice with kindness that there is 'judging' going on. Just being aware of hearing or listening, seeing colour and form, thinking, feeling or whatever arises.

Buddhist psychology speaks of four fields or foundations of mindfulness, which have been depicted by the historical Buddha in the Satipatthāna Sutta or *the discourse on the cultivation of mindfulness*. In all Buddhist traditions, this teaching is considered the most concise text on developing mindful awareness.[2]

We can invite you to practise the first of these four fields or abidings in mindfulness: namely *kāyānupassanā* or awareness of the body. This can be practised in different ways. You can realise this during walking meditation by being aware of the walking body or the movements of the feet. When eating, brushing teeth, going to the toilet and carrying out other daily activities, this can be practised by being aware of what you are doing, or when you are aware of the posture you are in – for example standing or lying down. You can also practice awareness of the body in sitting meditation when you are aware of the breathing movements, for example in the abdominal area or in the chest, or when you are aware of the whole sitting body breathing. There are some very practical reasons why the breath is used as a primary object. Firstly, the breath is always present in our lives, both during the day and at night. In this sense, the breath can be considered an inner friend or ally that we can always fall back on in this life. Especially when we have lost our bearings, making contact with the breath can bring a fundamental peace.

Participant: *The phrase 'And then you can go back to the safe haven of the rising and falling of the belly' often gave me such reassurance!*

Contemporary neuropsychology often uses the term 'interoception', which can be described as the ability to sense signals from one's own body, which is conducive to well-being. The breath can function very well as a 'detective' and give us information about how we feel. Sometimes, for example, a troubled breath can help you become aware that you have become anxious or angry.

Struggling with the breath

Many people, ourselves included, notice that when we start to bring awareness to the breath a familiar inner pattern occurs: the tendency to want to control everything. This pattern is highly developed in many of us and this is understandable from an evolutionary perspective. It reflects a need for security, namely to get and keep a grip on our capricious and vulnerable existence. So although this urge has a very valuable side, it has disadvantages as it costs a lot of energy and can easily grow into an unhelpful habit pattern Many meditators are inclined to judge this inner controller negatively at the beginning but it is actually wiser to congratulate yourself at moments when you notice it as you are becoming aware of something that probably does not only play a role during the retreat.

Noticing this pattern patiently and compassionately, with an understanding inner smile every time it happens, often creates space and will allow the breathing movements to become more natural again. Sometimes it may also give space to temporarily allowing the awareness to be more with the whole body, so that instead of the rising and falling of the abdomen or the chest, you are aware of the whole sitting, breathing body as a basis, almost as if the body breathes itself.

The movements of the breath do not necessarily have to be very deep and slow, however they are naturally occurring in the moment is totally okay. This is aptly expressed in a Chinese proverb: 'You don't have to push the river, it will flow by itself'. Trust in the fact that the breathing movements can present themselves in many forms: slow, fast, deep, superficial, short, long, medium, deep in the abdomen, more in the chest or elsewhere.

We automatically become intrinsically aware of something very fundamental in our lives by quietly observing all these variations, namely that everything is constantly changing. In Buddhism, this is referred to as a valuable existential insight: everything is impermanent. This wisdom, which will be highlighted on Day 4, grows naturally just by watching the breath movements. That is why the Buddha called awareness of the body very commendable and beneficial (*kusala*). As one of my teachers often said: 'We go back to nature'. With practice we come home to the nature of things, and that gives us inner peace and space.

Mindfulness is being on good terms with everything

We invite you to practise the first field of awareness when standing, walking, lying down and during everyday activities such as eating, drinking, putting clothes on or taking them off, opening a door or going to the toilet. As a basic practice you can be aware of the standing posture, the walking or strolling body, the physical movements and activities you are performing, but the practice does not have to become tense and rigid. The awareness of the breath movements may be regarded as a basis when sitting. But every time something else arises, it doesn't mean you've gone off track. You don't have to seek out other experiences, but every time you notice that another sensory stimulus, a thought, a physical feeling, a mood or emotion clearly arises, then the recognition of that experience can be noted, not as a disturbance but as a new experience in the present. All experiences can be integrated in this way and used as a rewarding object of awareness, as and when they become apparent. In this sense, mindfulness is all encompassing, it excludes nothing. And if at any time you find that something disappears of its own accord, fades or slips into the background, or if you sometimes feel that you have somehow become stuck in the practice, then you can always quietly reconnect with the breath movements, or to the sitting, breathing body.

Benefits of walking meditation

As walking meditation is often undervalued, it is perhaps useful to list some of its benefits here:

- Walking meditation or going for a stroll with mindfulness stimulates blood circulation and helps you sit better afterwards.
- It stimulates digestion and prevents constipation.
- It promotes physical fitness.
- Research indicates that walking meditation offers relief from anxiety.[3]

- Walking meditation appears to reduce depressive symptoms.[4]
- In alternation with sitting meditation or doing work that needs to be done seated, walking meditation stimulates inner clarity and flexibility.
- It promotes rest at night and brings more joy into the practice, especially if it is made clear that it may be practised in a playful, relaxed manner.
- We can appreciate having a body and the possibilities it gives us much more.
- It provides a balance between the energy and concentration factors in the practice, which allows meditative insight to grow far better.

> Participant: *While I was practising relaxed and attentive slow walking, I was overtaken (!) by an elderly lady with a walker. She stopped to look at me. I realised that I – much more than she does – have the freedom to go where I want ... at my own pace and direction.*

We sometimes jokingly suggest that just practising sitting meditation is the new smoking. On the second day of meditation, we invite you not to loiter during periods of walking or strolling meditation, but to regard it as equally valuable as sitting meditation, and to explore the speed at which mindfulness can most easily be developed, sometimes leisurely walking outside, and other times, step by step, then more slowly.

> Participant: *At one point the 'relaxed slowing down' hit me. It gave me enormous pleasure to experience how – in full presence of the different parts of the movement – you could walk somewhere and observe how the old habit of 'wanting to get somewhere' tried to compete with the pleasure of moving hurriedly in the now.*

The value of regular inquiry meetings with a teacher

During *vipassanā* meditation retreats, times are usually scheduled when you can share experiences with the retreat leader(s) individually or in small groups. In Thai, this conversation is called *sorb arom*, which can be translated as 'exploring the (meditation) object'. In English, the word *interview* was often used in the eighties. Nowadays it is sometimes explained as 'group or individual practice sessions with the teacher'. In this book, we decided to call it 'mindful inquiry meeting with the teacher'. We want to discuss this extensively in the following pages, because we think it is a very valuable element in a retreat.

We ourselves could easily go on a retreat for a longer period without the guidance of a teacher or retreat facilitator. However, we always look for a centre or situation that offers this option. In some centres, it is offered daily, in others every few days, depending of course on the availability of the teacher and the experience and needs of the participants. Sometimes we look forward to such a conversation, but often we experience it in the same way as 'going to the dentist'. We then experience a tension in advance, which of course can also be acknowledged. Yet we always notice how important these meetings can be, not only from the position of participant but also from the position of facilitator. You could also call them coaching conversations, as the general intention is to promote all the processes of awareness and growing meditative insight and to help the meditator to develop compassion and experience insight. Several valuable aspects can be identified in this mindful dialogue, they are not placed in an order of importance below but they highlight different angles.

Discovering pitfalls and blind spots in the practice

Meditation is a wonderful thing. It seems very simple and in fact it is. Perhaps it is even so simple that in no time at all we fall into familiar patterns and then unconsciously magnify something or approach something as a disturbance in the practice. Often, just verbalising what we encounter in the practice is clarifying and enlightening: what was implicitly present is made explicit. Sometimes this can also lead to what the Buddha called 'putting unhelpful ideas straight'.

The most difficult object of awareness

In my days as a monk, I (Frits) and a young monk from India once visited Ajahn Jumnien, a very friendly and approachable teacher who lives in Wat Tam Sua near Krabi. We asked him what he considered to be the most difficult object to observe. I expected him to answer 'sleepiness' or something similar, as I had many struggles with this myself at the time. But no, he answered without thinking for a long time in Thai: kwahm kit – ideas, beliefs. Gradually, I came to understand more and more why he said this. After all, we are often so identified with inner convictions about ourselves and the world that we hardly realise this.[5]

One of the functions of meetings with the teacher(s) is that, through interpersonal contact, we can be made aware of unhelpful beliefs that we might otherwise remain in for an unnecessarily long time. For example, a meditator recently discovered the value of walking meditation, whereas he had always thought that this was primarily for physical release and to be able to sit properly again.

Checking motivation and commitment

For most meditators, it is a huge quest how to wisely deal with dedication and the use of energy in a retreat. For example, it was very helpful for both of us at the time to be told that we don't have to try so hard and that we can really do the practice with a relaxed attitude rather than seeing it as needing strenuous effort. A good friend and retreat teacher in the Netherlands, Joost van den Heuvel Rijnders (2017), sometimes says that in using effort we can go for the full 60 percent. And sometimes it can be helpful to put a little more energy into the practice and sit a little longer, for example, or to switch to a slightly more detailed walking exercise. Ajahn Chah (2001) compared meditating with driving a car. Sometimes we have to move a little more to the left, sometimes to the right, sometimes a bit quicker, sometimes a bit slower, practice develops skill. Here a retreat teacher can act as a supportive co-driver.

Supporting meditative insight

During a meditation retreat, we walk a path that leads to liberating insight, that passes through various stages of deepening. We become aware of what Buddhism calls the three universal characteristics: impermanence, unsatisfactoriness and uncontrollability. This awareness process is not intellectual but develops in an experiential way that goes beyond reason. This process sometimes requires some extra encouragement and explanation. In South-East Asia, for example, there is talk of a so-called 'mat rolling-up phase', in which meditators feel that the process is not going well suggest deleting because repeated in the same line. I don't think this would affect the layout. Usually, the experiences are not pleasant at all. In fact, this phase is fully part of the process of advancing insight, but without good guidance, we could easily drop out here, roll up the meditation mat and go home or think that 'we are not doing it right'.

Supporting processes of healing

As human beings, we encounter all sorts of things such as illness, loss, conflicts or dilemmas. These difficult human themes occasionally come to the fore during retreats. In theory, we could always just name these and every time this happens, inner space is created. Yet we have noticed, and we also see with retreat participants, that mindfully verbalising what is going on often widens perspective. It is said that 'to name is to tame'. Being able to name something gives space to address it wisely and compassionately. Sharing is healing, it often lets air in to name something sad or painful out loud, which makes it easier for the practice to continue. This is supported by researcher Brené Brown (2007), who has investigated problematic shame. She identifies sharing the painful in a safe environment as one of the most valuable medicines against unnecessary feelings of shame.

In South-East Asia, 40 years ago, there was little room for this; we were supposed to name emotions only as emotions, without going into the content. However, we have noticed that many teachers have started to give more space to these processes and realise that this can be very healing, liberating and supportive in the practice.

Of course, it is important to keep the cultivation of mindfulness central, so that meditation does not become a form of therapy.

The understanding of common humanity

The term common humanity stands for a form of insight that goes beyond 'my world'. For example, it was very reassuring for us to hear that we are not the only ones who encounter a lot of sleepiness. The realisation that we are 'not the only one on earth experiencing something troublesome' has a soothing effect, which can also create more space in dealing with what we easily experience as disturbing or embarrassing. One of the valuable aspects of mindfulness is that it is on good terms with anything. Being regularly reminded of this fact seems to make the practice much smoother and softer.

To promote and deepen this awareness of shared humanity, we therefore offer participants not only individual meetings – of about 15 minutes per person – but also an occasional longer group meeting with the teachers of about an hour. Less experienced meditators in particular seem to gain more understanding and compassion from this, so that the practice can become more profound.

Meditatively relating to physical discomfort

During a retreat, you will be asking a lot of your body, just by sitting still and walking slowly seven or eight times a day. An important part of a meeting with a teacher is to explore how sitting and walking are experienced physically and, if for example knee or back pain gets worse, to explore what is sensible to do and what not to do. In addition, as a participant you may already have specific health problems and adapting wisely to these can be an important part of a regular inquiry meeting with a teacher. A meditative ability that the Buddha called *yoniso manasikāra*: 'skillful assessment' or 'wise attunement' can be used for this.[6]

The inquiry meetings can serve as a valuable opportunity to check how discomfort is handled and whether it is necessary to give extra supportive advice. Sometimes there is a physical complaint or limitation, which should not only be looked at but also needs extra care and wisdom. Sometimes there can also be 'meditation *dukkha*', whereby meditators encounter discomfort as a manifestation of the growing meditative insight that 'there is suffering'. We will return to this later in this book.

The content of an inquiry meeting

What can be discussed in a mindful inquiry meeting with a teacher? First of all, it can be helpful to know that as a retreat participant, you only have to talk about what feels safe and appropriate for you; that you can decide what you talk about and what you prefer not to talk about. An inquiry meeting is a valuable opportunity to ask questions and discuss doubts about the practice. We ourselves were quite cautious in the beginning about asking questions during a meeting with a teacher. However, we both gradually realised that this is an unhelpful learning attitude and began to practise 'stepping over the threshold of diffidence'. Perhaps the following credo fits well with this: 'There are no silly questions'. Not asking questions despite the fact that they clearly concern you is however silly.

Check your attitude

When I (Frits) was meditating in Myanmar a few years ago under the guidance of Sayadaw U Tejaniya (2016a, 2016b), I often heard him say during group exchanges: 'Check your attitude'. What he meant was that we can also be mindful of the state of mind of the moment and the attitude with which we meditate. How is the inner attitude? We can meditate with a gentle and patient attitude or with an impatient attitude, with a relaxed attitude or with a perfectionist attitude, interested or bored ... noticing the inner attitude of what you are experiencing and sometimes checking the inner tone with which you are aware and naming it accordingly appears to be a very valuable field of attention.

Looking back we can conclude that our inner attitude in the first years of meditation was very ardent and the motivation was 130 percent. For example, when walking we would do our utmost to be as detailed and attentive as possible, then when sitting we would often be exhausted and fall asleep. By becoming more aware of these two extremes, more of what Buddhist psychology calls *vīriyupekkhā* naturally arose: balance in the dedication with which we meditate.

An Asian proverb says: 'Tension is who you think you should be; relaxation is who you really are'. We have often noticed how hard many people can be on themselves, we have been so ourselves too. By paying more attention to inner patterns in the practice and by sharing this with a retreat teacher, you can gain insight into your inner attitude in meditation and experience more inner space and freedom.

> Participant: *I sometimes encountered a lot of impatience and restlessness when sitting in silence. The question "How is your attitude towards impatience and restlessness?" in an individual inquiry meeting helped me. I became aware that I was actually quite hostile in my practice and then began to become more allowing, thinking of the poem 'The Guest House' by the Persian poet Jalal ad-Din Rumi, in which all guests are kindly received.*[7] *Paradoxically, in the next meditation(s) I hardly felt this impatience any more, but instead felt a deep inner calm, a peaceful feeling.*

Reporting on one's own experiences

It may very well be that during a retreat you encounter no specific questions or doubts. This does not mean that an inquiry meeting with a teacher would then be pointless. An exchange during a meditation retreat should not be seen as therapy, where the content is mainly about life's problems. Perhaps it is more comparable to a handover report in which nurses, at the end of their shift, report on the ins and outs of patients

Reporting about the sitting meditation

You can for example indicate whether you had an easy or a difficult day and report specific experiences concerning sitting meditation, for example whether you can easily feel the movements of the breath in the abdomen or in the chest. The retreat teacher may then ask exploratory questions, such as whether the rising and falling movements of the breath are long and deep or short and fast, whether the rising and the falling movements are consecutive or whether there is a small pause after the falling movement. Does the breath flow by itself or do you tend to influence the breathing process? Which is easier: being aware of the movements of the abdomen/chest or being aware of the whole sitting, breathing body?

In this way, you can also indicate whether sitting is physically easy or whether you encounter a lot of discomfort, how you have dealt with this, whether you have only been aware of discomfort or whether you have also named it as a sensation, whether you have changed the posture in case of discomfort or whether you have remained seated with it. How have you related to inner reaction patterns, such as worry, desire or impatience?

Another valuable theme may be how you have related to thoughts. It can always be included here that insight meditation is actually a phenomenology: a study of phenomena. The word *vipassanā* means 'to see differently'; we take on a different perspective in the practice, going beyond the content of thoughts and feelings and viewing them more as changing phenomena. For example, in the practice of mindfulness, it doesn't matter whether a judgement about something or someone is constructive or destructive; you only have to notice: 'there is judgement'. You can then report, for example, whether thoughts are easily recognised as thoughts and whether there is patience in noticing thoughts. And what happens to thoughts when you recognise them; do they continue or disappear? Is naming them as, for example, 'thinking', 'judging' or 'planning' helpful or not?

And what kind of emotions and states of mind have you encountered? How did you relate to them? Has there been mindfulness with sensory perceptions such as hearing, seeing or smelling? In this way, you can explore and describe experiences of bodily sensations, physical sensations, thoughts, states of mind and sensory stimuli during sitting meditation.

Reporting on walking meditation and daily activities

Other valuable topics for exchange are walking or strolling meditation and being mindful in daily activities. Themes that might be mentioned here include:

- Do you walk slowly or a little faster? Which is most helpful for you?
- What do you perceive? The movements of the foot or more the whole walking body?

- How do you relate to thoughts, sounds and the like while walking or while taking a mindful walk?
- How is your awareness when getting up, sitting down, eating, drinking, brushing your teeth, going to the toilet, dressing, undressing, washing, showering and the like?

Specific life themes and suggestions for further practice

Finally, issues from daily life can always be discussed if they become evident during the retreat. Sometimes a retreat facilitator will only provide a friendly listening ear, sometimes he or she can give you specific practice suggestions or points of attention for during the practice. They might suggest for example, to relax a bit, to experiment with specific suggestions for walking meditation, to explore alternatives such as cycling meditation when a physical limitation prevents someone from doing the walking meditation. Or to pay more attention to decision-making processes that precede actions we take while eating or in the bathroom or how jogging can be integrated into the practice in a wise way if this is desired. A mindful dialogue with a retreat teacher is an opportunity to receive meditative care and advice.

Befriending discomfort

Many participants experience a certain amount of tension in advance of an inquiry meeting with a teacher. For this reason alone, a regular meeting with the meditation teacher can be of value. This may reflect a familiar pattern in interpersonal contact in daily life as well. It gives you the opportunity to learn to see and name this pattern of, for example, fear of failure, insecurity or the urge to prove yourself; internally or sometimes out loud when meeting a teacher. You train what in psychology is also called voluntary exposure which is a very valuable practice. You learn to be more at ease with discomfort. In addition, a regular mindful exchange with a teacher can also serve as a valuable exercise in mindful communication. As a retreat participant, you can already recognise the preparatory thoughts and inner dialogue preceding a practice meeting at the moments when this happens. Then practising mindful speaking and listening during the meeting itself and finally being aware of the effects or echoes of the meeting afterwards. In this way, we train ourselves in kind and mindful communication through a regular mindful sharing with a teacher, individually or in a group. Loesje, a well-known Dutch fictitious girl who writes posters with critical and/or humorous texts and sticks them in public spaces, puts it so well 'Everyone accepts me as I am. Now it is my turn'.

Mindful inquiry with the teacher on Day 2

More experienced participants we know from previous retreats are often advised at the beginning of a retreat to skip the inquiry meeting on the first full day of meditation and come on Day 3 for a first individual inquiry meeting with the teacher. We do invite participants for whom it is quite new to be on retreat and participants we do not know yet on Day 2 and if possible individually. We try to schedule everyone at least once every two days and new retreat participants every day for an inquiry meeting. The first meeting will of course be to get to know each other and to pay attention to specific 'settling-in problems'. For many, fatigue and stress-related symptoms, such as headaches and nausea, come into play in the initial phase. At the end of the meeting, we explore what would be a desirable format for the meeting for the rest of the week. Less experienced meditators are then suggested to alternate, i.e. to meet in a group of four to eight participants – depending on the number of people attending the retreat – one day and individually the next. In addition, there are always participants who have a clear need for an individual inquiry meeting and then daily or once every two days.

Evening introduction – Reactivity and patience

In the evening in an extensive talk, often called a Dhamma-talk, we touch upon a number of aspects related to the practice of meditation. We incorporate experiences we have listened to during the inquiry meetings. This talk can be understood as a guided sitting meditation or as a time to sit comfortably, listen with awareness and sometimes make a note as needed. In both cases, mindfulness can be further developed. The second day is often experienced as difficult, that is why on the second evening we pay extra attention to 'relating wisely and compassionately to reactivity'.

Story – The dung heap

This story is inspired by and builds on a story by Ajahn Brahm (2005). Imagine the following: you have just bought a beautiful house in a new neighbourhood, on the outskirts of a bigger city. You are very happy with this house and live there happily with your family. After a busy week at work, you cycle back home on Friday afternoon and are surprised to see a huge pile of dung on the pavement right in front of your house. As an experienced meditator, you might think 'shit happens'. But you may also encounter other reactions, which Buddhist psychology describes in detail as five common forms of reactivity:

Option 1. You think, 'I don't deserve this. I want to enjoy life and not be involved with all that smelly manure'. You just manage to get past the dung heap into your house, quickly collect some clothes, money, bank cards and your passport and arrange a last-minute weekend flight to a pleasant southern European resort. You then indulge in all kinds of pleasures all weekend long and hope that the problem will be solved by Monday. This represents the reactivity that can be referred to as desire and attachment.

Option 2. A deep anger and dissatisfaction wells up inside you, first of all directed at the person who dropped this dung heap on your doorstep. Because neighbours have no idea who did this, you also get angry at the neighbours. Or you get angry at yourself, for being stupid enough to buy a house in this stupid neighbourhood.

Option 3. A deep weariness and paralysis overwhelms you. You barely manage to squeeze past the dung heap and lie down on your bed, not feeling up to anything and sinking into lethargy and dullness.

Option 4. A strong sense of worry, fear and anxiety comes over you. You start worrying about what your neighbours will think of you and feeling guilty towards your family, being concerned for them and for your own health if you have to live longer in that stench. This sense of threat makes you uneasy.

Option 5. All these forms of reactivity make you doubt. About your choice to live here, about your own functioning, about the meaning of life. You are left with feelings of hopelessness and powerlessness.

This story reflects possible experiences during this second day of meditation. You may have experienced option 1 in a longing for home, in missing loved ones, in longing for a bed while feeling tired or when all kinds of erotic fantasies occurred to you. You may have felt option 2 at times when you felt dissatisfied, impatient or angry. Perhaps you experienced option 3 in the form of tiredness and dullness, in falling asleep again and again when sitting down, or in not liking the practice and feeling lethargic. Option 4 may have manifested itself in the form of restlessness, worry or guilt about something in your home or work situation. While you may have been confident in signing up for this retreat, you may have experienced option 5 at times when you were unsure whether participation was the right choice, or in doubting whether you would survive this retreat week.

As we tell this story we sometimes ask you to raise your hand and show the appropriate number of fingers if you recognise these options. We see many fingers showing all the options outlined, as all these forms of reactivity are very human. The 'truckload of dung story' does have a happy ending. After all the forms of reactivity have passed through you, you suddenly remember that you have a large garden behind your house and that this garden has hardly been cultivated. You have sown some seeds, but that is all. Realising that the dung heap dumped at your doorstep has no apparent owner, you grab a bucket and patiently scoop up bucket by bucket the manure and scatter it over your garden as compost. Thus, beautiful flowers and nutritious vegetables can emerge from the manure – like lotus flowers from the mud.

We encounter difficult things in many ways, in daily life and, of course, also during a retreat. The Buddha described this as a shared humanity: there is *dukkha*. In the monastic translation of this term, the word is usually split into two compound words. *Du* means disgusting or repulsive, *kha* refers to emptiness or absence of beauty, constancy and pleasure. In the broader translation, *dukkha* is described as 'that which is difficult to bear' or as 'that which moves with difficulty', like a cartwheel moving with difficulty through loose sand. Other suitable translations are 'unsatisfactoriness', 'pain', 'stress', 'vulnerability', 'torment' or 'suffering'. *Dukkha* implies everything that is burdensome, oppressive, conditional and subject to change (Koster, 2004). According to Buddhist psychology, the first thing we experience is directly palpable suffering: *dukkha dukkha*. Examples are physical pain, states of mind that feel unpleasant, mourning or being confronted with an undesirable situation. But the unsatisfactory is also automatically wrapped up in the fact that pleasant things are also not permanent. It is then called hidden suffering: *viparināma dukkha*. For example, you can suffer because you have had to say goodbye temporarily to your partner or children and now miss them. Finally, Buddhism also speaks of life pain or *sankhāra dukkha* and this refers to the conditioned and impermanent nature of everything in life as a source of discomfort. After all, there is always something that demands wise attention: work, health, family, relationships. And just when the wheel of life seems to be running smoothly, we receive another tax assessment, one of the parents suddenly needs a lot of care or we have to deal with a virus that spreads through the world in a destructive pandemic.

Discomfort is an inevitable part of life, we all experience pain and suffering. The moment we experience one of the above five forms of reactivity, we go from trouble to double trouble. If we then condemn the reactivity, it even goes to triple trouble. It is then as if we have scooped up the dung from the pavement, smeared ourselves with it and walked into the house with it.

Vertical and horizontal practice

The five types of reactivity described above are usually represented in Buddhist psychology as *nīvarana*. This word is traditionally often translated as 'hindrance'; unfortunately, this is a term that easily evokes a negative attitude. If we translate this word more precisely, we end up with 'that which is limiting inner freedom' or 'not excelling' or 'not shining'. In our opinion, this is a perspective that can bring about a much more neutral attitude. The word 'hindrance' can easily lead us into the pitfall of a practice in which an ideal state is pursued. We then practice, as it were, with a hidden agenda. That which arises is not okay or not okay enough and needs to be 'better'. This attitude can become constrictive, because unpleasant feelings are simply part of life and will always arise. The higher and more beautiful the ideal image we have of ourselves and our experiences in the practice, the more frustrating the practice becomes when we encounter a lot of resistance, anxiety, restlessness, fatigue or sadness instead of feelings of peace and joy.

A patient and kind recognition of this idealistic way of practising can bring about a shift to a practice in which everything you experience in the moment can be integrated into the practice and can be 'put in a cradle of compassion'. You could also say it's more about a pragmatic 'horizontal' practice that aims to connection with what is happening, rather than an idealistic 'vertical' practice that aims to perfection.[8] We hope it goes without saying that horizontal practice doesn't necessarily mean spending the whole retreat in the lying position. It's just a metaphor.

> Participant: *During the walking meditation I suddenly realised that I could welcome impatience. That immediately took the fear out of my agitation.*

So, mindfulness is about integrating what we experience, where all experiences are given understanding and compassion. There is no need to fight desire, erotic fantasies, resistance, fatigue, restlessness, anxiety or doubt frenetically, but rather to use them as a valuable field for mindfulness, ultimately just as valuable as feelings of peace or the movements of the breath. We are very glad that in the secular Interpersonal Mindfulness Program (IMP) the word 'hindrance' has been changed into 'limiting habit',[9] we also often speak of five 'thieves of the heart' or five challenges.

Here, besides kindness, a second perfection is more than welcome, namely the perfection of *khanti* or patience; patience in the form of tolerance and forbearance. Fortunately, this virtue has been receiving more and more positive attention in society in recent years. After all, aggression, racial intolerance and domestic and random violence have increased considerably and our lives have become frantic. Everything must be done quickly and on time, and impatience reigns supreme. In addition, we grow up with a kind of idea that we can shape the world entirely according to our wishes. In practice, this idea of social engineering leads to much frustration, especially at times when it becomes apparent that we do not have everything and everyone under control.[10]

Dealing with frustration

A young woman once participated in a seven-day retreat. Her motivation turned out to be a feeling of powerlessness. She had two young children and noticed that she sometimes felt like smacking them because of her frustration and anger. She did not want to hit the children, but sometimes she noticed this tendency and was, at least internally, very angry. Talking about it was taboo as she was ashamed of it. During the retreat she became acquainted with a less heavily focused attention, which will be dealt with in the next chapter. She also learned to acknowledge compassionately and at the same time look objectively at the anger and impatience and at her reactions to them. Ten weeks after the retreat we received her evaluation form with the short and powerful statement that she experienced much more space in the contact with the children.

You don't have to be patient to start meditating, but by learning to relate to all the vicissitudes in a retreat in a wise way, more tolerance and patience usually develop automatically. Certainly, in the early stages of a retreat, we often encounter impatience, because at the beginning the experiences can often be unpleasant.

Washing long-worn socks

We sometimes use an image to illustrate the above in the evening talk. Imagine that you have been wearing the same socks for a year. You go jogging with them, you wear them day and night, you never change them. Until perhaps you notice that they have become so smelly that you have to do something about it. Because you don't have a washing machine, you make a bucket of warm to hot water. You put detergent in it and then put the smelly socks in the water. What happens to the water? It turns brown and gooey, of course, and releases an unpleasant odour. This is what happens when we put ourselves in the wash and go on a retreat. We start to feel the tiredness of a hectic life and often the unconsciously stored tension and stress that comes out.

Fatigue

Many report feeling a strong fatigue in the first few days. In this case, we often invite a so-called 'three-track policy'. The first track is to regularly make time and space for rest and, for example, to take an extra nap after a meal, or to go to bed earlier. Allow yourself this. It is not always easy to be human; one of the valuable functions of going on a retreat is to pause and rest. When following the second track, we invite you, if the fatigue and dullness gets stronger, not to do the walking meditation slowly but to make it an effortless, relaxed walk with mindfulness. The third track is to quietly contemplate and internally notice the fatigue as it manifests itself, as 'tiredness, tiredness', 'dullness, dullness', as 'nodding off', as 'sinking in' or 'waking up' – every time fatigue or dullness manifests itself while sitting. The invitation is not to see it as a disturbance but as a valuable object of awareness.

Many meditators feel at the beginning of a retreat as if they have lifted the lid on a cesspool or feel like a mop. In fact, this is very healthy and can be compared to a physical cleaning process. Sometimes it is also accompanied by sweating a lot, not having a very pleasant body odour, having to defecate or urinate more often or feeling very cold or very hot for a few days. Because we usually experience such experiences as unwelcome or threatening, impatience or the desire for more pleasant experiences easily arise. At such times, it is advisable to name the impatience or desire each time it manifests itself clearly. It can bring inner peace and acceptance when we understand that the unpleasant experiences are meditatively very healthy. They may be a sign that meditative cleansing processes are taking place, like a detoxification process.

We sometimes make a comparison with a thrift shop, where people can buy second-hand things. People who don't see the value in objects any more, will go and leave old or used clothing, books and other things at the shop. They consider these worthless. However, new customers who visit the shop will be very happy to purchase these second-hand materials. In a similar way, mindfulness takes advantage of the difficulties that can arise during a retreat and considers these as valuable objects for cultivating wisdom and compassion. This attitude can bring us to a life with more joy, connection and well-being.

Meditative journaling

Through the silence, being attentive without looking for new stimuli, all kinds of processing and healing processes start to occur naturally. Old residues of grief and mourning, disappointment, guilt and remorse are (finally) given space to show and be felt, especially if such feelings have had little room in daily life. We come home, as it were, to what the Dalai Lama sometimes calls 'the ocean of life's sorrow'. It is therefore quite familiar to us that going on retreat can touch upon sorrow and 'thawing tears' to occur in some people. The kind acknowledgement of these feelings proves to be very healing, like a postponed grieving process that can now take place. One participant put it succinctly on an evaluation form: 'Processing the death of a child … my rucksack has become lighter'.

> Participant: *The longer I am silent, the more unfinished business comes to me.*

Sometimes meditators are in resistance when they hear this talk of suffering, as if there are no beautiful things in life! Of course, life also brings very beautiful and pleasant moments and experiences, and these can be very evident during the initial phase of a retreat for some. In any case, it is good to know that there is nothing wrong with you whatever occurs. Most meditators, however, experience more of the 'inner goo' and unpleasant smells at the beginning of a retreat, and this is usually related to the closer acquaintance with the very first teaching of the Buddha: 'There is *dukkha*'. Life brings stress and discomfort. As an English poem of unknown source very aptly expresses

> *It's easy to whistle when life goes by like a song,*
> *But a man worthwhile*
> *is a man that can smile,*
> *when everything goes dead wrong.*

Sometimes meditators think that going on retreat has caused the suffering and get the urge to give up. We know from experience we can be confronted by inner challenges in a retreat. It requires a great deal of courage, patience and wise perseverance and if you can muster up enough of these, a retreat can be very fruitful and we often hear this in the evaluations that participants send us afterwards.

Homesickness

I (Frits) tried two or three times during my first retreat to sneak out. At first I thought I was going crazy from restlessness and wanted to give up. Fortunately my teacher encouraged me to start naming the aversion to the restlessness and to take it a little easier. Only then did I realise how hard I was being on myself all the time. A few days later, thoughts about my home came

> up as a theme, accompanied by all kinds of feelings of regret and guilt because I hadn't connected with my parents for a long time – I was 21 years old and didn't have a good relationship with them. I suddenly felt homesick and wanted to go home. Fortunately, the retreat manager persuaded me to wait a few more days and to visit my parents after the retreat.

Revealing is healing

It can be reassuring to realise that during a retreat we are not creating *dukkha*; it is already there. It's just that we become more aware of it and we start to feel the pain, the restlessness, the stubbornly judging mind, the sadness, the tiredness, and so on much more. We start to experience a miraculously liberating paradox. On the one hand, we become more aware of the reality that there is suffering. But on the other hand, by acknowledging it and also patiently, objectively observing and noticing it, we are not completely fused with it. It is merely observed, as if we were noticing someone else's complaints, which gives rise to an enormous space. In mindful inquiry meetings, we sometimes ask whether it would make sense for a friend who is not usually a complainer to talk to you about something that has been bothering them for a long time. As a rule, the answer is yes; the friend puts the problem on the table and can then take a better look at it. Often we do not even need to respond because the mere act of speaking out loud about something that would otherwise be kept inside makes enough space and can add an insightful dimension: revealing is healing. And this is precisely the expansive quality that arises with mindfulness. By acknowledging and naming the things that keep passing by, a subtle inner space is created that has an insightful effect. We become, as it were, our own psychologist or life coach. We don't achieve this by putting a lot of energy into interpreting and analysing our meditation experiences, but by simply being present with what we experience, acknowledging and not identifying with them. In this way, we develop freedom within suffering. Or as the Buddha once said: 'I teach one thing, namely suffering and the end of suffering'.

Kindness meditation – Yourself, a benefactor and loved ones

We usually conclude the second day with a sitting meditation, drawing your attention to the possibility of practising kindness meditation in the second half of this last sitting period. The emphasis here is first of all on sitting with awareness, then making room for a kind or compassionate wish for yourself and then integrating a benefactor into the practice. A benefactor is someone who embodies wisdom and compassion for you, and who would wish you well if you met him or her. It can be an important person in history, such as Mother Theresa, Nelson Mandela, the Dalai Lama or Martin Luther King. It could also be an important person in your own life, such as a teacher or a grandfather or grandmother who was always there for you. Or you can integrate a loved one into the practice. Someone from your family or circle of friends, a beloved colleague, someone who is living or who has already died. Imagine that this person who is important to you or dear to you is in front of you, connect with him or her, and then gently repeat kind wishes, e.g. 'May you experience safety', 'I wish you happiness or wholeness' or 'May you be at ease'.

Such general kind wishes can be very appropriate, but you may also find that a more specific wish that spontaneously arises is more appropriate. In this way, you can involve several beloved persons or even favourite pets in the practice. If it is helpful, you can sometimes put one or both hands on your belly or heart area for a while and take the wish to heart physically, as it were. In this way, you can sit for a while, with kindness and mindfulness. With the wise words about patience by Rainer Maria Rilke (1929) in *Letters to a Young Poet:*[11]

One must allow things their own quiet undisturbed development
which comes from deep within;
which cannot be forced or accelerated by anything...

One must have patience with the unresolved in our heart
and try to cherish the questions themselves, like closed rooms
or books written in a strange language.

It comes down to living everything.
If we live the questions we may live slowly but surely
without noticing, one day towards the answer.

Notes

1. *The Comedies of Plautus* was published in 1881 by George Bell and Sons in London and translated by Henry Thomas Riley (1816–1878).
2. Various free downloadable English translations of the Satipatthāna Sutta can be found on internet or in *Satipatthāna* (2003) by bhikkhu Anālayo.
3. See https://journals.sagepub.com/doi/10.1177/0890117117744913 for a study of the effects of a short bout of walking and meditation on anxiety among young adults.
4. See https://liebertpub.com/doi/10.1089/acm.2013.0205 for a study on the effects of walking meditation on depression, functional fitness, and vascular reactivity.
5. Ajahn Jumnien's life story can be found in *Living Dharma* (2010) by Jack Kornfield.
6. In Insight Dialogue and in the Interpersonal Mindfulness Program, as described in our book *Mindful Communication* (2023), the fourth guideline for interpersonal mindfulness practice refers to *yoniso manasikāra* and is called 'attune to emergence'.
7. See also page for this famous poem.
8. See *Mindfulness-Based Compassionate Living* by Erik van den Brink and Frits Koster.
9. In our book *Mindful Communication* (2023), Erik van den Brink wrote a chapter on the Interpersonal Mindfulness Program (IMP).
10. Allan Lokos (2012) has written an interesting book on this topic called *Patience. The Art of Peaceful Living.*
11. See R. M. Rilke (1929) Briefe an einen jungen Dichter (own translation)

Chapter 3

Being aware in a relaxed way
Day 3 – Mindfulness and generosity

On Day 3, we cover awareness of bodily sensations, focused and receptive attention, and how to practice yin and yang compassion. We describe the value of relaxation in walking meditation and introduce standing meditation. We cover mindfulness of thoughts and generosity as a next perfection.

Take rest. A field that has rested gives a bountiful crop.[1]
—Ovid, Roman poet (43 BC–AD 17)

Participants often experience the first two days as difficult. After waking up, sitting in silence and mindful movement lying on the mat, after breakfast on Day 3, we guide kindness meditation in order to help participants unwind. In the previous chapter, we used the metaphor of washing some old socks, so we can think of the kindness meditation as the fabric softener. We invite participants to casually place more emphasis on the practice of kindness at times – when sitting or walking – connecting the wish more closely to themselves. But once in a while, it can also be very appropriate to make a 'detour' to a kind wish for a dear one, afterwards returning to the practice of mindfulness.

Mindfulness of physical sensations

A part of the body or bodily sensation is always available as a grounding object during the retreat. Whilst walking or running, attention can be directed to the movements of the feet or the awareness of the whole walking or running body. When sitting or lying down, we can be aware of the breathing movements or of the sitting or lying body, when standing, we can sense the standing posture, when carrying out physical actions, such as eating, drinking, going to the toilet, taking a shower, going up or down the stairs or opening doors, the moving or performing body can always be observed as an anchor just by simply being aware or lightly accompanying it by a subtle naming. In sitting, for example, as 'out', 'in' …'out', 'in' … or as 'rising', 'falling' …'rising', 'falling' … But when you use this naming technique, allow it to happen only very lightly, as a gentle whisper confirming what is happening in the moment. Perhaps you can experiment with not seeing the sensation as 'mine' but as a human experience that we do not need to claim as 'me' or 'mine'.

So, we can use the expansion and contraction of the abdominal wall or the chest for grounding the attention, but there is no need to get obsessed with this, seeing it as the goal of the practice and therefore as an onerous task. Every time something else arises clearly of its own accord or takes over as it were, then this new experience can become the focus and we can note it as an experience, as long as it arises clearly. There is no need to regard anything as a disturbance as all experiences are valid and can be integrated into the practice. You will often encounter physical discomfort, for example, itching, tingling, tension in the back or a numb leg. The Buddha called this part of a second field of awareness, next to body awareness: *vedanānupassanā* or awareness of bodily sensations.[2]

Many retreatants experience the beginning of a retreat as physically more demanding. Apart from the physical 'loosening' of stress and tension, the body has not usually got used to the rhythm of the retreat by the third day. You will always be able to notice all kinds of discomfort in various forms and degrees anyway. Having a body has a beautiful side, because it enables us to fulfil all kinds of wishes and needs but it also has a darker side, because it does not always function smoothly.

For example, you may notice numb legs or some back or knee problems. You will need to have patience here too so that these sensations or reactions to them are not seen as a disturbance but as an object of meditation each time they occur. Sometimes, for example, a numb leg may give rise to anxiety or irritation. Our meditation teacher Ajahn Asabha from Myanmar often gave a very simple suggestion to notice what is in the foreground in the present. Sometimes that is the physical sensation itself, at other times the reaction. The awareness is with both experiences. The American meditation teacher Jack Kornfield, author of, among other things, *The Wise Heart* (2015), says the following about this:

> "I always thought that – I should meditate like a samurai warrior in order to become free. But now I understand that we can also practice like a devoted and caring parent of a newborn child. It requires just as much energy but has a completely different character. It is more about compassion and presence than having to overcome an enemy in a fight."

Focused and receptive mindfulness

It can also be valuable to realise that we can be mindful in different ways, distinguishing between focused mindfulness and receptive mindfulness. Sometimes it can be valuable to focus our attention explicitly on something. In daily life focused attention is very helpful in performing a complex task like writing an important text. On retreat reorienting and focusing can be very helpful, for example when you feel that you have lost your way. You can then bring your attention consciously to the movements of the breath and this will help you to focus to reset internally. However, if you have the idea that you should always be doing this, going on retreat can become quite exhausting as it will take more effort.

When we practise receptive mindfulness we don't specifically focus our mind on an object but we are simply aware what happens by itself and acknowledge what we receive through the senses. When we practice focused attention there will be more 'doing-mode', when we practise receptive mindfulness there will be more 'being-mode'.

However, many people experience physical sensations in a focused 'doing-mode', usually unconsciously and with a hidden agenda: 'If I focus my attention on this discomfort, maybe it will go away'. Unfortunately, mindfulness is not a magic 'Harry Potter wand' with which we can perform all kinds of disappearing acts. Sometimes something disappears spontaneously and of its own accord when we observe it, but often it does not. And the intention of mindfulness practice is not to make things disappear, but rather to notice what is happening and maybe relate to it a bit differently.

> Participant: *I've experienced that my tinnitus – though present – can also fade into the background and I can be at peace with it.*

You can develop awareness of physical sensations, just being aware of them, or if you find that this supports the practice, lightly naming them as experiences. If a word like 'pain' easily arouses a rather negative reaction or connotation in you, then you can explore a more neutral-feeling word and name the experience, for example, as 'feeling' or as 'sensing'.

Yin and yang compassion in sitting with discomfort

Kristin Neff and Christopher Germer (2019) talk about 'yin compassion' and 'yang compassion'. Sometimes it is possible to practise the courage and fortitude of 'yang compassion' or 'fierce compassion' as it is sometimes called in Tibetan Buddhism. You then decide to sit quietly with the discomfort you are experiencing and do not immediately change your posture. It might be reassuring to know that we have never experienced a numb leg not waking up any more after sitting for 30 or 45 minutes. And doing the bowing meditation after a sitting period, preferably with curled toes, usually gets the blood circulation going again in no time.

However, sometimes we need the gentleness of 'yin compassion', for example when you notice that you are too hard on yourself. Or when you have varicose veins or another physical limitation, or when your legs or knees start to ache more often while walking. Then you will need the courage to be gentle with yourself. In a feedback form, a participant expressed concisely how yin and yang can be related like communicating vessels.

> Participant: *And I signed up for an extra individual practice meeting on the last day without hesitation. To me, those are great examples of yang and yin compassion: brave outward, gentle inward.*

Be careful of 'No pain, no gain'

Most retreat leaders will agree about the value of a little discomfort. However, for many there can be a tendency to be 'strong and tough', seeing a retreat more as an opportunity for practicing 'no pain, no gain' and doing the sitting meditation with the idea of having to sit through everything. We do not subscribe to the idea 'the more you suffer, the more liberated you become'.

For us, it was very enlightening to hear one of our teachers, Ajahn Somsak, say that the purpose of sitting meditation is not to sit as properly and obediently as possible, but to develop awareness. We have already mentioned this on Day 1, but when a physical sensation becomes unbearable or when there is a genuine physical problem, then it is good to realise that you can always change the posture. It will be helpful though, to notice the inner struggle and/or the desire to change the posture first. Then, the bodily movements can be observed and noted, as a mini-practice of 'mindful movement', until a new sitting or lying posture is found. In this way, you might practise 'yin compassion' by abandoning the posture, but you don't lose the most important thing in a retreat, which is being mindful.

Walking meditation – A relaxed attitude and standing meditation

On the third day, we invite you to continue with the advice given earlier, with an extra emphasis on being relaxed when walking. We like to remind participants here of the two modes of focused and receptive attention as described above by inviting retreatants to do the walking meditation in a relaxed and receptive way. Sometimes conscious focusing can be very valuable to collect the scattered mind, but in general, it does not have to become an onerous concentration exercise. As one participant put it, 'I learned how to stroll'.

Insight does not always need to be hard work

Early on, we were urged by some teachers to do our best and 'anchor the attention deeply in the now-object'. It was very liberating to meet Sayadaw U Tejaniya in 2006. He made it clear to me (Frits) in a very simple way that for years I had unconsciously been trying much too hard. At first this refreshing perspective was quite painful but at the same time very liberating: insight is not necessarily gained by extreme effort.

Finally, we would also like to point out the possibility of standing for a while, for example at the beginning of a period of walking meditation or when you notice that you have started to practise on automatic pilot. Standing can also be of value when waiting in line for a meal buffet or sometimes as an alternative to sitting in case of dullness or specific physical limitations. The sense of standing can be perceived as coming from within for example, the contact of the feet with the ground, specific (leg) muscles needed for standing, the awareness of weight that can sometimes be light and other times heavier, or simply an awareness of the whole body standing.

If standing takes place for a longer period of time, then the breathing movements can also naturally come more into the foreground. In which case, just observe the breathing movements, while at other times observing the awareness of the standing breathing body and at moments when other experiences, such as seeing, hearing, thinking or feeling present themselves, then these can be acknowledged as experiences. In this way, we can practise 'standing with awareness' for a short or sometimes a longer period of time.

I (Jetty) sometimes advise participants for whom standing still for a longer period of time can become difficult or painful to gently move their body weight back and forth with relaxed attention from one leg to the other like a meditating elephant. This proves less stressful than standing completely still and can sometimes offer a valuable alternative to walking or running meditation.

Inquiry meetings – Searching for an inner balance

Naturally, all sorts of themes arise in the inquiry meetings on Day 3. One of the things that many participants are dealing with, besides the fatigue that is still present for many, is the search for an inner balance and encountering something in themselves that can playfully be called 'the hard worker'. This pattern naturally has a very valuable side and ensures that we can function and perform well. However, the dark side of that is when it makes us exhaust ourselves. Often, it is a pattern with which we are so caught up in internally that we do not see it clearly. That is why we often have meditators do two experiments in an inquiry meeting.

Exercise: Two experiments

Close your eyes and sit down comfortably, with your hands on your thighs. We are going to do two small experiments, not choosing in terms of 'right' or 'wrong', but rather inviting you to see what you experience.

Experiment 1

We would like to ask you to bring all the attention that you have ready at the moment into one of your two hands, so that you crawl, as it were, all the way into that hand, right into the fingertips. Then, very slowly, inch by inch, raise that hand and arm about half a metre, staying with all your attention in that hand. You can also name this, as 'lifting', 'lifting'; while staying completely and with all your attention in that hand. When the hand has been lifted about half a metre, you can move it slowly downwards again in the same way, while staying completely and with all your attention in that hand. With all your attention, lower the hand or arm until the hand is again resting on the leg. You can then sit for a moment without having to do anything, being aware of the resonance of this first experiment.

Experiment 2

You can now slowly raise your other hand half a metre. But you do this in a different way: not focussing all your attention into the hand, but just being aware of the wish to lift that hand, as if the hand goes up by itself. All you have to do is to be aware that there is an upward movement. When the hand and arm have been lifted about half a metre, you can bring them down again in the same way, without being completely in the hand, but merely being aware of the downward movement, until the hand is resting on your leg again. You may feel the resonance of this second experiment for a while and open your eyes again.

Meditators can experience significant differences in the two styles of observation. We often hear things like 'The first experiment felt very heavy, whereas the movement with the other hand felt as light as a feather'. Or 'It took a lot more effort to lift the first hand, it felt very heavy'. 'I had no idea where I was during the first experiment, I was completely absorbed in the hand'. 'I felt quite tense and I also noticed that I tensed all kinds of muscles in experiment 1. 'I found the first experiment very tiring'.

When I (Frits) then ask which observation style is most often used, for example in walking meditation, most meditators report that they are initially inclined to observe as they did in the first experiment. This is how we ourselves started. I sometimes say, jokingly, that it's a miracle that I didn't burn out in those early days. I was so motivated and wanted to do my best so much that I was just trying very hard, without really and evenly observing what was happening. We find that when they start 90 per cent of all meditators have a tendency to try much harder and to concentrate more deeply than necessary. It is also in our nature to do our best, to try to do everything as perfectly as possible and this can be very helpful, e.g. in writing a book. On the other hand, it also has a downside, and we believe that the unconscious tendency to put in extreme effort and concentration are important inner factors that can exhaust and burn us out.

It is usually very liberating for meditators to hear that they do not need to focus excessively and do their utmost to get and stay completely with the foot, belly or whatever anchor is the focus of our attention. It is enough just to be aware of the movements and to note them lightly, and this of course also applies to the awareness of sounds, smells, physical sensations and other experiences.

In other words, sometimes it can be helpful to focus the mind, especially when performing a complex task. However, the more relaxed awareness shown in the second experiment may be sufficient for the practice of insight meditation. As my first meditation teacher once put it with a smile during a lecture to western health professionals: 'Western people are always looking for depth, but actually in *vipassanā* meditation we are doing something very superficial'. The paradox in this approach is that much more 'natural' or existential insight can arise if we do not focus deeply but are naturally aware of what is happening.

> Participant: *For the first time, lighthearted, playful, soft and friendly in attention and awareness. The relief, I have put away my samurai and wonder – can it really be like this?!*

In management training courses participants are often advised to take half a day off each week and just do what they feel like doing. It is precisely at such moments that a shift appears to take place from driven doing and being focused to a relaxed meta-perspective, and then new possibilities suddenly become visible of their own accord. For many people, the greatest creative insights take place during holidays. Psychologically, this has everything to do with the shift in emphasis that takes place at such moments, from the focused, willpower-driven observation (first experiment) to the broader awareness that something is taking place (second experiment). In insight meditation, you don't have to worry about whether or not you are concentrating hard enough. Simply being aware of what is happening to or within us and possibly naming or noticing it internally as a phenomenon, is the right amount of concentration. This moment-to-moment concentration, which in Pali is called *khanika samadhi*, is light in nature and can easily move from object to object. It is supple and pliable. It can be compared to someone who is surfing the sea waves, always using and riding the highest wave that comes along.

Different views in Dhamma-land

There is some disagreement on this subject and we have come to recognise two different currents. In one school teachers adhere very clearly to the Visuddhimagga. This great commentary was written around AD 400 by the Sinhalese monk Bhadantacariya Buddhaghosa. It was translated into English by bhikkhu Ñanamoli under the title *The Path of Purification*. The book is considered in the Theravada

Buddhist tradition as one of the most detailed and respected reference works in the field of meditation. The author beautifully gives clear definitions of all kinds of mental factors. In this way he, for example, describes mindfulness as a mental capacity, first analysing the root of the word and using the term *saranti*, which implies 'remembering'. As a characteristic of mindfulness, he mentions the Pali term *apilapana lakkhana*. This term was translated by Ñanamoli as 'non-floating' and therefore as 'plunging into the object'. The function of mindfulness, in this description, is 'non-forgetfulness', while it manifests as 'protection' and as 'a state of mind in which an objective field is confronted'.

Teachers generally agree on most of the elements of this definition. 'Remembering' is fairly unanimously explained as remembering what is happening in the present. Non-forgetfulness is explained as now-awareness or presence of mind. The manifestation as protection refers to not doing stupid things or letting accidents happen from lack of awareness, from not paying attention in traffic, for example. It also refers to the absence of craving, hatred and ignorance in every moment of awareness. We will pay much more attention to this later in this book. The last aspect, somewhat cryptically worded as 'confronting or being face-to-face in relation to an objective field', refers to witnessing what is occurring in the present, without identifying with it, having to repress it or going into the content of what is experienced.

Teachers of the former movement express this active aspect much more explicitly and actively. Sayadaw U Pandita from Myanmar, for example, would describe this as 'attacking the object without hesitation'; he sometimes made a comparison with soldiers, who overcome the enemy troops in a lightning attack. There is then a much more active aspect in this than merely being aware of what is happening at the moment. Teachers who adhere to such an interpretation then often add to this by describing the term *apilapana lakkhana* as 'not wavering or staggering but sinking or diving into the object' in other words, plunging into the object.

The German monk and scholar bhikkhu Anālayo (2003) observes in his book *Satipatthāna*, that this is possibly much more a description of focused attention, in other words mindfulness with a large dose of effort and concentration.

Teachers who appear to belong to the other camp, such as Ajahn Asabha, Ajahn Somsak and Sayadaw U Tejaniya have always recognised the value of the Visuddhimagga in their guidance, but have not taken it as their main guide. Rupert Gethin (1992), for example, observes that Buddhaghosa may have misinterpreted the word *apilapeti*, which refers to diving or sinking into the object. This is much more a characteristic of focused concentration, whereas the original scriptures use the term *apilapati* (or *abhilapati*). The second term means 'to remember something or someone'; just as we might give a friendly reminder. So different interpretations or translations are possibly the cause of much confusion in the *vipassanā* world.

We found the above knowledge very helpful as it confirmed our suspicions that we were putting far too much energy into being as focused as possible. This realisation has made space for much more playfulness and relaxation in the practice and we also see this in retreat participants. Perhaps it can be compared to learning by job shadowing. In many professional training courses, this is part of the training. Potential or new employees are asked to accompany an experienced professional and are allowed to observe and sometimes ask questions about the work but they have no responsibility and do not have to do anything themselves. This may illustrate the right attitude when we meditate, relaxed and balanced. We need not judge. We need not push anything away. We do not need to focus especially hard. All we have to do is contemplate and make it our art to do this continuously, from waking up to going to bed. We learn to live with effortless effort.

Caring for the body

In addition to the regular enquiry meetings with Frits about the meditation practice, I (Jetty) provide daily consultations for participants who are struggling with physical posture. All they have to do is to put their name down on a list. From a professional background as a physiotherapist and also from my personal experience with a vulnerable back, I explore one-on-one with participants how the practice can become accessible. I have noticed that many participants find it difficult to take care of their limits in this and can harm themselves. I first explore the physical posture, listen to what exactly the complaints are, and then suggest possible adjustments, such as sitting on a lower cushion or the use of an extra cushion under one or both knees, how to hold the hands and arms in the case of shoulder problems or how sitting on a meditation bench can become easier. I also invite people with back problems or who are struggling with autoimmune conditions to regularly do part of a sitting period or the whole sitting period lying or sitting on a chair. We have noticed that many appreciate this very much and also give us positive feedback about this in evaluations.

> Participant: *I don't ask for help easily so I had to cross a barrier, but it was really special how the practice suddenly became a lot easier after a small suggestion from Jetty.*

As human beings, we have limitations and blind spots. We can't perceive our own sitting position well from the outside and can often detect something in someone else more easily than we can in ourselves. Therefore, we offer this extra physical care and find that it contributes to a much smoother meditation process.

Evening talk – Relating to thoughts and generosity

Even the third day is not easy for many, but as a meditator, you may notice that there are more periods when the mindfulness is just there, without having to make any effort. This is what American meditation teacher Joseph Goldstein (2016) calls 'spontaneous' or 'unfabricated' awareness, because it arises naturally. In addition, there are times when you practise meditation more as a technique and you are then engaged in 'fabricated' awareness. Both are valuable; sometimes it comes naturally and sometimes it takes a bit more effort. However, in general, the invitation for this day is also to meditate with minimal effort, so to put less emphasis on trying to achieve something and more on bringing kind attention to what arises by itself.

In this talk, we would like to draw attention to an area of life that is probably very often in the foreground, but which has been less addressed in the guidance so far. The Buddha summarised this area as *cittanupassana*: awareness of mental processes. This area then forms a third field or abode for awareness, after the body and feelings. This third field could be distinguished into three fields of experience: thoughts, states of mind and inner patterns or attitudes – mindsets which arise from and are related to thoughts and states of mind.

Three characteristics of thoughts

When we ask average people what they associate with the term 'meditation' they often mention things like 'freedom of thought', 'letting go of thoughts', 'being zen' or 'not being in my head'. The average person seems to experience about 45.000 thoughts in a day; many cultures live under the influence of the French philosopher René Descartes (1596–1650), who said 'Cogito, ergo sum': 'I think therefore I am'. The rational has taken an important place in our way of life, while at the same time, many people suffer from it. You will encounter all kinds of thoughts in a retreat for example planning, remembering, judging, fantasising, explaining, talking to yourself, brooding. If your intention was to finally stop thinking, this is of course very disappointing. You have started meditating out of a desire for a quiet life and only come across unwanted inner chatter, pondering and arguing. This is also how we started out: as restless, tyrannised by thoughts jumping all over the place. They appear as a purely mental process (mental thinking) but sometimes also as an image (visual thinking) and have specific characteristics.

Thoughts are very fleeting

Thoughts often arise very quietly, without us realising it. Just like cookies on the internet, which slip into a computer or laptop invisibly. And when we notice them, they often immediately evaporate.

Thoughts can have an intoxicating power

Until I (Frits) started to have more ethical awareness, I did a lot of fishing as a boy. I could distinguish different kinds of fish. Some fish were very easy to catch; they seemed to see the bait and take the bait impulsively. Other fish seemed more cautious. They first swam around the hook but were then enticed to bite. A third and final category seemed to see the bait, but also the fishing line in the water and the silhouette of the fisherman on the bank. They were intelligent enough not to take the bait and just swam past it.

If you now see the bait as thoughts, then it can be said that we as humans are usually like the first category of fish. We unconsciously get directly caught up in the contents of thoughts that occur to us. If a thought has a pleasant atmosphere, then this may be pleasant, then we dream about a nice holiday or something entertaining. What makes this tricky is the fact that our entire nervous system is programmed by evolution to fight off a possible threat as quickly as possible than to find deeper happiness.

The American neuropsychologist Rick Hanson (2009, 2014) states that our brain works like Velcro for negative experiences and Teflon for positive experiences so they don't stick. This is also called the default mode network in our brain. It causes us to be more inclined to fret, grumble, complain and think up doom and gloom scenarios, even when this is not necessary, and that happy or even blissful thoughts are less absorbing. In secular mindfulness training it is often said: 'Thoughts are not facts'. What is actually meant is that although thoughts can sometimes reflect facts, or shared realities, their content is not always very reliable. We are quick to believe in the truth of the content of a thought, such as 'I am no good', 'I will never do well enough' or 'It is my fault'.

We cannot control thoughts

We do not appear to be able to control thoughts. They often, if not most of the time, just come up, whether we want them to or not. Just try not to think about a pink elephant for a minute. In a way, thoughts are like mosquitoes in the bedroom. If we don't have a mosquito net or other defences they will keep coming at us. And even if we chase them away, they just come back, because they cannot help but seek blood. In a way, thoughts are like mosquitoes. The more we fight them off, the more they bother us. We can get away from real mosquitos by crawling under a mosquito net but this is not possible with thoughts.

Thoughts and relationality

Whether we like it or not, thoughts come up; they are part of life. The question is what do we do with them? The Buddha often spoke about following a middle way, not repressing anything but at the same time not being overwhelmed by what we experience. Jon Kabat-Zinn, the founder of the eight-week mindfulness training Mindfulness-Based Stress Reduction (MBSR), regularly calls mindfulness a training in 'relationality', emphasising how we relate to everything and how we can be with integrity, with wisdom and with kindness to ourselves and to others'.

This can also be linked to the many thoughts that come to mind. We can regard them as unwanted mosquitoes or troublemakers in our life and try to 'pick them off' or get rid of them constantly, or we get completely caught up in the content of the thoughts and thus end up in a frenzy of brooding and compulsive thoughts.

In the second case, we quietly integrate them as a field of awareness each time a thought arises, without needing to do anything else but just to acknowledge them as thoughts passing by.

> **The rat family**
>
> *When I (Frits) was meditating and studying as a Buddhist monk in Southeast Asia, I once stayed for three months in a meditation centre in Thailand during the rainy season. Near me, on the edge of the centre, was a beautiful little wooden hut. It was surrounded by a stream and an attractive bamboo forest; I thought it would be lovely to stay there.*
>
> *When the monk who had meditated there left after the rainy season, I saw my chance and asked permission to stay there for a few more months. This was granted and with great joy I moved into the beautiful hut. Around eleven o'clock in the evening, I went to sleep. About an hour later I was woken up. Above my head I heard a very loud noise. I did not know what it was and felt unsafe. It was noisy all night I didn't sleep a wink.*
>
> *The next morning, I went on an alms round and came back to eat. I looked at the ceiling on the veranda again and suddenly saw a large rat tail through a little gap in the ceiling. I felt a great deal of panic and nausea. I had always considered rats to be the most frightening creatures. All kinds of scenarios ran through my mind, most of them about planning to leave. Then suddenly another reaction came up. The rat had undoubtedly moved in here before me. If I gave the rat food, he would surely not attack me, maybe it would spare my life. I fished a piece of meat out of the alms bowl. With knees wobbling, I stretched my arm up and held my slightly shaky hand with the piece of meat between my fingers close to the hole in the ceiling. After a few seconds, a rat's snout appeared and to my surprise and relief, the rat did not bite! It only sniffed at the piece of meat and then withdrew.*
>
> *'Ah, lucky it is not a meat-eater ', I thought. While I had always thought that rats preferred (human) meat, this rat did not like meat. Somewhat relieved, but certainly not relaxed, I grabbed a green bean from my alms bowl and decided to give it another try. To my great surprise and excitement, the rat did not bite me this second time either. It sniffed again at the food, took the bean very calmly with her paw between my fingers and withdrew again. I was totally moved.*
>
> *From that moment on, I started feeding the rat every day. My fear and loathing disappeared more and more and at night the racket above my head bothered me less and less. A couple of weeks later a very small rat suddenly dived down through the hole in the ceiling and shot away across the veranda. That night it was completely silent; the family had left. I missed them and never forgot the adventure.*[3]

Viewing thoughts as small flows of energy and information

Professor of psychiatry and author Daniel Siegel (2011) describes how, as a medical student, he could not find an answer to what a good definition for the human psyche might be. After many years of searching, he defines the mind as 'an embodied relational process that regulates the flow of energy and information'. This definition fits very well with the mindful handling of thoughts. We do not have to fight them or follow their contents, but we can develop the ability to greet them as small flows of energy and information, without having to grasp or fight these flows. Mindfulness is not about stopping thinking but about noticing what is going on in the moment, in body and mind, so thoughts can be used as a valuable field for awareness. You can merely be aware of them, or if this helps you to be aware, you can very lightly accompany the awareness with a subtle inner noting. In this way, you can create, as it were, inner folders for thoughts that you name, such as 'judging', 'planning', 'remembering', 'commenting' or simply as 'thinking'.

With a limited understanding of peace, you will be looking for moments when you feel very peaceful in the practice. If you are lucky, this will happen once in a while, but probably less often than when you meditate with a broader understanding of peace, which is being at peace with what is happening to or within you at the moment. When you approach 'your' thoughts in this way, they no longer get in the way, but are transformed into a useful object of meditation. According to Buddhist psychology being aware of thoughts is just as valuable as being aware of the breath or of emotions.

In this way, we can befriend ourselves and life in general. Thoughts are then allowed to simply be there and can be integrated into the practice, each time acknowledging them as a phenomenon of awareness. Paradoxically, they then appear to become calmer and less tyrannical. Inner freedom is the result.

> Participant: *At a certain point it became clear to me that what I encountered was always trying to solve or analyse with my mind. When I started to notice this simply as 'thinking', 'thinking', 'thinking', I very easily came back to the breath. So it was very simple, while it had always seemed so complicated to me!*

The power of generosity

The third of the ten perfections ties in nicely with the story above: generosity or *dāna*. In Buddhism, this virtue is much talked about; in the classic list of ten perfections, it is even mentioned first. The Buddha gave the reason that ordinary people, even when they have never meditated, can still experience a glimpse of inner freedom or enlightenment if they feel the joy and lightness of heart that arises when they are generous. Generosity can be practised in many ways. In Asian countries, for example, it is practised in the generosity of lay followers towards monks and nuns and in the great hospitality felt in the culture. We can also practise it when we support a good cause financially or by volunteering, when we give wise counsel or attention, when we magnanimously give someone the right of way in traffic, when we encourage someone, when we forgive ourselves or others for something, and sometimes even when we kindly set ourselves or others limits.

In Buddhist psychology, generosity is defined as an altruistic attitude from which we give and are thus, at least temporarily, free from desire and attachment. Usually, we live like flies that are irresistibly attracted by the wonderful smell of a fly strip and then cling to it and lose their freedom. Desire has such stickiness and generosity is free from it. Generosity is not coercive or claiming and manifests as a non-clinging presence. The direct cause for generosity is the availability of something that we can share.

> Participant: *Suddenly I realised that I may carry this baby in my belly for a while. And that I will take care of this child. But it is not only my child. It is for all of us. I am slowly giving it to the world. It makes me sad, but I also find it very beautiful.*

Generosity brings lightness to life and often comes back to us spontaneously, without us wishing it. Three types of generosity are described in Buddhist scriptures: giving like a beggar, a merchant and like a king. In the first case, it is giving something that you wanted to get rid of anyway, which is the easiest form. In the second case, we are talking about strategic giving, with the hidden desire for a good name, fame or wealth, for example, wrapped up in it. It is an investment in the future. There is nothing wrong with this in itself. The Dalai Lama, for example, once said that kindness to others is a healthy form of egoism. If we are always blunt and disrespectful to our neighbours, they will be less inclined to help us when we need help. What goes around comes around.

If we give like a king or queen, we do not need anything in return and we give because we have more than enough and want to contribute to the happiness of others. It goes without saying that the last form of generosity is the most admirable. One of the special characteristics of the meditation process is that it focuses on developing awareness, but in a very natural way, other beneficial factors also flourish. Just like loving-kindness, generosity has two forms of expression, an active and a subtle non-active form. The active form expresses itself as generosity in possessions, gifts, compliments, in giving blood to a thirsty mosquito and the like. This form is called *dāna*. The subtle and more inner form of generosity manifests itself more in the meditation process, namely as the non-attaching, non-identifying or non-clinging awareness of what arises. This form is called *alobha* in Buddhist psychology: the state of being without desire, grasping or clinging. This can be understood in different ways.

Generosity in every moment of awareness

For example, when we are subconsciously absorbed in our thoughts, we could be said to be identified with them. We are then completely absorbed in them and attached to them; we are mesmerised by their content. The moment we recognise them, however, we are no longer in them, there is just the sober observation that there is thinking. The fascination and absorption dissolve at that point, there is freedom from identification. This is not the same as letting go. In our opinion, this term often causes confusion. If someone is brooding or obsessing about a problem that is difficult to solve in daily life, we tend to say 'Let it go!' It's easy advice but most of the time it is counter-productive because in addition to struggling with the problem, you also struggle with being swallowed up in it. Letting go is therefore a term that we ourselves seldom use. In fact, you could say that we learn the art of not having to let go. Letting go is hard work and often a struggle. The more we try to let go of thoughts, pain or emotions, the more frustrating and tense the practice can become. There is often also a negative judgement involved; we try to let go of something because we consider it undesirable or disgraceful.

It can be a relief not to have to put so much energy into trying to let go of what arises. Therein lies also that acknowledging attitude again: we may brood, grumble, judge, enjoy and be attached. When we acknowledge all that, and just notice objectively, a natural letting go takes place automatically. The perhaps unconscious identification with it is somehow terminated or steamed off, just like a stamp that is steamed off from an envelope by a stamp collector.

Mindfulness as a means of unblocking

During one of the first retreats we conducted at our home in Ezinge (the Netherlands), the drain pipe of the kitchen sink became clogged. After diagnosing the problem, we grabbed a mechanical unblocker and started trying with all our might to unblock it. To no avail, nothing happened. Then we remembered that somewhere in the house we had a small bottle of liquid unblocker. We carefully poured a dash of this into the drain, let it soak in and the clog resolved itself, without any extra effort on our part. Mindfulness has the same effect as this liquid unblocker, only it is more ecologically friendly. So in the meditation process you don't have to work hard to let go of anything, simply noticing what is in or to you at the moment automatically creates space.

> **Exercise – A hand in front of the eyes**
>
> *We sometimes illustrate the above with a simple exercise. We ask you to hold one of your hands directly in front of and against your nose and forehead, with the palm facing the face. We invite you to look at this hand (option A). Then we ask you to hold the hand half a metre away from your face and look at it again (option B).*

We ask a few questions at the end of this short exercise:

- When could you see the hand better as a hand, in option A or in option B?
- When did you experience more spaciousness?
- When was it easier to see something else when needed?

Usually, these questions are answered with a realisation that seeing the hand from a distance (option B) is much easier and gives more space than when you hold the hand right against your face.

This is a simple illustration of how mindfulness works. Speaker, researcher and author Megan Reitz (2018), once described mindfulness in a webinar as an intimately detached presence. Mindfulness does not push away anything or try to detach, but simply notices that thinking, hearing, feeling or whatever is taking place. The identification or symbiosis with the object is automatically released and there is a movement from 'my experience' to a more generous 'there is an experience'. Inner space is created.

Some objects, however, are more captivating than others. Occasionally you may encounter thoughts or emotions that involve a stronger enjoyment, attachment or identification. If you do not name this reactivity when it is evident, as a variant of aversion or impatience, you will remain stuck with the attachment itself. Until this stickiness is clearly recognised and noticed, for example as, 'enjoying', 'cherishing', 'being absorbed in the thought', 'attachment' or 'identification'. By noticing this clinging, inner space is automatically created. Sometimes the perceived object disappears, and sometimes it remains clearly present for a while. But that does not matter; it may be contemplated as long as it clearly present by itself.

Meditating with a hidden agenda

Another manifestation of generosity in the practice is a selfless or detached awareness. There is a link here to the focusing that we talked about earlier in this chapter. When we focus on something, it is often because we have a particular interest in it. We think it is more important than other experiences, there is preference. Another possibility is that we focus with the desire to see it as clearly as possible and thus to 'meditate well', or we practise in a way that Joseph Goldstein aptly calls 'meditating with a hidden agenda': 'If I just observe and name it properly it will probably go away!' or, 'I hope this experience lasts'. When you recognise such a tendency, you can name it 'pushing away', wanting to hold on or simply as 'agenda'.

Often we also focus because we have been taught to work hard or because in a strange way we want 'value for money'. By noticing such kinds of desires and expectations in a non-identifying way every time they clearly appear, a cooler, less heated and more detached observation gradually develops. In this way, we can practice generosity, which loosens or can cause desires and attachments to evaporate.

The credit card

I (Frits) feel very fortunate to have had much guidance from Ajahn Asabha, who died in 2010 at the age of a hundred, and who was once sent by the Mahasi Sayadaw to teach vipassanā meditation in Thailand. When we talked, he spoke Thai with a Burmese accent and I spoke Thai with a Dutch accent; this way we could always communicate well.

This story happened just after Ajahn Asabha moved to a new meditation centre, after he had lived for many years as abbot in Wat Vivek Asom, a beautiful meditation centre near Chonburi.[4] I wanted to continue meditating under his guidance and went on retreat at this new centre in 2001. I didn't know anyone else there, but on the first day I decided to leave my passport and money with the centre's manager for safekeeping. That was a relief, partly because I was allocated a room which had no lock. Just before the retreat, I had received a new credit card in the Netherlands. I was very pleased with this beautiful gold coloured card and decided not to hand it in. After all, I did not know anyone and did not know how my money was kept, even though the manager seemed to be a very trustworthy woman. So it felt safer to keep the card with me when I would go to the restaurant. The first few days I kept the card in my pocket but at some point I realised that I was very attached to that card. As an extra exercise of detachment, I decided to just leave the card somewhere in the room. But during the next meal in another building, I became restless. There was a little boy who often played in front of my meditation hut and seemed to be somewhat mischievous. 'Soon that boy will look into my room and steal the card', I thought. And then he would probably pass the card on to his father or uncle, who probably maintained contacts with the Chinese mafia in Thailand. My suspicion was growing, but so was my relief when the card was still in my room. I felt a bit tough that I had dared to do this. But for the next meal, I was still worried and decided not to just leave the card there, as, I was making myself very vulnerable. So I decided to take a middle course and hid the card in the toilet; that day I went to the dining room with a detached and calm mind.

> *But the next day I saw the little boy playing again and he seemed to be looking at me with curiosity. 'He is probably planning to steal the card', I thought. So I just took the card back to the dining room but then I felt discouraged. What a coward I was. I couldn't let go, I probably wasn't strong enough to make progress. So I hid the card again, but this time in another, even more clever, place. For the next week, the card kept popping up as a mind-object and I thought of one hiding place after another. The meditation process itself went quite well, the teacher was satisfied. But my awareness kept losing power because of the inner and outer fussing about this card. After a week I was so fed up with this that I took the courage to simply bring the card to the manager. I gave her a good cash donation of the money she was keeping for me and gave her the card as well.*
>
> *Then peace returned, I had practised generosity by simply letting go of the awkward hassle of the card by handing it over. The little boy suddenly didn't look like a dangerous potential criminal at all anymore, but just a friendly playful boy who didn't bother me at all.*

All expressions of generosity are valuable, large and small, in society and in a retreat. The Buddha once said: *Sabbadānam Dhammadānam jināti* – the gift of Dhamma transcends all gifts. Indeed, every moment that we are aware in an acknowledging, non-satisfied way, we are practising the generosity that is entwined with the practice of *vipassanā* meditation. Every moment that we are mindful, we are practicing this form of generosity, and there is a movement from 'ego system' to 'ecosystem'.

Kindness meditation – Self and loved ones

We end day 3 highlighting how we can also be generous in kindness, by sharing a kind wish and by being generous in love towards ourselves and towards one or a few loved ones.

Notes

1 *Ars Amatoria Bk 2*, Translated by Henry T. Riley in 1885 and available from Project Gutenberg.
2 The word *vedanā* is often translated as the feeling tone that can be sensed with all our experiences. In Chapter 7, different feeling tones will be explained more specifically.
3 Source: *Mindfulness-Based Compassionate Living* by Erik van den Brink and Frits Koster (Routledge, 2015).
4 This new meditation centre is called Wat Bhaddanta Asabharam and is located near the town of Ban Bueng in Thailand; for more information, see www.watbhaddanta.com.

Chapter 4

Becoming at ease with impermanence

Day 4 – Inner patterns and wisdom

On Day 4, we cover mindfulness of states of mind and impermanence. We give further instructions for walking meditation and describe rigidity and inner patterns as themes in the individual and group meetings about the practice. We present the RAIN model and wisdom as the fourth wholesome virtue.

Nothing endures but change.[1]

– Heraclitus, ancient Greek philosopher

In a guided meditation exercise in the morning of Day 4, we invite you to sit with awareness and offer yourself a kind wish; to place yourself, in the words of a Tibetan meditation teacher, 'in a cradle of kindness'. There is also space for a kind wish to loved ones, and we invite you to include someone in the practice from time to time throughout the day, to whom you have a more neutral attitude. It could be someone you don't know at all or only superficially know and who you don't explicitly like or like, but who you don't find annoying or unfriendly either in other words- a 'neutral' person. It is almost impossible to find someone for whom your feelings are exactly neutral and that is not necessary. It may be a participant who crosses your path or passes by during the walking meditation, someone sitting next to you, a casual passer-by in a car or on a bicycle, the patient, paramedic and driver in an ambulance which you hear from a distance.

Even if you do not know these people, they are part of the human family. As the Dalai Lama aptly puts it, 'I have never met anyone who was a stranger to me', so from time to time you can wish something kind for these persons for a short or a longer period.

> Participant: *In the context of the kindness meditation, in our minds we could also greet the people we met in the corridor or outside in the garden during the retreat and wish them something kind in silence. I did that – every time – and it gave me a pleasant feeling. It made me happy every time.*

DOI: 10.4324/9781003519072-5

Noticing the inner weather report

You can then focus on sitting with mindfulness, and let there be kindness in your gaze, while you are mindful. Sitting with awareness allows you to be aware of the breathing movements again to ground yourself. There is no need to seek experiences other than the rising and falling of the abdomen or the chest. But whenever something else comes up, then this can kindly be acknowledged.

In the previous chapter special attention was paid to how we can see thoughts as thoughts. We can then add another field which also belongs to the third abiding of mindfulness, namely states of mind. We encounter all kinds of moods and states of mind in our daily lives, and of course in a retreat as well. These are sometimes happy, sometimes sad and sometimes enthusiastic and inspired, sometimes disappointed or bored. Sometimes they are full of energy and sometimes tired. When the word 'emotion' comes up, most people think of the four 'big emotions': angry, happy, scared or sad. However, it also refers to more subtle moods, such as doubt, trust, impatience or enjoyment. Sayādaw U Tejaniya's one-liner 'check your attitude' as mentioned earlier, not only invites us to be aware of the current inner attitude, state of mind or mindset but also to regularly check the 'inner weather report': what mood is present now? All moods and states of mind are allowed to be there, whether they have a pleasant, unpleasant or neutral feeling tone.

Acknowledging and possibly naming the state of mind in the present creates inner space, as research into labelling by Matthew Lieberman et al has demonstrated.[2] The inner space that this creates is concisely expressed in a statement attributed to the Austrian neurologist and psychiatrist Viktor Frankl: 'There is a space between stimulus and response. In that space there is a choice to choose our response. In our response lies our growth and our freedom'.

Wisdom and the law of mortality

> Participant: *I watched how moods can alternate so quickly and how they also 'dissolve' or 'evaporate' if you continue to look at them with gentle kindness ... experiencing different states of mind and really deeply experiencing that they pass away again, like clouds that come and go. Thus I experienced both sincere gratitude for life, longing for the end of the retreat and listlessness in the face of practising within one and the same sitting session. The ability to give up the will to control was something I had never experienced so strongly and was a learning moment that I will certainly take with me into 'real' life.*

Therefore if we are sitting with an awareness which is gradually becoming steadier, a fourth perfection will grow naturally: wisdom or insight (*paññā*). This insight is not based on thoughts but on the direct clear observation, through which we get more insight into very basic universal laws, such as changeability and impermanence, which we encounter everywhere in our lives. This meta-understanding, called *anicca* in the Pali language, grows in the awareness of the breath movements and how they are always in motion. How a rising movement arises, grows and ends again and a descending movement also arises, grows and, as it were, falls away. Modern science recognises that all the cells or building blocks in our body are constantly renewing themselves and that a continuous process of birth, ageing and death is taking place in our body.

This is like all the seasons of our lives in a nutshell, again and again. We can observe how the breathing movements are sometimes fast and sometimes slow, sometimes deep, sometimes shallow, sometimes clearly perceptible and sometimes less so, how sometimes a small pause after an ascending or descending movement is perceptible, or how an ascending and/or descending movement seems to take place in small stages.

In watching the breath movements over and over again, an intuitive understanding of changeability and impermanence develops. But this also manifests itself in other ways besides just in relation to the breath. Thoughts, physical sensations, different moods and sensory stimuli keep arising, being present and falling away, coming and going. By being aware of this wondrous ever-changing landscape in a non-judgemental way, we automatically become more familiar with the transience in our lives. This is beautifully expressed in the poem 'In the morning' by Anita Holleboom:

> *In the morning*
> *if the call of*
> *a distant stranger*
> *dies away in feathery silence*
> *I feel death*
> *so peacefully near.*

Research shows that mindfulness helps us develop psychological flexibility and this is a skill that cannot be learnt cognitively, but only through practising. Cultivating inner flexibility is a well-known theme of the teaching the Mahā Parinibbāna Sutta concisely formulated by the Buddha as follows: 'All conditioned things are impermanent, they arise and fall away. Being at peace with this gives a special kind of happiness, the happiness of inner freedom'.[3]

Participant: *I was carried away to a sad experience in the past. I first tried to get rid of the sadness by telling myself that it was over, the person had already died, he was no longer suffering, and so on. Frits pointed out to me that I could also just name the feeling – in this case sadness. The next day I had a similar moment and I continuously named it: 'sadness, sadness'. That was liberating and gave space. The unpleasant feeling – because that is what I thought it was – was present in all its intensity at first, but ebbed away automatically after a few minutes. It felt better than trying to talk it away.*

Unwinding with choiceless awareness

The 16th-century Spanish mystic John of the Cross expressed another aspect of impermanence in the following statement: 'Tenderly now I touch all things, knowing that one day we will part'. You may be able to bring this tenderness into your practice in sensing the movements of the breath, in sensing the movements of the feet in the walking meditation or in whatever you experience from moment to moment.

We invite you to regularly practise for some time without trying to come to back to the breath during the sitting meditation. This will help you be able to see the impermanence in all experiences more clearly. This can be uncomfortable if you are used to returning to the breathing movements as quickly as possible after having recognised another experience, for example, a sound or a physical sensation, at least at first. Yet we often hear that it brings much more peace and relaxation into the practice. After all, it is an inner unwinding in the form of being aware of something for as long as it is in the foreground. The impermanence of all experiences also becomes much more visible, that is, the emergence and disappearance, the sliding into the background or 'evaporation' of what is occurring. This can have a very broadening and deepening effect, especially during periods when the practice is relatively easy and effortless. It is called 'choiceless awareness' in secular mindfulness training. After all, you do not choose what occurs, but simply notice what occurs naturally and stay with it as long as it is present.

You can always reconnect with the breathing movements at times when something has resolved or faded by itself and when nothing else clearly arises, or use the movements of the breath to reset internally when choiceless awareness is no longer desired or helpful.

Walking meditation – More advanced instructions

We invite you to continue to walk outside with mindfulness and also to find yourself a path for walking inside at other times, going back and forth step by step. If you find this slower step-by-step walking easy and is resonating well with you, we suggest dividing the steps into two stages for a while, just being aware of the lifting and putting down of the foot. You can either simply be aware of this or possibly combine it very lightly with a subtle inner noting, such as 'up', 'down', 'up', 'down'. This works more easily if the steps are smaller. However, it is not compulsory and should only be practised at times when this can be done in a relaxed way. It is not that wisdom comes as we walk slower; we invite to you flexibly tune into what form of walking or running is most appropriate for you in the moment.

In addition, we invite you to be aware of your overall physical and inner posture from time to time, and to generally aim for a relaxed upright bearing including a relaxed head position. The gaze of the eyes may be soft and directed downwards between three and ten metres. The primary intention is to be aware of the movements of the feet or of the walking or running body but without interpreting other experiences as disturbances. Every time there is something else, for example hearing, listening, seeing, smelling, thinking or feeling, then that new experience can be recognised as an experience.

Finally, we warn against a tendency that we sometimes see in meditators after a few days. The idea creeps in that walking is primarily in the service of sitting, of being able to sit properly. Meditators then tend to shorten the walking period, and to concentrate on the 'real work of sitting'. This might be understandable but does not usually prove helpful for inner balance and the development of meditative insight. The Greek philosopher Diogenes once said 'Solvitur ambulando' – 'It is solved by walking'. In the mental health and coaching world, 'walk and talk' conversations are increasingly being viewed these days as a good way of meeting and discussing difficult themes. Therefore, we occasionally remind participants that walking meditation in a retreat is at least as valuable and insightful as sitting meditation and to therefore continue with it diligently until the bell for sitting is rung.

Inquiry meetings – Inner patterns

Two things often come out clearly in interpersonal inquiry meetings. The first is a lack of kindness towards oneself, which often manifests itself in being very strict either regarding thoughts, specific feelings, experiences other than the breath, or regarding physical posture, and so on. When we encourage participants to notice it first of all with kindness and to explore how befriending can come into the practice, they usually 'thaw out' gradually and start to allow themselves to sometimes change the posture or to sit with an 'okay' in all experiences. This is often accompanied by tears, which is a bit like water melting in a natural thawing process.

Playing Bingo

Self-judgement is common for many retreat participants and is often experienced as an unwanted and irritating obstacle to developing wisdom and compassion. When we encounter this, we sometimes ask in individual and group inquiry sessions what it would be like if a surgeon were to skilfully suck the capacity to judge out of your brain. This is usually not considered desirable as we would then be unable to make even simple decisions.

We also sometimes ask if you have ever played bingo. And if so, how do you feel as a participant when you find the number called out by the bingo master on your card? Connoisseurs of this game almost always like this, you score and can 'tick off' the number on your paper. If this happens often enough and your card becomes full, you can say 'Bingo' and be rewarded with a prize. Usually, this is not a great prize but it has made it a classic party game.

We can relate to the judgemental, condemning and commenting mind in a similar way. When we have a negative attitude towards these kinds of thoughts, there is a lack of compassion and not much joy, while we actually encounter something very human, namely the judgemental mind.

What about bringing playfulness into the practice by playing bingo when becoming aware of the judging mind? Instead of regarding judgemental thoughts as negative, you can say 'bingo' every time you notice the judgement – about your appearance, your functioning, about others or about this book, for instance. Of course, you don't have to deliberately start judging in order to score well, but actually, every time you notice a thought as a thought, something worthy of congratulation is taking place. After all, when you notice the judging mind with recognition and with a sense of common humanity, there is mindfulness and the capacity for compassion and sympathetic joy grows. The practice can become playful and you can say 'bingo' or 'Ah, there's another one', every time you notice that you are making a judgement. We find that this offers relief to many participants.

Inner patterns

The second theme that often comes up, which is related to the harshness mentioned above, is that all kinds of inner patterns come to light, either during practice or sometimes by talking about them in the group or individual inquiry meetings. If we make a top-ten of frequently mentioned patterns during retreats, we arrive at the following:

1 'I have to do it perfectly'.
2 'I must not fail'.
3 'I must be in control'.
4 'I must be strong'.
5 'I must be patient'.
6 'I am responsible for everything'.
7 'If I rest, I rust'.
8 'I prefer to count myself out'.
9 'I am not good enough'.
10 'Everything is about recognition and appreciation for me'.

These patterns are often formed in us in early childhood in dealing with difficult or painful situations or circumstances in our family or at school and they may have been the best survival strategies at the time.

Playfulness in relating to an inner pattern

We develop these ideas and start storing them in our system, just as favourite websites can be stored on our computer. The only difference is that with internet favourites, we can consciously choose which sites to save and which to discard again. We store our 'life favourites' unconsciously and develop such a strong symbiotic relationship with them that we are hardly aware of their existence. That is why it is said: 'We often see things not as they are but as we are'. So as human beings, we are conditioned by the above patterns and we take them with us into our practice, and try very hard to be mindful without omitting anything. Another pattern might be that we start feeling very uncomfortable because we are all in silence and the other participants are not talking or looking at us. Such vulnerable patterns prove difficult to observe at first, precisely because we are so 'fused' with them and live completely in and from these mechanisms.

We often explore the disadvantages and the advantages of these patterns together in the individual and group inquiry meetings. The disadvantages are usually clear, a perfectionism pattern can lead to exhaustion for example. Understanding the advantages can often be more difficult, but when we look carefully we might find out that the pattern can actually be beneficial. If we always put other peoples' needs before our own, it means we are also highly socially sensitive and intelligent. The legendary Dutch football player Johan Cruijff once put it very simply: 'Every disadvantage has its advantage'.

We sometimes suggest starting to name an inner familiar pattern, as an extension of noticing a thought as a thought. After all, 'to name is to tame'. Rutger Bregman (2021) describes the 'Homo Ludens' and the importance of playfulness in learning something. To encourage a little lightheartedness, we therefore invite you to regularly search for a playful nickname or image, inspired by a cartoon character, an animal, someone from a novel or a fairy tale or a film star. Here are some examples: 'Doom and Gloom', 'Speedy Gonzalez', 'Florence Nightingale', 'Madame Perfect' or 'Mister Control'. This can prevent a 'terminal seriousness' in the practice, as one participant once put it.

> Participant: *One of my conditionings I call 'Bob the Builder', it wants to constantly 'renovate' everything around me. Like I can do this better' or 'This has to be done differently.' Now I greet and recognise Bob with a smile and have a choice in how to deal with him.*

> Participant: *During an individual exchange with Frits, I spoke about two inner patterns: a dwarf with a pedantic finger (critic) and Cinderella's stepmother (judge). Only these were 'evil' figures and I was quite troubled by them. Frits*

advised me to reduce the power of these figures by making them smaller, i.e. a little dwarf and a little mother. In the end, the dwarf stayed and the stepmother became Miss Sour. How I look at them has changed completely by making them smaller, now I get a smile on my face every time I notice that they are there again. This is very pleasant to notice!

Evening talk – The RAIN model and uncontrollability

Look within yourself. Within you is a source of good that never stops flowing, as long as you do not stop examining yourself.[4]
 – Marcus Aurelius, Roman emperor and philosopher (121–AD 180)

In this talk, we want to pay attention to a model that brings together a number of ingredients of mindfulness: the so-called RAIN model. This model refers to the invigorating and vitalising value of water, and so similarly, the acronym RAIN names four valuable qualities that can be really helpful in the practice of insight meditation.[5]

R stands for recognising, realising or remembering the present time object. This reflects the most basic function of mindfulness, which is to become aware of what is happening to or within you in the present moment and possibly naming it as an experience.

A stands for acknowledging, allowing, affirming, accepting what is there at the moment. As the Flemish psychiatrist and mindfulness trainer Edel Maex very concisely says: 'Mindfulness is giving yourself the right to exist'.[6] All experiences have their value, a right to exist, and may be appreciated.

The American monk Ajahn Sumedho (2010), connected with the Thai forest tradition and former abbot of the Buddhist Amaravati monastery in England, often discusses the uncertainty that many Western people carry in their practice: 'Am I doing the practice right?' 'Am I putting in enough energy?' 'I'm probably not mindful enough'. There seems to be an old Western (Calvinist) pattern in this which American meditation teacher Tara Brach (2004) calls a trance of unworthiness. This delusion, belief or conviction can manifest itself in a deeply rooted conviction of not being okay. More subtly, this delusion manifests itself in the feeling of not being good enough. The A of RAIN invites more openness and trust in what is happening. This does not mean, however, that we should be resigned to everything we meet in life. This will be addressed elsewhere in this book.

I stands for investigating or interest with care, for a kind curiosity. The I of RAIN implies an open and friendly exploration and interest. This interest does not relate so much to the 'why' of what we are experiencing it is simply about what is happening. It is less focused on the content and more on the process of what we are experiencing. Without having to judge directly, we explore what happens from moment to moment during meditation. We may then become aware of the many astonishing fluctuations in experience, whether in the body or the mind. In that sense, you can call insight meditation a very direct worldview, with which we learn to look at ordinary life with awe.

Sometimes the I of RAIN can create extra space which is especially helpful when you encounter something difficult in the practice that turns out to be very 'sticky', such as a conflict or quarrel with a family member or a colleague. If you have already patiently named the experience yet it keeps returning, then an open inquiry question may be very helpful. Simply ask yourself a question: 'What is actually going on here?' Or 'Is there something underneath all this?' These are not so much 'why' questions but questions that invite you to look again at what is going on. Inquiry like this can help us to see past anger to an underlying emotion such as hurt, powerlessness, uncertainty or disappointment. In this way, what is sometimes poetically called 'the original face' in Zen Buddhism can be understood here in a small way.

> Participant: *I always thought I suffered from the taboo of anger, in the sense that others forbade me to be angry. But actually, sadness is my taboo, not only showing it but even feeling it.*

N as the last letter in RAIN stands for a non-clinging, non-claiming, non-grasping, non-attached or non-judgemental awareness. The N reflects a quality of mindfulness that has not yet been much named. Mindfulness is aware, has something kind but also expresses an attitude of non-identification or non-fusion that creates a subtle inner space where we are not completely absorbed in what we experience. Here it is good to point out that the word 'not' is often interpreted as a rejection: 'So I may not identify or be attached'. Therefore we use the word 'non', which is more gentle and we get words like non-identification, non-attachment, non-clinging, and so on. This invites a softer atmosphere, where attachment, identification or judgement is not wrong. We experience this N when we are aware of an experience as it naturally occurs, without trying to repress it or hold on to it. We then behold an experience as an experience, with an inner attitude that does not require us to judge, grasp or possess. The N could also be signify the word 'natural'. Tara Brach, who works a lot with the RAIN model, introduces another valuable aspect, naming the N as 'nurturing' with self-compassion.

Aspects of wisdom

> *Realise that, like a bird needs two wings to fly, wisdom and compassion need to be developed simultaneously.*
>
> – Buddhist saying

This beautiful saying shows that mindfulness is not completely without intention, and that being mindful, which in the metaphor can be understood as the body of the bird, brings all kinds of valuable qualities to fruition. Two of these qualities that are being nurtured are very explicitly named here: wisdom and compassion. Compassion already received attention on Day 2, therefore in this talk, we will pay more attention to the wing that is called wisdom.

According to a description in Buddhist psychology, wisdom, or *paññā* in Pali, investigates and penetrates the reality of things. It sheds light in the darkness, creates clarity and is a wholesome medicine for misunderstanding, confusion or ignorance (*avijjā*).

The wisdom of the information technology specialist

A toddler will have very little understanding of what is possible with a laptop. This is the level of understanding of someone who is totally unfamiliar with meditation and other contemplative methods. An adult has a much greater insight into the various possibilities of a laptop and can work with all kinds of software programmes. This is comparable to someone who has started to develop mindfulness. But they will be at a loss when the laptop crashes. An IT specialist has a transcendent understanding, not only of the software but also of the hardware. Therefore, they may be able to repair the laptop if necessary. This can be compared with a meditator who has more experience and meditative wisdom. In Pali literature, several synonyms are given for wisdom. The most common are *vipassanā* (insight), *dhamma vicaya* (investigation of phenomena), *ñāna* (level of insight), *vimamsa* (discriminating wisdom) and *sammā diṭṭhi* (wholesome understanding). Just as a diamond has many facets, wisdom appears to have many layers and forms of expression. We will mention some of these facets below.

The wisdom of common sense

This is the wisdom where we use logical and down-to-earth power of reasoning to explore whether something is right or wrong. In Buddhist psychology, this refers to a fundamental discernment between what is beneficial and what is not. This enables us to see and follow a path in life that leads to greater happiness, insight and harmony. This basic insight ensures that you calmly consider the various possibilities in a dilemma and it can motivate you to walk a spiritual path. Without this insight, you would never have started meditating.

Awareness of previously unconscious processes

You can call insight meditation a journey of discovery or a 'discovery-channel', where you become aware of experiences that were previously unconscious. This insight begins with the growing awareness of how little we really know about ourselves. A large part of our mental and physical experiences take place unconsciously, yet they have control over us without us even noticing. When we practise insight meditation, previously unconscious, mental and physical processes are slowly but surely discovered and 'mapped out' and we automatically gain a deeper understanding of the situations we find ourselves in.

> Participant: *On the first day after the retreat I had a meeting with the works council of our orchestra. They asked me a question about how I would give feedback on undesirable behaviour by a colleague. They didn't even wait for an answer from me and eventually everyone started talking at cross purposes. I sat back and thought, "What do we have here?" I then also said what I saw happening and that I was upset about it. Dead silence and a member of the works council who said: 'That's giving feedback!' After this we had a nice conversation. This would never have happened if I hadn't been so aware in that situation and that was clearly related to the retreat.*

Therapeutic insight

By becoming more aware and understanding, we also automatically become more aware of all kinds of inner patterns, vulnerabilities and sometimes grief processes that have not been given enough attention. Naomi Remen, author of the bestseller *Kitchen Table Wisdom* (1997) states that it seems that people often suffer from burnout or depression because they have had or taken too little time and space to be tired or sad. Meditation is not a form of therapy, but a therapeutic healing process does take place in many ways and this is often intensified during a retreat.

Existential wisdom

At this level, three laws or universal characteristics, *tilakkhana* in Pali, of human existence are clearly revealed. The first two shared human facts have already been named: impermanence (*anicca*) and unsatisfactoriness (*dukkha*). We now want to pay special attention to the third side of the 'triangle of life': uncontrollability (*anattā*).

Disappointment as a friend

Uncontrollability refers to the inability to control or shape impermanent and unsatisfactory processes. Try not thinking for half an hour and you will be disappointed very quickly. Even though we don't want to get sick, we don't seem to be able to fully control the ups and downs of our bodies. We sometimes experience enormous emotional ups and downs or lie awake at night worrying without wanting to. This can be difficult especially for people who have grown up in a very individualistic culture, where we get the idea that everything can be controlled.

In psychiatry, where I (Frits) worked for many years, there is often talk of delusional thinking as part of specific disease symptoms. For example, one speaks of a paranoid delusion when people start to believe that there is a conspiracy against them. We can suffer from a guilt delusion if we blame ourselves for everything. In a somatic delusion, we live with the conviction that there is something seriously wrong with us physically, and in a prophet delusion we can even believe that we have been chosen to proclaim 'the true teaching'.

We can all get caught up in delusions, even when we are not actually psychiatric patients. In this sense, the Buddha sometimes used the term *vipallāsa*, which is possibly best described as a human distortion or distortion of reality, as a suffering-inducing delusion or distortion that can arise through the senses, thinking and beliefs. He mentioned four distortions:

1 We easily interpret things as permanent that are ultimately impermanent. We then suffer (unconsciously) from a so-called delusion of permanence. In that case, if you live with a reasonably healthy body and then suddenly get a serious diagnosis, you are completely devastated.
2 We interpret things that do not *really* bring us real happiness as joyful and happy. One example is the so-called Christmas delusion, in which the media lead us to believe that everything at Christmas should be completely perfect and in harmony with everyone else, including a harmonious and joyful family Christmas dinner.
3 We interpret that which is ultimately not completely pure and beautiful as ideal, pure and perfect. This delusion arises, for example, when we are in love with someone and on cloud nine.
4 A final distortion that is mentioned is the so-called control delusion, in which we start to believe that we are in control and can control everything. And the more we unconsciously believe in this delusion of control, the more frustrated we become when things do slip through our fingers or when we are unexpectedly caught off guard by things we didn't want to happen.

Susan Gillis Chapman, author of *The Five Keys to Mindful Communicating* (2012) calls disappointment a friend. After all, disappointment wakes us up from an unrealistic expectation or dream and confronts us with the uncontrollability we encounter everywhere in our lives. In meditation practice, we encounter uncontrollability everywhere: in dealing with thoughts, feelings, in dealing with unexpected noises in the meditation room, and so on.

Wisdom in uncontrollability

Some meditators interpret the concept of uncontrollability as fatalistic. However, there is a paradox in the practice. Once we become aware of uncontrollability we become better able to deal with it wisely. This was regularly expressed in a subtle way by one of our teachers, Sayādaw U Tejaniya (2016a, 2016b). When in a group inquiry session one of the participants frequently complained about something, he often said with the smile of a Mona Lisa: 'Yes, it is as it is'.

This is beautifully expressed in the so-called 'serenity prayer': 'May I have the serenity to accept what I cannot change, the courage to change what I can change and the wisdom to know the difference between the two. Tuning in mindfully and with wisdom refers to *yoniso manasikāra* or 'clear understanding' mentioned on Day 2. When we understand we can't control things, we can better attune to the circumstances in the present and assess what is possible and wise and what is not.

Working with dilemmas

Many meditators come to a retreat with a life dilemma, for example: 'Do I want to continue with this job or with this partner? I think I would like to have children but I haven't decided if I really want them'. Every stage of life appears to bring up questions that cannot be answered immediately. Our basic stress system does not like dilemmas as they make us feel unsafe, we would prefer to have clarity immediately. Our thinking mind is therefore quickly activated and starts looking for solutions. This can sometimes work well, but in the case of a large and complex dilemma, it can also cause a lot of rumination and even sleepless nights. This can also happen during a retreat and this can be quite frustrating, especially if you have come on retreat with the hope and intention of finding an answer.[7]

> ### Separating with awareness
>
> *For me (Frits), whether or not to separate from my ex-partner was my dilemma. We had lived together for almost ten years and had already noticed that the relationship was no longer working so well, until she fell in love with a neighbour. When I heard and realised this, all kinds of feelings came up in me: anger, resentment, fear, jealousy, insecurity. It was definitely not a good time. My first instinctive reaction was to repress the feelings, my second instinctive reaction was to act them out immediately. I had very unpleasant nights worrying. Suddenly I realised that for years I had been talking about the valuable fruits of insight meditation, but that this was now a real test or trial of my practice. Could I now use all those principles of mindfulness myself? Fortunately, my partner was also a meditator and we decided to just give everything some more time. It was not an easy period for either of us. I encountered many painful emotions and old patterns, such as a deep-rooted tendency to resentment and fear of abandonment. In the beginning I could sit with it for a long time and not see beyond it, but gradually I noticed that there was more and more inner space, each time acknowledging this. New perspectives naturally emerged for both of us, perhaps precisely because we did not try to force a solution. We did separate after a year, but in a very harmonious way and have remained good friends ever since.*

Dilemmas and pondering over them clearly show uncontrollability. Whether we like it or not, the thoughts keep returning to them and repeating all kinds of inner records. We often recommend adjusting the expectation of finding an answer during a retreat in such cases. We often give an alternative definition of mindfulness, inspired by Ellen Langer (2014); you could also describe mindfulness as 'keeping all options open, as long as this is wise and compassionate'. When there is more space for playfulness, we also recommend noticing such inner repetitive records with a gentle smile: 'Ah, there's record number A, B or C again'. In this way, we can also find more spaciousness in relation to a dilemma.

Kindness meditation – Micro-moments of positivity resonance

The American researcher Barbara Fredrickson (2017) conducted research with her team into the effects of the practice of kindness meditation. She wanted to explore the phenomenon of 'love' more closely, but not so much the romantic part of it. She defines love as a 'micro-moment of positivity resonance'. The word 'micro-moment' shows that love in this definition is not a matter of always or never, but can happen at the moment when you share a smile in silence with a stranger in traffic or with a meditator who is otherwise unknown to you. The word 'positivity resonance' refers to an inner vibration or resonance. This can be experienced interpersonally when you feel a beneficial vibration in relation to another person. However, it can also be experienced intrapersonally, that is, only within and towards yourself, when you allow a kind wish to resonate and a gentle or tender smile to be given space towards yourself as a vulnerable, imperfect human being.

We invite you to continue the practice of love, first towards yourself then towards loved ones and perhaps then also towards one or some other persons in your life. We end Day 4 with the poem *Control* by Rachel Holstead, which beautifully expresses the uncontrollability in our lives.

Control

We seek safety in control,
in putting things in place
in setting things up
in holding on tight.

But really, the world will turn as it will
and all we must do is grow older
and, someday, pass away.
And the more we pretend
that this is not so,
the less time we have for really living.

*Can it not be beautiful,
this slow tuning in with the world,
this slow settling into our skin,
this careful tending of the light within?*

*By feeling this raindrop,
we are alive.
By watching that wave break
and hearing its sound on the shore,
we are alive.*

*By watching the sun come up
and hitting the snow on the mountain,
which is not how it was yesterday
and is not as it will be tomorrow,
and is only now,
we are alive.*

*Let us not find ourselves at the end
thinking 'what happened?'
but just be here, and here, and now, and now
each moment deepening our wisdom
and refreshing our hearts.*

Notes

1 Heraclitus is quoted here by Plato in Cratylus, 401d which is available from Project Gutenberg. Translated by Benjamin Jowett (1817–1893).
2 See https://pubmed.ncbi.nlm.nih.gov/17576282/#affiliation-1.
3 This is a free translation of the following Pali text: *Aniccā vata saṅkhārā. Uppāda vaya dhamminō. Uppajjitvā nirujjhanti. Tesaṃ vūpa samō sukhō.* This passage is often recited by Buddhist monks when someone has died; it reminds us of the impermanence of life.
4 From *Meditations* by Marcus Aurelius in the public domain and available from Gutenberg.org.
5 In the early 2000s, the acronym RAIN was introduced in America by Michele McDonald, where the four letters stand for: Recognition, Acceptance, Investigation (or Interest) with kindness and Non-identification. Many Western meditation teachers use this model in their teaching.
6 See Chapter 5 in *Mindful Communication* (2023) by Frits Koster, Jetty Heynekamp & Victoria Norton (editors).
7 Maggie Jackson has written a valuable book on insecurity called *Uncertain. The Wisdom and Wonder of Being Unsure* (2023).

Chapter 5

The art of living: Relaxed commitment

Day 5 – Mindfulness in daily activities and compassionate breathing *(tonglen)*

On Day 5, we talk about dedication or commitment as the fifth perfection or component of integrity (Andersen Stark, 2020). We pay attention to curiosity and awe in the practice of walking meditation. We explore informal practice and explain the practice of compassionate breathing (*tonglen*) as an additional support. In the evening talk, we address the question 'Who am I?'

> *Men go abroad to admire the heights of mountains, the mighty waves of the sea, the broad tides of rivers, the compass of the ocean, and the circuits of the stars, yet pass over the mystery of themselves without a thought.*[1]
> – Augustine of Hippo, theologian and philosopher (354–430)

We are now about half way through the retreat. In the morning guided meditation we invite you, first to sit paying mindful attention to each moment and then to wish yourself and perhaps one or more loved ones something kind. From there you can continue with mindfulness meditation. We propose an open, flexible practice where you are not consciously choosing between the practices of insight meditation and kindness meditation. Giving space to both can really strengthen the practice. Someone once asked the well-known Indian meditation teacher Dipa Ma[2] whether she should practice mindfulness or *mettā*. Dipa Ma gave her the following answer: 'In my experience, there is no difference. When we are really loving, then we are also mindful, right? And when we are really mindful, is this not also the essence of love?' So also on this fifth retreat day, you can sometimes drop into playfully emphasising kindness meditation towards yourself and sometimes towards someone dear.

You can also occasionally wish something kind to someone passing by on a bicycle or in a car, another participant or a cow or a horse in the field. In this way, you can sometimes lightheartedly give space to micro-moments of love or positivity resonance towards strangers whilst being mindful of what effect this has on you. Remember it is always possible to return to the simplicity of just being aware while walking and sitting.

Commitment as a virtue

You are now off to a good start as a retreat participant, like a steam train that starts slowly using a lot of energy to build momentum, but which gradually begins to run more easily. After starting the talk with kindness meditation, we turn to a fifth perfection: dedication or commitment. This factor or companion in the practice, which in Pali is called *vīriya* and which is also often translated as effort, ardour, zeal, devotion or dedication, is indispensable in the practice. When we have struck the right balance with this factor we can call it a perfection. In daily life, however, it is quite an art to find and maintain this inner balance.

Finding the right level of effort

Sometimes external factors make us exert a lot of effort in daily life, for example, a deadline that must be met or an increased workload caused by the illness of a colleague. However, 'efforting' is sometimes also driven by an inner pattern, such as a great sense of responsibility, a strong desire for perfection, fear of failure, insecurity or because we have been taught 'if you rest, you rust'. This kind of pattern can drive us to unconsciously demand a lot from ourselves. On the one hand, diligence is a virtue and it can be an important quality which 'enhances wellbeing', as Joan Halifax writes in her book *Standing at the Edge* (2019). On the other hand, it can also take a huge amount of energy and can be exhausting in the long run. Finding the right level of effort or the right balance is truly an art.

Often the way we meditate is a reflection of how we behave in daily life. During meditation, this high level of effort reveals itself for example when we find ourselves obsessively naming everything. Even when the rising and falling of the abdomen or other meditation objects are not very clear, we still make a lot of effort to make the meditation experiences as clear as possible. Or we strive to name or register all the tiny experiences, objects that disappear so quickly when we recognise them, that they have faded away before we have a chance to identify them. If there is pain, discomfort, an unpleasant emotion or unwanted thoughts, we can put a lot of energy into trying to get rid of or changing these unwelcome experiences.

Another sign of a high level of effort when practising is accompanied by a focus on attention, as discussed on Day 3.

Finally, a high degree of effort can also easily arise when we have become very inspired or motivated during meditation. It feels pleasant and so we can easily forget to integrate this into the meditation process by simply making the pleasant feeling state of mind the object of attention. This can get us into a blind pursuit of wanting to get the most out of our meditation and tempt us into not being present with our experience.[3]

If you realise you are 'efforting', don't condemn yourself for it. It is just an inner pattern that is probably deeply embedded; just use these signs of effort as an object of meditation. You can just name it and congratulate yourself for recognising it. For example, if you notice that you are trying to stop or get rid of pain, agitation or unpleasant thoughts, you can name this tendency as 'trying', 'trying', 'condemning', 'impatience' or 'rejection'. Or if you find that you are resistant or afraid to allow yourself to be tired, dull or tense, name this pattern as 'resistance', 'fighting' or 'fear'. You don't have to feel peaceful or wonderful, you are fine just the way you are. Sometimes a good-natured nickname can also be very helpful here: for example 'Ah, there's Mr Good-for-nothing or Miss Perfect again'.

If you feel enthusiastic, motivated or inspired, you may just note this as simply a state of mind. By integrating excessive effort into the practice as an object of meditation and registering it the moment you recognise it, inner space will naturally arise. As soon as we see a pattern clearly, we are no longer unconsciously trapped in it.

> Participant: *This retreat has made it very clear to me that I am always trying very hard – also in daily life – and I think that causes a lot of my fatigue... I am definitely going to keep practising and I am also extremely interested in anything else that might be connected with it.*

A low level of energy

The other challenge in energy management is when we try too hard and find this level of effort is not sustainable. We feel tired after work or at the end of the day and have no desire or inclination to do anything. Often, we do not even permit ourselves to be tired; we ignore the tiredness and start to force ourselves to do things. When we do this in everyday life, it all too often results in a situation where we become exhausted or even burned out.

Struggling with sleepiness

Many meditators have difficulty relating skilfully to sleepiness, and we have often struggled with this ourselves. From a psychological viewpoint, sleepiness can be as a defence mechanism, whereby you unconsciously do not want to feel pain or sorrow and therefore allow yourself to sink into sleepiness. This is only one possible explanation. Sleepiness can also have other causes:

- You may have just eaten; the energy in your body is used for digestion and this causes your mental state to temporarily become sluggish.
- You have slept badly, which makes you tired and drowsy during meditation.
- You have, perhaps unconsciously, exerted yourself a lot for a while, resulting in low energy.
- Pleasant experiences are not carefully recognised and are used as objects for meditation. This causes first inertia and then dullness of mind.

- There is a temporary loss of dedication or commitment, so that the concentration can easily come to dominate. We will go into this in more detail in the next chapter.
- Individual disposition also plays a role. Some people have a highly developed ability to concentrate by nature or on the other hand are easily discouraged when there are difficult experiences to handle. This can lead to a greater tendency to inertia, lethargy and sleepiness.

Headbanging

I (Frits) was usually very diligent in the practice. I did the walking meditation very slowly and I observed very carefully all the sensations of lifting, moving through the air and putting the foot down again, step by step with enormous dedication. Then when I sat down, it was as if the practice collapsed like a jelly pudding and I was mostly sleepy and rocking to and fro or headbanging as a hip-hopper once called it. I spent many months in Thailand and Myanmar in this way.

Working with sleepiness wisely and compassionately

Whatever is causing it, sleepiness is a challenging meditation object to work with skilfully, because it is so difficult for us to become aware of it. Perhaps it is helpful here to take a detour to some research done by American psychologist Kelly McGonigal (2015) on stress. She found that she and her contemporaries grew up in a culture where stress is usually viewed as something negative. Chronic stress can be immensely depleting and is therefore definitely not desirable, but in essence, stress also has something positive. 'A gem cannot be polished without friction, nor a human perfected without trials' as the Roman author and philosopher Lucius Annaeus Seneca used to say. Stress signals alert us that something important to us is under threat. Stress therefore has several facets. McGonigal defines stress as 'that which we experience when something we care about is at stake'.

Such an open and non-judgemental attitude may also be helpful in relating to sleepiness, dullness, inertia and lethargy. If you were unwell, you would take care of your health, so in this case, just take care of the sleepiness or fatigue and respectfully integrate it as a meditation object. See it as a challenge, on the one hand, to accept the experience of sleepiness as a meditation object, while on the other hand trying to name or register it as soon as it comes into the foreground. In this way, you can be aware of inertia, dullness, sleepiness, lethargy, the light, 'woolly', heavy or tired feeling as a meditation experience and name or register it. All the symptoms of low energy or sleepiness such as yawning, moving back and forth or little jerking movements of your body during short moments of falling asleep can be used as an object of meditation and noted.

If you have been following this advice for some time, but nevertheless continue to sink into sleepiness, you may wish to try one or more of the following strategies:

- Begin by mindfully and slowly massaging your head and neck with your hands. You will then give yourself some extra stimulation.
- Notice the intention to open your eyes, and then open your eyes in a mindful manner. Note the seeing, and meditate for a while with your eyes open and looking down at the ground a few metres in front of you. When your eyes become heavy, just note that again.
- Look with awareness at sunlight or artificial light.
- Change your posture, stand for a while or start practising walking meditation. If sleepiness is frequent, it is even advisable to walk for five or ten minutes longer than sitting during such periods.
- Be moderate in eating. This often helps against feeling sleepy after mealtimes.
- Go outside and walk and/or sit. This will allow you to get some fresh air and other invigorating stimuli. If our participants become sleepy while practising walking meditation, we sometimes suggest walking backwards as safely as possible. However, this may be discouraged at some centres because of health and safety concerns.

If none of this works and the sleepiness remains dominant, just sit with it. If you fall asleep sitting up, you will find that you wake up automatically. It is not disastrous to fall asleep; in fact, a short nap during meditation can be very refreshing and may recharge the 'energy battery'. It is a persistent phenomenon and often requires a lot of patience and creativity to learn to work with it. Therefore, finally, a last suggestion of the Buddha in the Anguttara Nikāya[4] to one of his most devoted disciples, the Venerable Moggallāna, when he struggled with recurrent sleepiness and had already tried everything: 'But if that does not get rid of the sleepiness, then you can lie down on your right side, like a lion, putting one foot on the other foot, attentive and clearly aware, with the intention of getting up again in the back of your mind. And when you wake up, you should get up without hesitation and think: I will not surrender to the pleasure of lying down and resting, to the pleasure of sleep! Thus, Moggallāna, you must practise yourself!'

Relaxed commitment

Through meditation, we can gradually learn to restore inner equilibrium and realise a new state of energy, which is also called *vīriyupekkhā* or equanimity of commitment and effort. This form of equanimity focuses on the effort with which we are observant and invites a practice that is between the two extremes of too much or too little effort. It refers to a relaxed commitment to mindfulness and balanced energy management. Here we develop two aspects, which are in harmony with each other and bring balance to our lives. On the one hand, we cultivate an open receptive attitude to what arises, which means you don't need to change anything. Everything you experience or encounter at this moment may be there. Pleasant, unpleasant, neutral, spectacular, boring, peaceful or restless: everything is okay as it is. You do not have to calm yourself, make yourself happy, relax or be free of resistance.

On the other hand, we can maintain a very subtle activity coming from this acceptance, which is to note or label in a light way what is in the foreground in the moment. This effort is minimal which means this practice can be done with relaxed concentration, without having to fight, magnify, change or judge anything. And if you recognise a subtle mode of doing, then it can be noted again. Just being aware or possibly allowing the awareness to be accompanied by a subtle inner noting such as 'thinking', 'feeling', 'chaos', 'peace', 'tiredness', 'restlessness', 'impatience', 'hearing' and 'listening' serves as an inner confirmation: this is what is happening now.

If these states do not quickly dissolve or disappear of their own accord, there is no need to try to make them disappear or to approach them with harshness. In this sense, mindfulness is not a 'vanishing act or a magic wand' but just being aware of what is happening in the moment. It is enough to note it or label it in a soft, lighthearted way and be in contact with it as it presents itself and remains in the foreground, accepting that it is there without having to eliminate, change or hold on to anything. It is enough to notice it as it presents itself to us, as long as it is clearly recognisable.

If you notice that something dissolves or disappears of its own accord, and if at such a moment something new does not immediately present itself to you clearly, then that is a moment when you can once again be aware of the rising and falling of the abdomen and possibly name or note these processes again very lightly, as 'rising', 'falling', 'rising', 'falling', or as 'out', 'in', 'out', 'in'.

In this way, you can learn to mindfully and kindly improve your energy management. You can learn to be more aware of signals of tiredness, of forcing yourself or not respecting boundaries. You are learning the art of being and of making friends with life as it manifests itself in the moment. You can discover and cultivate relaxed concentration and this may help you develop a less exhausting lifestyle in daily life.

Walking meditation – New instructions and curiosity

We invite you to continue in the same way with the walking or strolling meditation and, if it suits you, to explore some new aspects. The first suggestion is to experiment with dividing a step into three small stages, namely 'lifting', 'moving forward', 'placing down' or 'up', 'move', 'down'. And if this becomes tiring or you feel it is making you feel a bit tense, then it is always possible to go back to a simpler form, as outlined in the previous chapters. After all, it is not the case that the more detailed your awareness of walking, the more insight there will be.

Curiosity

I (Jetty) had covered all the windows with cloths in my meditation hut so that I would not look outside during the walking meditation. However our Thai teacher Ajahn Somsak made it clear to me that curiosity is a very valuable quality. After all, without curiosity we cannot learn and develop as human beings. It just becomes oppressive and tiring if we have no choice but to follow it automatically all the time like a slave. He therefore advised me not to cover the windows but instead to keep the eyes slightly closed during the walking meditation, with the gaze 5–10 metres in front of me looking at the ground and without having to focus on anything in particular, and then to simply name the urge to look as 'curiosity', without actually looking at the object of curiosity. So, not seeing it as an unwanted disturbance but as a very healthy inner drive to learn and to notice it with kindness and mindfulness as curiosity. He also suggested following curiosity mindfully when it becomes irresistible and then really integrating it into the practice by noticing it as 'watching'. I noticed much more relaxation in the days that followed.

Participant: *In an inquiry meeting, I asked the question to what extent people with a lot of meditation experience are different from people with only a few years of experience. Well, you can call this 'curiosity', said Frits. I replied with 'Yes, that's right. But can you also give me an answer to the question asked?' Frits: 'I just gave you an answer'. It was a beautiful insight into my analytical 'wanting to know everything' way of thinking and the confrontation with another perspective.*

Awe of the senses

There is an old saying that curiosity is the beginning of wisdom. Therefore you can also include the quality of curiosity or awe in being mindful. In hearing a sound, for example, we can notice all sorts of things. Sometimes we just hear a sound and we can note this as 'hearing'. At times the feeling tone can be striking, so that it can be noticed, as a 'pleasant, unpleasant or neutral feeling' when listening. At other times, curiosity about what you hear is added and you can notice 'listening'. Often, an interpretation of what causes the sound you hear has already been formed, as e.g. a 'car' or a 'crow'. Who knows, it might not be a crow but a pigeon that has been cooing hoarsely. That is why you do not have to label it as a 'crow' but you can observe that 'interpretation' or cognitive framing is taking place. Perhaps an associative thought or a reactive emotion, such as irritation or enjoyment, immediately comes to mind when you hear it. In that case, this can be noted as 'thinking', 'irritation' or 'enjoyment'. Thus, you can be aware of what is happening when you hear, see, smell, taste, feel touch or physical sensations, experience thoughts or emotions beholding experiences in the present moment with awe. You don't have to go looking for anything and you can just be aware of the basic sensory experiences, acknowledging in a relaxed manner whatever is most prominent from moment to moment: the sense experience, the feeling tone, interpretation, thought or feeling.

Mindfulness on the toilet

To sharpen your awareness, we also invite you to consider daily activities as an integral part of meditation. One of our teachers, Sayādaw U Kundalabhivamsa from Myanmar, used to have western meditators listen to cassette tapes with teachings translated into English in his meditation centre in Yangon in the afternoons. One of these tapes describes in beautiful old-fashioned English how to pass a bowel movement with awareness. We are going to repeat the instruction in detail here, if this example is not appealing you can of course always consider performing another routine activity in a similar way, for example mindfully brushing your teeth.

It starts by noticing the urge. Then we can notice the desire to mindfully seek out a toilet. We may notice the opening of the toilet door, the entering, the opening of the trousers or the raising of the skirt, the lowering of the pants and, if we are ready, the sitting down. With a bit of luck, Mother Nature will then do her job and we will be able to notice the descending and exiting of the stool, the sensation of the sphincter and the feeling of relief if the operation was successful. Sometimes Mother Nature needs a little help and there is a need to push a little; this too can be noticed. If any thoughts, sounds, smells or other sensations are noticeable in between, these can of course be noted. Then the intention to take the toilet paper, the unrolling, tearing off and folding of the paper. Then the wiping off until we can note with relief that the operation has been completely successful and the toilet meditation has come to an end. We may then notice the intention to flush, put the clothes in order, wash the hands, unlock the door and go outside feeling relieved.

This is an example of how we can develop awareness in everyday activities with relaxed attention. Both of us found being attentive in everyday activities very complicated at first, and have noticed that most meditators neglect it and think that meditation is mainly about the formal periods of sitting and walking meditation. Participants often mention in the evaluation forms how being attentive in daily activities gave them a lot of insight. This is confirmed by Buddhist scriptures, in which all kinds of situations are described in which someone did not come to a deep insight while walking or sitting but for example when washing clothes.

> **Energy management training**
>
> *During my first retreats, after the hot meals I (Frits) often experienced an indefinable tension in my head and neck, without understanding why. In the beginning I linked this to the very simple vegetarian meals for example only a cheese slice or cheeseburger that we took in an old Catholic monastery in the south of the Netherlands. Until, during one meal, I suddenly realised that I was only trying to be observant but I was exerting myself enormously and was actually concentrating too hard, without any open attention. When I realised this, it turned out that I could also be perfectly attentive with relaxed attention to the movements with the spoon or fork, the chewing, the swallowing and so on, without concentrating so hard and exerting myself. By being less focused on awareness, I could from then on also notice much more easily that there were sometimes sounds or other things in the foreground. Before, I couldn't perceive them because of the strong willpower with which I was meditating; now they could easily be noticed, as 'thinking', 'hearing', and so on.*

Routine actions like brushing your teeth, putting on or taking off clothes, eating or going to the toilet are not trivial. In fact, changes in bowel habits can be a sign of illness and noticing them can be very valuable. We invite you to be attentive in a relaxed and playful way during ordinary daily actions and to explore what is appropriate in the moment. Sometimes you can perform an activity quickly and with a more general mindfulness, other times you can choose to relax consciously and perform something more slowly. A pitfall with daily activities is to fall into extremes, either becoming inattentive or carrying out the daily activities excessively slowly and precisely. At the first extreme, we easily miss a great deal in observation, and when activities are performed very slowly we can easily become over-focused. Buddhism speaks of a middle way, which we can discover and cultivate on a retreat. In this regard, you could also call a retreat an energy management training.

Participant: *Washing up with attention together with another participant. Looking together in silence at the enormous mountain of dishes to be washed. Noticing different feelings and just starting. I pre-rinse, my dishwashing buddy does the washing up and I dry the dishes. After a while of mindful rinsing and drying, my dishwashing buddy throws cutlery into the water. Water splashes up and loud noises can be heard from the cutlery hitting each other. I look at my dishwashing buddy's face. Frustration radiates from it. Our eyes meet. She softly mentions how much she hates washing the cutlery. I whisper, 'Notice it' and look at her with a mischievous expression. At the same time, we burst out laughing. Washing up can be so liberating!*

Inquiry meetings – *Tonglen*

All kinds of experiences are talked about in the individual and group meetings. When we are leading a retreat, we never prepare such conversations and invite you as a participant just to wait and see what naturally comes up and to tune into it. When participants identify a dilemma or difficulty in their practice or life, we sometimes invite them to engage in an exercise, which is derived from an old tried and tested form or meditation, called *tonglen* in Tibetan Buddhism. *Tong* means giving or sharing, *len* means taking or receiving. We offer this practice as an alternative to kindness meditation. In the Mindfulness-Based Compassionate Living or MBCL compassion training, we have tried to make this practice more accessible and name it 'compassionate breathing'.[5]

> Participant: *By means of tonglen – a technique I know but had 'forgotten' a bit – I was able to look at an issue that is currently going on in my life with a different perspective (lighter, kinder).*

The exercise may seem strange at first, because as a participant you are invited to do something paradoxical which goes against your usual instincts. It therefore requires some courage, patience and willingness. Yet this exercise has been practised for centuries. It invites us to become more intimate with what we usually consider undesirable and to practise generosity by sharing what we would rather keep.

This 'wonderfully paradoxical' practice is described below, as we sometimes offer it in a little group or individually in a meeting. However, we always offer it with the warning to only join in if you feel comfortable with it. If you are new to it, we recommend not to start with a very painful theme right away, but with something that feels manageable.

4

Exercise: Compassionate breathing with a difficulty

We invite you to find a sitting posture, noticing physical sensations, thoughts, sounds or the mood or emotion you are experiencing. Acknowledge whatever experience is there.

Then connecting with the breathing movements as they flow by themselves and effortlessly sitting with mindfulness. The next exploration may require a bit of courage and willingness, therefore it can be good to know that you always have the choice of pausing or stopping, and simply sitting with mindfulness. You also don't need to try very hard to achieve something or to get rid of something, you may allow yourself a relaxed attitude.

In this exercise we welcome you to an old meditation practice that may be helpful in exploring a difficulty, for example a conflict or a struggle, a dilemma, a disappointment, a worry or simply the tiredness or tension that you might be experiencing at this moment. There is no need to explore the most pressing issue in your life. It is fine to explore something stressful that feels manageable in the moment.

Be mindful of how this affects you. If you are feeling enough space to continue, you may imagine that this difficulty is being placed in front of you at a distance that feels safe, so that you can examine it. Then exploring if there is a sensual quality that you can easily image, feel or associate in relation to this difficulty. What does it look like? Is there a specific colour or does an image come to mind that symbolises something of the feeling around the theme you are exploring? Is there a sound, an unpleasant smell, a bitter or sour taste that goes with this difficult theme? And how does it feel physically? Is there any tightness? Or is it feeling heavy or hard? Explore the emotional atmosphere surrounding this theme, for example is there any tiredness, fear or anger?

Then invite yourself to an experiment that might seem paradoxical. Imagine that you have a lot of inner space to take in and welcome difficulties, and that in moments of breathing in you carefully welcome little bits of the dark smoke or colour, the image, the unpleasant smell, the physical tension or the emotional atmosphere that you are experiencing in relation to this difficulty.

You may be compassionately mindful of how that affects you.

If you wish to continue you may open yourself to a wholesome or helpful alternative, and on moments of breathing out you can share that with the outer world. For example, if you are experiencing a dark colour, then receiving this dark colour with the inhalation, and on the exhalation sharing something light with the outside world. If you are breathing in an unpleasant smell or a bitter taste, then imagining that you are breathing out something sweet. If it is hardness or heaviness that you are inhaling, then exhaling relaxation or softness. If you are breathing in anger, tiredness or sadness, sharing peace or kindness with the out-breath.

These are just a few examples, we invite you to experiment and find your own way of practising, not with the intention to get rid of a difficulty but as a way of tenderly and more intimately exploring a difficulty that is there already. You might say welcoming little bits of the mud of life breathing in and opening for a lotus to be shared breathing out.

How is this affecting you physically, emotionally and mentally? How is it affecting your relationship with the difficulty you are exploring? Whatever experiences come up they are okay and allowed to be present. Just sit like this for a short time, being attentive to what arises or is touched in this practice.

Resilience

When the wind of change blows, some build a wall, others a windmill.
– Chinese proverb

If this proves to be a valuable practice for you, then we invite you to add it to the retreat as an extra supportive practice, as a helpful alternative to the kindness meditation. It does not need to be practised for very long; doing it for few minutes can be very liberating.

The practice of tonglen can be compared with a psychological flu shot. A vaccination trains the immune system by taking in a fragment of a virus. In a similar way, when we take in a small amount of something painful, we can boost our inner resilience. The important thing here is to do this in small, manageable portions, giving yourself time to connect with a beneficial response to the theme you are exploring.

> Participant: *For a long time I had an underlying feeling of dissatisfaction. During an inquiry meeting with Frits, he guided the exercise whereby you breathe compassionately towards what you are struggling with. On the penultimate day, the unpleasant feeling surfaced more strongly. I imagined that I was gently breathing in what was unpleasant and breathing out kindness towards the unpleasant. I noticed that it softened by itself. Suddenly I realised that the unpleasant feeling was part of who I am. Through the exercise, my attitude towards the side I dislike, such as frustration, dissatisfaction and envy, changed. I have come to accept this side of myself more.*

Sometimes there can be an uncomfortable distance between ourselves and someone else, or we feel dissociated from a painful part in ourselves. Or we may find ourselves working with clients or colleagues where we sense a lot of tension but where words don't feel appropriate. There may be illness or dementia in the family or bereavement and the grief associated with it. All of us are familiar with the pain and suffering on the news these days. We can practise tonglen or compassionate breathing informally in daily life in all sorts of moments like these. This can be very supportive, especially in circumstances where we feel helpless, hopeless or powerless. It enables us to stay connected and be mindfully and compassionately present without using words. We don't need to sink into 'empathy fatigue' and can feel more inner balance in the face of uncontrollable or unavoidable circumstances. At such times, this practice can also feel like 'breathing with equanimity', referring to a perfection that we will explore further in Chapter 7.

The practice of tonglen or compassionate breathing can thus help us cultivate a different attitude to pain, stress and discomfort. This is sometimes expressed in Buddhism as: 'There is a suffering which leads to suffering and there is a suffering which leads to the liberation of suffering'.

Evening talk – Who am I?

May you see what you see through other eyes.
May you hear what you hear with other ears.
May you taste what you have never tasted before
And may you go beyond yourself.
– Masai blessing

In the previous evening's talk, we paid attention to the concept of *anattā* – uncontrollability. In Buddhist psychology, however, this term also refers to an aspect of egolessness or 'non-self', stating that in the ultimate sense, there is no ego, self or fixed identity governing our lives. Life is made up of countless mental and physical phenomena that are interrelated in a cause-and-effect process and can be compared to a river, which is essentially made up of millions of water droplets. The idea of a 'self' or an 'ego' arises through identification with what are essentially transitory and unsatisfactory processes, which we interpret as 'mine', 'mine' or 'I'. This interpretation is understandable from an evolutionary standpoint. It is an attempt by a vulnerable system to get and keep a grip on the environment and to feel more responsibility and care, for example when having children. This 'identification', which meditation teacher Christina Feldman (2017) pithily refers to as 'selfing', is something that can even be observed in small children. It starts with 'my doll', 'my jeans' and 'my rock band' to 'my car', 'my status', 'my house', and so on. This is a habit that also takes hold of the inner world and can lead to 'my belief', 'my guilt' or 'my body'.

Although it is very understandable, this kind of identification also has a dark side. It can lead to a strained attempt to control things that in a deeper sense do not belong to either me or others, but are just a part of ordinary shared human experiences. We try to control the river of life because of this illusion, often in a way that causes tension and stress. Even though we can influence the stream or river of life to a certain extent, beneficial or otherwise, ultimately all these mental and physical processes are impermanent and uncontrollable.

Who owns the clouds?

You must have lain on your back on a lawn and looked at all the clouds that drifted by. Who owns the clouds? Do they belong to you? Do they belong to the neighbours? Do they belong to the Netherlands? Or did we buy them from Germany, or borrow them from England? Presumably, you can't answer that question and conclude that they don't belong to anyone. However, they can be perceived as changing clouds and weather conditions that emerge from specific conditions, drift by and disappear. Similarly, we do not need to distinguish all the different moods as 'mine' or 'my neighbour's'. We can be aware of them as moods without a possessor, as shared human phenomena.

It is healthy to distinguish between conceptual reality and ultimate reality. For example, you might go to a bank to take out a loan. If the bank employee asks you your name, you might say: 'Oh, you know, names are very relative. What you see here is more of a mishmash of physical and mental processes that are constantly in motion. Actually, we can't really give it a name, it is all non-self'. We suspect that it might then become quite difficult to take out a loan. In ordinary everyday life, it may be wiser to speak of Frits, Jetty or whoever. And also to be able to say: 'This is my passport' or 'This is my child'. In the same way, in kindness meditation you can let a kind wish flow to yourself, knowing whom you are sending the wish to.

The notion of non-self as a more expansive concept refers to an ultimate wisdom; a deeper meta-perspective behind ordinary human experiences and this is also the deeper meaning of the word *vipassanā*: to see differently. Here we are going to see phenomena as phenomena, as also suggested by the fourth abode of awareness: *dhammānupassanā*. You may notice that the word *dhamma* is written with a small d; this refers to the phenomenological aspect in the practice, which has been mentioned several times in this book.

The five constituents of human existence

The Buddha distinguished human life into five constituents that make up the personality. Just as we can deconstruct a car into an engine, wheels, chassis, seats and the like, so we can divide human existence into the five elements:

- The body. This includes all the material or physical matter, organs and tangible aspects of our body.
- Feeling. According to the Abhidhamma,[6] feeling consumes or experiences the object as pleasant, unpleasant or neutral. It is much more elementary than an emotion such as joy or sorrow, which is why it is often referred to today as the feeling tone associated with what we experience. Feeling, as it were, 'tastes' the object as pleasant, unpleasant or neutral and is a very determining factor in our functioning. In Chapter 7, we will discuss the different feeling tones and their conditioning effects in more detail.
- Cognition. This quality, also called cognitive representation or discernment, enables us to distinguish the qualities or details of an object. For example, in a moment of visual awareness, we can distinguish a man, a woman or a specific colour. Cognition can also express itself as a (positive or negative) judgement about what we perceive. Finally, this quality plays a major role in memory. Cognition has the function of creating a recognition anchor or sign and in this way creates a frame of reference. It manifests itself as the interpretation of specific characteristics of the perceived object. Cognition is also present in small children, but not yet strongly developed. All kinds of concepts still have to be formed and their knowledge of vocabulary is still limited. As we grow older and the intellect develops, discernment becomes a strong factor, allowing us to increase our ability to distinguish, interpret, assess and store in our memory.
- Concomitants or companions of sensory awareness. This includes all kinds of conditioned states of mind, emotions and abilities that can be experienced. Examples are sadness, anger, devotion, joy or trust; classically, this aspect of human existence is often referred to as 'mental formations' or 'conditionings'.

- Sensory awareness. This refers to very direct and basic sensory awareness, by which we can see, hear, smell, taste, feel and/or think.

The Buddha named these five ingredients of human existence as *pañcupādānakkhandā*: the five constituents or aggregates to which attachments are made. This division in five constituents breaks the illusion of a 'self' and this brings a liberating inner space.

> **From 'my pain' to 'there is discomfort'**
>
> *I (Jetty) tried to call an unpleasant feeling in my leg or back 'my leg', 'my back' or 'my pain' for a while. I then noticed that it bothered me much sooner and more; after all, I was being attacked by an unpleasant feeling. Being more neutrally aware – there is 'discomfort' or 'feeling', 'sensing' made the discomfort much more bearable and less likely to evoke all kinds of reactions in me.*

Many participants tell us that they find it very helpful to occasionally name phenomena as phenomena, as 'thinking', 'feeling', 'hearing', and so on. This not only sharpens our attention but also brings us more naturally into the mode of non-self. Here, thoughts are not taken personally but as small streams of energy and information. As thoughts, which are neither mine nor anyone else's but just as human experiences that pass by and can be recognised as experiences.

Participants often ask a few questions about the concept of 'non-self'. First of all, 'Who is observing?' Buddhist psychology gives a very simple answer to this: mindfulness is observing and mindfulness is not mine, nor is it anyone else's, but simply a mental quality with which something can be observed in the present moment.

Another question that is often asked is: 'What's in it for me' Possibly, this healthy question can be answered very simply: as we come to understand more about the 'transparency' of our experiences, a greater flexibility will naturally arise.

> **Sometimes the mindfulness goes on holiday**
>
> *Ajahn Asabha mirrored the notion of non-self once very beautifully when I (Frits) kept trying to do a meditative cleaning task very attentively, but often found after a while that I would fall into an automatic pilot habit. During an inquiry meeting with the teacher I expressed my frustration about this. All he said was the following: 'Well, maybe you don't have to take it so personally. Sometimes the mindfulness goes on holiday'. I noticed that this brought much more kindness and therefore also more depth to the practice.*

The famous physicist Albert Einstein expressed this perspective very well: 'The true value of a human being can be found in the degree to which he has attained liberation from the self'. Dogen Zenji – a 13th-century Japanese master – expressed this more poetically: 'To study the way is to study the self. To study the self is to forget the self. To forget the self is to remove the boundaries between ourselves and others. To remove the boundaries between ourselves and others is to become enlightened by all things'.[7]

The poem *Air dancing* by Rachel Holstead may also tie in with this:

On the beach yesterday,
a massive wind
blew spray from wave,
sand from shore,
separating
the very particles of being.

We are nothing more
than a momentary
assemblage of atoms,
forming and reforming.
Nothing but a movement
of air and matter
blown by the currents
of the universe.

Yesterday, the wind blew me asunder
leaving nothing but air dancing
on the shore
and I was nothing
but emptiness and connection.

Kindness meditation – A difficult person

In the kindness meditation, we invite you to let a kind wish flow to yourself and to loved ones and to pause regularly and be aware of how this affects you physically and emotionally, giving and receiving in one person.

Then if you feel the space for it, you can make inner contact with someone with whom you have a difficult relationship in one way or another. You can have compassion for yourself and only choose someone with whom you feel you have enough space to explore the relationship. Perhaps this person has hurt you or treated you disrespectfully, or you easily get into a competitive relationship with this person. Perhaps it is someone who annoys you or makes you feel insecure or uncomfortable. If you cannot find anyone, you can count yourself very lucky. If you do find someone, imagine them standing or sitting in front of you, preferably at a distance that feels safe for you.

You can leave it at that; if you feel ready to continue with the exercise, then you can reflect that this person, like everyone else, is vulnerable and encounters loss, pain and grief and is trying to find their way through the ups-and-downs in life and is making mistakes or doing stupid things in the process. This is not usually done intentionally.

You can then, if you feel the space to do so, start by gently repeating a kind or understanding wish, with the rhythm of the breath or separately, perhaps a wish for peace, the best possible health, or wisdom, whatever fits but preferably a wish with little self-interest.

This exercise is certainly not meant to justify disrespectful behaviour, but addresses the vulnerable, non-perfect human behind this behaviour. And sometimes a wish in the 'we' form can be very appropriate.

If you have found the practice of compassionate breathing suits you well, and if you have the space to do so, then you can also turn your attention to the person with whom you have a difficult relationship in the tonglen practice. You can then tune in to the suffering part of this person. This person can for example experience a lot of sadness, or feel unloved, lonely or insecure. You can imagine that you have a lot of space within yourself. You can then breathe in the painful quality that belongs to this person and open yourself to a beneficial quality that you can breathe out again and again, as long as you feel it is appropriate.

If you find that it helpful, you can move one or both hands towards your heart or abdomen in a receiving movement whilst breathing in the painful qualities, moving them out again in a giving gesture to the outside world whilst breathing out the beneficial qualities.

How does this affect you? Acknowledge what you are experiencing, with kindness for all experiences. Sometimes, however, this practice can be difficult and brings up old anger, bitterness or sadness. If so, you can always go back to sending kindness to yourself, as you are the one suffering from the difficult relationship. You can wish for security or inner space and put one or both hands on your heart or belly as a support, apply the practice of compassionate breathing to the pain or sorrow you are experiencing at the moment or you may wish to temporarily return to simply being aware.

Participant: *As I am quite a perfectionist with a highly developed tendency towards self-judgement, I had to think of the paradoxical wish 'I allow myself to be imperfect'. That gave me some space! Then a wish for someone close to you. I had to think of the same thing: to grant that other person also to be imperfect. And then a wish for someone with whom you have a more difficult relationship. I was reminded of growing up in a neglectful environment and saw my parents before me when I could say to them at that moment: 'I give you permission to be imperfect'. That gave a lot of kindness to my attitude towards them and for a moment that could exist alongside the sadness and anger I can feel towards them. It felt healing.*

The practice of compassionate breathing possibly gives a deeper meaning to a poem of Jalal ad-Din Rumi, well-known to many mindfulness practitioners: *The guest house*. Rumi compares being human to being a guest house, where we can welcome all guests, including those who bring suffering and stress. When we welcome them, we can learn to see them as messengers who come to tell, teach or show us something valuable.[8]

Notes

1 From *Confessions* Chapter VIII translation by E. B. Pusey 1909 and available from Gutenberg.org.
2 See *Dipa Ma. The Life and Legacy of a Buddhist Master* by Amy Schmidt (2005).
3 This pitfall in the practice will be addressed more specifically on Day 6.
4 The Anguttara Nikāya or *The Numerical Discourses* of the Buddha form part of the old scriptures of Buddhism.
5 The eight-week secular MBCL training was developed by Frits Koster and Erik van den Brink. The training offers a continuation of MBSR, MBCT or an equivalent mindfulness-based programme. MBCL is described in *Mindfulness-Based Compassionate Living* (Routledge, 2015) and *A Practical Guide to Mindfulness-Based Compassionate Living* (Routledge, 2018). See for more information www.mbcl-international.net.
6 Abhidhamma literally means 'Higher Dhamma' and refers to the more academic study of phenomena in Buddhism. For an introduction to this fascinating and detailed analysis of human existence see *The Web of Buddhist Wisdom* by Frits Koster (Silkwormbooks, 2015).
7 Two books about *anattā* or 'non-self' that we can recommend are *Emptiness* by Guy Armstrong (2017) and *Seeing that Frees* by Rob Burbea (2015).
8 See https://community.mindfulness-network.org/course/view.php?id=39 for a webinar about the practice of compassionate breathing – with explanation of the psychological mechanisms in this practice and exercises of compassionate breathing in relation to ourselves and others.

Chapter 6

The power of simplification
Day 6 – Moments of intention and cultivating integrity and gratitude

This chapter highlights simplification and truthfulness or integrity as the next two perfections. Three motivational systems and five spiritual powers are introduced. We pay attention to following a 'programme without a programme' and to integrating intentions or decision-making processes into the practice.

I have only three things to teach you: simplicity, patience, compassion.[1]
— Lao Tzu

We often let the sixth day of a retreat be an 'extra practice day'. There are only inquiry meetings with the teacher at the request of the participants themselves – with a sign-up list. In the guided meditation in the morning, we invite participants to practise a sixth perfection: *nekkhamma*. This word is classically translated as 'renunciation' and in the Buddhist tradition, this is connected with the decision of Prince Siddhartha to renounce the ease and pleasure of his life of prosperity as a prince and to live as an itinerant ascetic, as was and is still often done in India. In fact, you are practising this already by going on a retreat or in daily life, when you practise meditation, or take a walk during a busy working day. Another translation we find appropriate for this quality is 'simplification'; this quality can be cultivated in many ways and can give the meditation process much more power.

Simplification in the practice

As Lao Tzu once said: 'I have only three things to teach you: simplicity, patience, compassion. These three are your greatest treasures'. For example, in sitting meditation you can practise 'simplicity in the posture'. If you recognise that you easily tempted to change your posture and to move more often, you can experiment with just sitting without moving and watching whatever arises. The effect is stillness in the posture, and this can sometimes strengthen the practice.

> **Fishing and the art of stillness**
>
> *As mentioned before, when I (Frits) was young – and until I started to develop more ethical awareness, I went fishing a lot. I noticed that the fish came and stayed closer to me the less I moved; fish are frightened by a lot of movement. In a similar way, insight and healing processes come into view better when we quieten down and 'simplify our movements' and only move when necessary – and then, of course, with awareness.*

Simplification can also be developed during walking meditation. If you notice that you often change places and walk here and then there, it can give you peace of mind to resolve to walk in one place for a period of time and to keep on walking there. If thoughts and impulses come up to do something else or to walk somewhere else, then this may be noticed with kindness, without acting on it, just keeping to the task at hand.

We can also practise this in daily activities. For example, you can feel free to skip a daily shower or shave or cut back on your consumption of tea or coffee.

We know that this can sometimes meet with resistance, so we add another form of abstention to the examples. Giving something up can also be practised with inner patterns. If you notice that you tend to be less than conscientious, then acknowledging and renouncing this 'laziness pattern' can be very helpful. If, on the other hand, you know you are very stern with yourself during practice, then kind observation and consciously giving up this 'harshness pattern' can be very valuable. In all cases these are merely suggestions, we invite you to experiment with them. In this way, you can become your own retreat coach.

Different forms of concentration

It is good to talk a bit more about the value of concentration (*samādhi*). This factor has the characteristic of not being scattered and distracted. Concentration has the effect of collecting or concentrating the consciousness in one object, it manifests itself as a calm unification or one-pointedness of mind, as the focus or magnifying glass through which something is perceived. Concentration is a valuable asset in our daily life; it enables us to easily perform our tasks and provides inner peace. This is why Sayadaw U Tejaniya (2016b) also refers to this quality as stability. Buddhist psychology describes three types of beneficially directed concentration, namely:

- Access concentration (*upacāra samādhi*).
- Deep, full concentration (*appanā samādhi*).
- Momentary concentration (*khanika samādhi*).

The first two types are mainly developed in meditation forms where the emphasis is on realising calm and blissful forms of absorption or *jhāna*. Such a level of concentration can be achieved by focusing the mind on one specific preferred object and excluding all other objects. In the initial stage in the Abhidhamma, this is called *upacāra samādhi* (access concentration), when deeper absorption is realised it is called *appanā samādhi* (absorption or full concentration). There are many valuable forms of meditation to be found in all wisdom traditions which teach this kind of practice. In Buddhism, these are often called types of *samatha* or tranquillity meditation.

The third form of concentration belongs to the practice of *vipassanā* meditation, in which the development of mindfulness or awareness is central. It focuses on what is occurring in the present moment, without a preferred object and without having to concentrate deeply on what is perceived. Therefore in *vipassanā* meditation, there are many more objects, because any physical, mental, emotional or sensory experience is suitable as a meditation object. A light momentary concentration is sufficient here, always maintaining a non-dissociative space around the object, by being internally aware of what arises and possibly naming or registering this as an experience. This third form of concentration develops little by little and grows in strength slowly but surely, without becoming dominant. Mindfulness remains the strongest factor, whereby flexibility in moment-to-moment awareness creates a clearer focus and leads to deeper insight.

Both types of practice are very valuable and in retreats that we lead ourselves we make use of both types. Indeed, kindness meditation fits more under the heading of tranquillity meditation, even though the goal here is not so much to realise deep states of absorption as to bring about inner calm and tranquillity. In the guidance, we therefore use it more as a valuable support for inner healing processes and the practice of *vipassanā* meditation. We invite you as a participant to freely explore both types.

Three systems of motivation

On this extra day of practice, we sometimes offer a model that can be helpful to assess the way you are practising. The model was developed by Paul Gilbert (2010) and distinguishes three basic emotion regulation systems. These are also called motivational systems: a soothing system, a threat system and a drive system. We present the cat as an example. If a cat feels safe and has eaten well, she will lie down in the sun or groom herself or another cat. She is relaxed; the calming system dominates at that moment. However, if she suddenly hears the barking of a dog nearby that she doesn't know, she will jump up and start hissing, with an arched back and a bushy tail. Her attention is then fully focused on the threat; the threat system is activated and on alert. When the danger is gone, she will lie down and relax again.

If she suddenly sees a mouse, she is again fully alert and focused, but the atmosphere is different from when she feels threatened. Now she is focussing on getting something, namely a reward in this case prey. This is also called the drive system. When she has caught the mouse and possibly devoured it, she will rest again.

This model provides a simple understanding of the hardware in all animals. And we humans are animals too, of course. We think it is a very helpful model, because it is non-judgemental. After all, we need all three systems to live and survive. If you didn't have a threat system you wouldn't survive the busy traffic in a big city; if you didn't have a drive system you would starve. And if you didn't have a soothing system, you would be completely exhausted.

> Participant: *If I noticed that I was trying very hard – from the threat or drive system – then the image of the three cats would easily make me smile. I then more quickly returned to the soothing system.*

The threat system may be the most powerful system and it feels unpleasant. After all, it is trying to warn us that there is possible danger, so it is no wonder that the threat system easily dominates and appears to be deeply embedded in the nervous system, as confirmed by Stephen Porges (2017), who introduced the term 'neuroception' into neuroscience. This term refers to the subtle and subconscious, autonomous activity of our nervous system, which, like a radar or a very subtle extra sense organ, constantly and subconsciously scans the environment to assess whether it is safe or threatening. It is therefore not surprising that the threat system soon comes to dominate over the other two systems.[2]

The threat and the drive systems cost a lot more energy and provide an interesting differentiation in the doing-mode mentioned earlier in this book. When animals do not need to flee or hunt, they will return to the calmness of the soothing system, the 'being-mode', to rest and recharge in order to be able to hunt or flee again. In humans, this is more difficult. Our new brain has given us unprecedented capabilities and made us the most creative and powerful species on earth. However, we also start to imagine all kinds of catastrophes with this same new brain. As Mark Twain stated: 'I've suffered a great many catastrophes in my life. Most of them never happened'. And we set ourselves all sorts of goals to achieve, even when we are on holiday. Paul Gilbert expresses this aptly: 'We are different from other animals in profound ways too, and this is both a gift and a curse'.[3]

Nurturing the soothing system with mindfulness

You will come across these three systems everywhere in your life including on retreat. You could formulate two intentions here: first, to wisely and compassionately relate to the threat system and the drive system, and second to develop extra space for the soothing system and to nourish it. We automatically create more inner space and connection with the 'being-mode' when, in a gentle, understanding way, we notice physical, mental or emotional signs of the threat and/or the drive system. In addition, the relaxed atmosphere of the soothing system can also be developed whilst sitting, walking, brushing your teeth and doing other activities in a relaxed and unhurried way. We then stimulate an atmosphere of well-being, playfulness and connectedness.

A programme without a programme

Ladybird flew to me
and landed.
She doesn't want to leave anymore.
– Haiku from an anonymous participant

We cannot force concentration, but we can facilitate it by creating favourable conditions and by operating from the soothing system. One way is to simplify the practice, as outlined earlier in this chapter. Another way mentioned in Buddhist commentaries is 'refreshing and making the mind happy and content'. For the first few days of the retreat, everyone is invited to practise with the retreat schedule. We invite you to make room for a 'programme-free' programme on the sixth day and not to have to follow the usual meditation schedule for one or more sections of the day. Of course, this does not necessarily mean that we will ask you to go online again and answer your emails or watch a film or sitcom on your mobile phone, but it does mean that you will have the freedom to leave the usual programme of walking and sitting for what it is and, for example, to go for a long walk and sit down somewhere for a while at a suitable spot on the way, without any time restrictions – except for the meals in the centre, of course. However, you can always return to the familiar programme if you wish.

> Participant: *When in an inquiry meeting I received the suggestion to leave the afternoon programme for once and do what I felt like, I felt uncomfortable at first. I went for a walk but did not know what purpose this served. Until I remembered that as a little girl, I had often played or lain carefree on a lawn. After the long walk, I sat down on a bench at the edge of the moor ... I have not felt so peaceful for years and will not forget this anytime soon.*

Five spiritual faculties

In Buddhist psychology there is often reference to five spiritual faculties or *indriya*, which blossom with the practice of *vipassanā* meditation; our meditation teachers regularly referred to these five beneficial qualities. Their growth cannot be forced, and in that sense, they are like grass, which does not grow faster when you pull it.

Faith

According to the Visuddhimagga, faith or *saddhā* is characterised as 'the presence of faith or trust'. Trust or devotion has a purifying effect and manifests itself as clarity, decisiveness and as a resolute attitude. A direct condition for the emergence of trust is the presence of what in Pali is called a *saddheyya vatthu*: an object that evokes inspiration or trust. Examples are:

- Seeing a Buddha statue or someone with a peaceful appearance.
- Hearing or reading the teachings of the Buddha or listening to wise advice in general.
- Realising that you are doing or have done something valuable for your own well-being and/or that of others.
- Maintaining friendships with other people who practise; this is considered very beneficial in Buddhist psychology.
- Experiencing the beneficial effects of meditation.
- Realising or reflecting on one's ability to cope in a wise way with difficult experiences in life, such as illness, pain, fear and grief.

Faith or trust is the basis for performing beneficial deeds, such as generosity, ethical behaviour and patience. It is also the basis for engaging in a spiritual path. When we start practising meditation, the trust may still be somewhat blind, which is also called *pakati saddhā*. After all, there is no real experience of meditation yet and you only have faith in someone who has told you about the beneficial effects of meditation or you have been inspired by something you have read. Over time, and certainly, in a retreat, a second form of trust gradually arises that is more derived from the practice of meditation: *bhavanā saddhā*. This deeper confidence supports the growth of the second spiritual faculty.

Dedication

Dedication or *vīriya* has already been introduced in the previous chapter. Dedication or commitment (engagement) has patience and perseverance as its characteristic; the courageous commitment not to give up in the face of difficulties and temptations on the path of meditation. Its function is to support and strengthen mindfulness. Commitment manifests as a firm and heroic determination not to give up on activities or undertakings prematurely or in the middle. It comes from confidence and a sense of urgency, from being confronted with the instability or uncertainty of existence.

Buddhist psychology describes four beneficial forms of commitment. They are often called the four 'right efforts' or *sammappadhāna*, they can be developed during retreat and in daily life.

- The first form is the commitment to handle and deconstruct unhelpful states of mind in a wise and compassionate way.
- The second form of commitment focuses on prevention of reactivity. This form of commitment is more subtle in nature and usually takes time to understand and use. Here, you become more aware of signs of, for example, anger, fear, sleepiness or inner patterns, which can prevent suffering.
- The third form is the development of beneficial, helpful forces that have not yet arisen. In fact, you realise this form of commitment every moment that you are attentive.
- The fourth and final form of commitment is called the further development of beneficial experiences. This is the kind of commitment that you can make if you have continuity of mindfulness and an inner balance, in which the practice can easily flourish.

Mindfulness

A balanced dedication supports mindfulness or *sati*. We have already written a lot in this book about this wholesome companion in our lives, so below is just a brief summary of the four fields of awareness:

1 The body – for example, the rising and falling of the abdomen, awareness of the physical posture, of movements made or actions performed.
2 Feelings – this includes pleasant and unpleasant bodily sensations, as well as the pleasant, unpleasant and neutral feeling tones experienced through other sensory and mental experiences.
3 Mental processes – thoughts, moods and inner patterns.
4 Phenomena – being aware of the arising and passing away of mental, physical and sensory phenomena and being aware of how we can cultivate inner freedom-enhancing qualities.

These four fields can be compared to four meadows that can be used by a cow to graze on. They can also be seen as the necessary foundations on which a house (of insight) is built. If these foundations are not firmly built, then the house can easily collapse. This example shows that the four foundations of mindfulness are all equally important.

Concentration

Mindfulness encourages concentration or *samādhi*, which, as described earlier in this chapter, brings stability and depth to the practice. As the Buddha once said: 'Those who have reached and established concentration see the world as it really is'. In the commentaries concerning the practice of (insight) meditation much attention is therefore paid to creating good conditions for the development of concentration. A link is made here to the maintenance of a healthy ethic, so that one is not unnecessarily plagued by shame, fear and guilt. In addition, the Visuddhimagga offers a number of suggestions for cultivating concentration, some of which we describe below.

Cultivating a healthy foundation

This means taking good and wise care of yourself in terms of health, hygiene and lifestyle, so that a healthy climate for meditation is created.

Balancing the five spiritual powers

This is perhaps the greatest art of meditation. The balance between commitment and concentration is of great importance. That is why it is generally advised to keep periods of walking and sitting meditation equal in length during retreats. Mindfulness is the most important factor in both walking and sitting; in walking we usually develop a little more energy and in sitting a little more concentration so alternating walking and sitting creates a good inner balance. However, this balance can sometimes be disturbed. For example, strong, persistent dullness often indicates too much concentration in relation to the available energy or *vīriya*. Practising a bit more walking meditation or general daily living activities attentively performed can then help you to restore the necessary balance. And when you feel a lot of restlessness, practising a little more sitting meditation may help to calm the mind.

Skill in the meditation object

In tranquillity meditation, this means unifying more and more with the object of concentration. In insight meditation, it means developing an ever-increasing skill and flexibility in being aware and noticing what arises within or around you from moment to moment. Patience is paramount for creating growth in the practice.

Encouraging yourself every now and then

This is particularly necessary at times of (prolonged) pain, reluctance, inertia or fear. You encourage yourself and resolve to stay put and continue with the practice for as long as it is possible to stay with the pain or the difficult state of mind without force.

Sometimes, motivating or inspiring yourself is also necessary to avoid inertia and lack of awareness. This can be achieved, for example, by reflecting on our shared humanity – that we all face or will face human suffering and are all subject to old age, illness and death.

Being content with circumstances

In the modern world, we are often used to having high expectations regarding food, clothing, living conditions, guidance, our own functioning and so on. In order not to fall prey to dissatisfaction, complaining and disturbed concentration, it is advisable to be content with the living conditions as they are at the moment. The conditions for perfect concentration almost never present themselves. Sometimes the food is less tasty or nutritious, sometimes you don't feel so well or you're just not in the perfect sitting position, sometimes there are distracting noises. Insight meditation could be formulated as the realisation of perfection in the imperfection of conditioned human existence. Instead of chasing an ideal image, you can also learn to reconcile yourself with the situation as it is now. If this is not helpful, name the dissatisfaction that has arisen. In this way, you can develop an attitude which was described by the Buddha as 'contentment with little'. This virtue is fertile ground for developing good concentration.

Directing the mind to develop concentration

This last suggestion invites you to plant more and more seeds of mindfulness into your daily activities and to increasingly integrate the practice of meditation into your life. It goes without saying that a retreat serves as an ideal basis for the fifth and final spiritual faculty to flourish.

Wisdom

Wisdom or insight is the fruit of the above four qualities and comes from concentrated attention. Wisdom or insight is not only an intellectual ability to put things into perspective, but also refers to a deeper intuitive understanding of reality as it presents itself in the moment, without using 'step by step' reasoning.

Mindfulness is the most important of the five forces mentioned in this chapter. Without awareness, it is not possible to bring and keep the other four *indriya* in proper balance. Achahn Asabha once compared the function of mindfulness to that of a prime minister, who is the hub of a team of five ministers, with the other four ministers having an individually specialised task and being coordinated by the prime minister. In traditional writings, mindfulness is also sometimes compared to a coachman who leads two pairs of horses – effort and concentration as a pair and wisdom and faith as a pair. If these pairs are not in balance this can be detected and corrected through mindfulness, so that the meditative faculties start to harmonise again and develop in such a way that they can be called five *bala* or powers. It is an art that can be learnt slowly but surely and that allows for greater independence in the practice.

Walking meditation – Catching the intention

In addition to the possibilities already mentioned on previous days, we invite you to freely experiment with an alternative way of walking on this sixth day. Here something can be integrated that you could call 'intentions' or 'decision moments'. Because on a very subtle level, an intention and decision takes place in every moment before we do something. This happens before we stand up, sit down, take something, say something, do something or cease to do something. This subtle inner 'yes' happens thousands of times a day, most of the time unconsciously, without us even realising it. During normal daily activities, such as showering, eating, going to the toilet and so on, it can be fascinating to recognise these subtle stimuli. During walking meditation, we invite you to notice the small decision to take a new step now and then. The decision or intention to begin and the decision to end or continue walking will be much more evident than whilst walking normally. When walking slowly naming 'left step, right step' can be done more easily. If necessary, the naming can be 'decide, left step' and 'decide, right step'. Or the 'decide' can be replaced by another word, such as 'yes', 'green (light)', 'intention', 'okay' or 'wish'. The word is less relevant here than the awareness that it is taking place; mere awareness is also fine. For many meditators, this subtle process manifests primarily as a cognitive 'yes'. There are, however, also participants who more easily recognise it as a physical process, namely as the very first physical beginning of a movement or activity. Both options are fine; in the second case, this can then be noted, for example, 'begin, left step', 'begin, right step'. We can recommend doing this in a gentle unforcing way, with a lighthearted attitude. If you notice getting tense while noticing intentions you may leave it out. Ultimately it is just a suggestion that may sometimes work well and other times not.

You will then often naturally become aware of other related processes as well, such as hesitation, doubt or indecision. Such subtle attitudes can also be included in the practice without needing to judge them.

From impulsive to meditative

Achahn Asabha often gave a very pragmatic suggestion to start noticing intentions and decision-making processes more often. His tip was an extension of the old wisdom of counting to ten first if you have a short fuse and have a painful mixture of 'impulsive and explosive' in your mental condition/state. Counting to ten first can then create space for more wisdom.

We sometimes invite you to try two experiments in a retreat:

Experiment 1

After reading this sentence, notice the decision to make a simple movement with your hand, arm, leg or foot, and then perform it with relaxed awareness.

Experiment 2

After reading this sentence, notice the decision to make another simple movement with your hand, arm, leg or foot, and then explicitly name this decision three times, as for example 'deciding', 'deciding', 'deciding', 'intention', 'intention', 'intention', 'okay', 'okay', 'okay', and then perform this movement with relaxed awareness.

Do you notice any difference between these two experiments? Many people find that the second experiment brings a little more space and unwinding; it is as if the awareness and the concentration are automatically more collected. Similarly, if you notice lack of attention when, for example, you are eating or using the bathroom, you can bring the suggestion of the second experiment into your practice for a while. It often feels somewhat artificial at first, but it can be a practical help when you are struggling with a high degree of impulsiveness or mindlessness in your practice.

If the integration of intentions becomes like searching for a 'needle in a haystack' or you notice that the practice is creating tension, then let go of this new suggestion. It is merely a suggestion that can sometimes be helpful and sometimes not. We keep inviting you to cultivate a relaxed, unforced way of walking or mindfully strolling, from the beginning to the end of the retreat.

> Participant: *At first, the suggestion of noticing decisions, for example, taking a new step in walking, drove me crazy. At a certain point, however, I also started to enjoy it and I noticed that it started to give me much more space. In daily life I am usually on edge. By becoming more aware of the 'just about to do' experience I can sometimes choose not to do something or to do it differently.*

Evening talk – Pleasant experiences and integrity

In the evening Dhamma talk, we pay attention to experiences that have not been addressed so far. Indeed, much attention has been paid to 'difficult' experiences, such as physical discomfort, emotions that feel unpleasant, unwanted thoughts. Many retreatants, however, also gradually begin to experience pleasant experiences, in all forms, frequencies and strengths of perception. It is not that this happens to all meditators; it depends on the circumstances from which you are participating, the facilities at the retreat, your familiarity with the practice of meditation and other factors. But the fact that such pleasurable experiences arise is a natural thing. During the preceding days of the retreat, a number of inner healing and wisdom processes have already taken place, causing you to experience a less burdened mind and a better inner meditative balance. Therefore, in a sense, they are fruits of the practice.

> Participant: *The next day I realised that a different kind of happiness emerges, a gentle inner radiance that no longer depends on drama or comedy.*

Pleasurable experiences

In Buddhist psychology, nine pleasurable experiences are specifically mentioned; for the sake of enthusiasts, the Pali terms are also given throughout:

1. You may start seeing lights, colours or all kinds of images while sitting with your eyes closed (*obhāsa*).
2. All kinds of insights may come (*nāna*).
3. Deep joy may arise. This is not so much the joy you have when a nice dessert is waiting for you at dinner, which of course is not wrong either. This joy, which is also called *vipassanā* joy, arises more from experiencing a carefree heart (*pīti*).
4. A strong sense of trust may well arise in you, trust in the teacher, in the practice and/or in yourself (*saddhā*), or a deep peace or serenity may descend upon you like a pleasant warm blanket (*passaddhi*).
5. You suddenly feel very happy, satisfied and at ease; a sense of well-being (*sukha*).
6. The pleasantness may also manifest itself in a powerful way, for instance, as a clear determination, steadfastness and motivation to practise (*adhimokkha*).
7. You suddenly feel very fit and energetic (*paggāha*).
8. Great and spontaneous clarity arises, awareness becomes effortless (*upatthāna*).
9. A very calm and balanced inner attitude arises amidst all the ups and downs (*upekkhā*).

All such experiences are quite understandable; as some weeds in the 'garden of life' have lost their strength more space naturally opens up and new valuable qualities blossom. There is nothing wrong with you if you have this kind of experience.

Under the spell of the pleasurable

There is a catch; we are a reactive species. When something feels unpleasant, we easily react with anger or discontent. The same mechanism takes place with experiences that are pleasant in our perception. We then become intoxicated by these pleasant experiences and unconsciously react to them. Therefore, these pleasant experiences are also called *vipassanā* pitfalls or *upakilesas* in Buddhist psychology, and this is made particularly clear by the tenth item in this list 10. Attachment (*nikanti*) arises, wanting to hold on to the beautiful experience for as long as possible. Sometimes this can make you not want to go to meals or participate in the walking meditation, for fear that this might disturb the deep peace. You start to long for that one beautiful experience and get disappointed every time that beautiful experience does not want to arise or appear again. Or you start to identify strongly with it: 'This is only my true core. All that restlessness I experienced before was probably the negative radiation of other meditators. But now I have discovered my true self'. You may start to feel overconfident or haughty: 'Look at me meditating well. The others haven't got that far yet', or you may become suspicious: 'I'm supposed to be looking at pain and suffering. This is very strange'.

All these forms of reactivity are quite understandable. But they are the reason why the above experiences are called meditative pitfalls. On the one hand, these are the fruits of a more peaceful mind and of the practice of meditation; on the other hand, we can easily become entangled in reactivity and the practice can stagnate, sometimes for years. In addition, pleasant experiences can easily blind us, as the following story shows.

The Ayurvedic Garden

We were on holiday in Sri Lanka a few years ago. During a taxi ride, we were persuaded by the driver to visit an Ayurvedic garden near Kandy. It was later in the afternoon; we turned out to be the only guests and were received like a king and a queen. The people showed us around the beautiful gardens and were full of praise for our interest and good looks. Before we realised it, we were lying on a massage table and getting a wonderful massage just like that. We felt wonderfully peaceful and were also allowed a look in the shop ... half an hour later we walked away happy and content. After about ten minutes, we woke up from this enchantment and wondered: what have we bought now? We turned out to have bought all kinds of expensive ointments, soaps and other attributes that were of no use to us at all and, moreover, were difficult to get on the plane with us.

We all sometimes fall under the spell of a pleasant experience; it can take years before we realise this. For example, for years I (Frits) was unconsciously caught in an enormous drive (number 6 of the meditative pitfalls) in the practice. During walking meditation I did my utmost to be aware of all details in a step; when sitting down I would sink into fatigue and dullness in no time.

The Buddha was once asked how he found deeper wisdom and crossed the 'flood' (of confusion). He replied poetically: 'It is in this way, friend, that by not halting and by not straining I crossed the flood'.[4] In this passage, sinking into dullness and being unconsciously blinded by the meditative pitfalls is expressed as 'standing still'. Fortunately, there is a very simple and also liberating way out of these pitfalls: be mindful of all experiences including pleasant ones and to the reactivity in them.

Being honest and truthful in the practice

Here the seventh perfection fits very well: truthfulness or realism, honesty or sincerity (*sacca*). In daily life, this virtue, can be very important. Sincere, honest people radiate more reliability and in the long run often get more done than people who lie. 'Honesty is the best policy' as the saying goes. This quality can be developed when we ask ourselves whether we are acting with integrity and not fooling ourselves and/or other people. One of the guidelines in interpersonal mindfulness practice is called 'speaking the truth'. Here the truth does not have to be described as an ultimate law, but more as an intention to speak out in a congruent and respectful way what you feel is right in the moment. One participant expressed the value of this as follows:

> Participant: *For a while I felt real, not fake. There was no difference between my inner life and the presentation to the outside world, I stayed more in harmony with myself. It is a form of loving myself, very nice.*

In mindful communication programmes, you can further develop this integrity in an interpersonal way. When you are on retreat, you can further develop this attitude in an intrapersonal way, by not magnifying one experience, while glossing over, condemning or pushing away another. In this, you can adopt the attitude of a judge who does not yet have to make a decision. He or she will first listen to all parties disinterestedly and impartially and only then, with as much integrity as possible, will he or she pass judgement. The N from the RAIN model in Chapter 5 can therefore be understood here as neutral or as a normal experience. The American meditation teacher Joko Beck and Smith (1995) express this aptly through the title of their book *Nothing Special*.

Nothing special

When we had talked about pleasant experiences and meditative pitfalls during a retreat a few years ago, an angry participant came to a group practice session the next day. She felt that something had been taken from her. It turned out that she had been meditating for many years and easily found herself in a peaceful atmosphere; the introduction to the meditative pitfalls had hurt her. When there was enough space to explore this further, she had to admit the following. She lived with her husband and two boys and always went upstairs to meditate for half an hour after dinner. When she came downstairs after meditation, she often felt an unpleasant split in the practice. She usually came out of meditation feeling very peaceful, but when she heard her two adolescent sons arguing and saw that her husband hadn't done the dishes yet, she immediately felt dissatisfaction and that often felt particularly painful. After the retreat, she emailed us to say that she had started to name the peaceful atmosphere in the meditation as an ordinary, not special, experience. Because of this, she had noticed that there was much more flexibility in the practice and that the gap between meditation and daily life had narrowed.

By integrating pleasant experiences as an object of meditation, more maturity and inner balance usually come into the practice. In the scriptures, this is even referred to as a specific deepening process which in the commentaries is described as 'purification through knowledge and vision of what is path and not-path' (*maggāmagga ñāṇadassana visuddhi*). This refers to an expanded insight, whereby in the practice a greater openness arises to all experiences – including those with a pleasant feeling tone.

> Participant: *I sometimes saw all kinds of images and colours with my eyes closed. It was a little disconcerting at first, and then also very reassuring to begin to look at these as normal phenomena, not to be caught up in them.*

Am I still allowed to enjoy myself?

The suggestion described above not uncommonly meets with resistance. Often we hear objections: 'Am I still allowed to enjoy myself?' This question can easily be answered: 'There is nothing bad about enjoying, awareness has no enemies'. In a retreat, however, the invitation is to treat all experiences in the same way, and thus to honestly acknowledge enjoyment, treasuring, wanting to hold on to, pride or desire as an experience in the now, without having to repress it or follow it. And we can also celebrate life in a very subtle way, as the following participant feedback shows.

> Participant: *I suddenly realised that to be aware of your breathing is basically to celebrate life. If you don't breathe, life is gone. Very simple. So you can celebrate your birthday every year, but for the same reason you can celebrate your life every day ... by paying attention to your breathing.*

Enjoying ourselves is a very healthy activity, certainly also in daily life, precisely because the default brain described earlier is already so focused on possible danger and coping with it.

That is why Rick Hanson (2009, 2014) often talks about 'taking in the good', and social psychologist and researcher Dacher Keltner (2023) speaks about the value of awe as a way to uncover everyday wonder as a vital force within our lives. He believes it is okay to consciously open ourselves up to the pleasant things that life has to offer. If you are rather strict with yourself, we often suggest that you go for a pleasure walk and while you are walking, open yourself up to the pleasant stimuli that present themselves through the senses.

Kindness meditation – Gratitude

In the last sitting period you are invited first to sit in silence and with awareness and then to give some space to a kind wish towards yourself and then to a kind wish towards one or some loved ones in your life This is a good introduction to the topic of tonight's talk which is 'gratitude'.

The invitation is namely to ask yourself the question: 'What can I feel grateful for in my life?' or 'What makes me happy in my life?' Even if sometimes you think your life is not going so well, some answers may come up that have to do with something that came naturally to you at birth, such as a reasonably healthy body, a talent, the environment or family you were born into.

Perhaps other responses arise, perhaps you feel joy or gratitude for people you have met in your life? A good friend, a teacher who meant a lot to you, children, grandchildren or a pet.

There may also be things that come to mind where you have done something beautiful or valuable that makes you feel grateful or satisfied. For example, a study you have carried out, a business you have built or a contribution you have made to put something beautiful into the world either recently or further back in the past. There may even be a memory of a difficult or painful period that has finally brought you to something new for which you can feel gratitude; a lotus that has emerged from the mud. Finally, there may be gratitude or appreciation for something you have discovered or developed in this retreat.

What can you feel grateful or happy for? You may also want to echo the question, 'What is it that makes me grateful or happy?' Explore the effect this question has on you, on your body, emotions and thoughts.

You can explore the inner landscape of gratitude for as long as you like. Or you may wish to sit with the reflection of the French novelist and essayist Marcel Proust (1871–1922): 'Let us be grateful to the people who make us happy; they are the charming gardeners who make our souls blossom'.

Notes

1 *Tao Teh King*, available from Gutenberg.org and translated by James Legge.
2 Porges, S.W. (2007). The polyvagal perspective. *Biological Psychology*, 74, 116–143.
3 From the foreword by Paul Gilbert in *Mindfulness-Based Compassionate Living* (2015) by Erik van den Brink and Frits Koster.
4 From the Oghatarana Sutta in the Samyutta Nikāya or *The Connected Discourses* by the Buddha.

Chapter 7

Recognising the feeling tone
Day 7 – Steadiness and equanimity in the practice

The last full day of meditation focuses on steadiness and equanimity as the last two perfections. Three feeling tones and their conditioning effects are covered and how to strengthen the five spiritual faculties. In the inquiry meetings, we look back over the retreat and also begin to look to the future.

Yesterday is history,
tomorrow is a mystery.
Today is a gift,
that is why it is called the present.
– Attributed to Eleanor Roosevelt among others and used by the old turtle in Kung Fu Panda

We have now arrived at the last full day of the retreat. Again, we invite you to start with a kind wish towards yourself and you can also regularly send a kind wish to a dear person at home or in your family. You may also include a 'neutral' person, for example, a meditator who is sitting or walking near you or someone who happens to be walking or cycling by when you are outside, a person you don't know very well. It can be nice to realise that there are millions of people we don't know very well who can therefore be integrated in this category. Whenever you wish, you can return to the simplicity of sitting, walking, lying down, standing, walking or acting with awareness.

Going to the end of the retreat with determination

This day usually brings new experiences. The mind starts planning for life after the retreat. This may be accompanied by joy, restlessness, anxiety or sometimes a reluctance to engage with something difficult in daily life. There may be a tendency to work extra hard or to sink into lethargy. There might be thoughts that are evaluating the retreat and these might be accompanied by joy and satisfaction or disappointment. The approaching end of the retreat may be accompanied by relief or some sadness. All these experiences are quite normal, because of our new human brain we have a sense of time and this affects us in many ways. Here the eighth perfection, steadiness or determination (*aditthāna*), can be very helpful. In the classical Buddhist scriptures, this perfection is often linked to the quest of Prince Siddhartha. After many years of practising as an itinerant ascetic, he decided to take better care of his body and to follow a path between harshness and rigidity on the one hand and pleasure-seeking on the other. When he had recovered sufficiently, he sat down to meditate under a big tree with a determined wish 'May my blood and flesh dry up and leave only the skin, sinews and bones. May I die but I not rise until I have realised the deepest wisdom'.

Now, you don't have to go along with this completely. However, perhaps this can inspire you to develop a quality of steadiness and determination, for example by setting a few intentions to stay with being aware while walking or sitting: 'In this sitting period I will sit still whatever happens' or 'This time I will stay with the path which I have chosen in this period of walking meditation'. If stimuli arise to move while sitting or to do other things during the walking meditation, then you can quietly acknowledge these without needing to act upon them. We have experienced time and time again both with others and with ourselves that the last day of a retreat can be very insightful. So you practise what the Buddha summarised beautifully: 'The Dhamma is lovely in the beginning, in the middle and at the end'. This means, among other things, that a retreat is not only fruitful in the beginning and/or in the middle, but that the latter part of a retreat can also be very insightful.

For example, meetings are often particularly prone to confusion at the end. Many people become impatient and do not listen carefully or make unwise statements. The end of a sitting period or the end of a retreat can be a very valuable training in retaining control by remaining with mindfulness in quiet contemplation until the end.

Three feeling tones and their conditioning effects

Today we invite you to integrate another field of awareness into the practice. Buddhist psychology assumes that all human experience is accompanied by a so-called feeling tone, a basic feeling or *vedanā* in Pali, that we do not choose but that arises naturally with the object of observation. Feeling is the factor that consumes or experiences the object. It is an elementary affective way of experiencing an object; feeling is thus much more elementary than an emotion such as joy or irritation (Koster, 2015).

We have already discussed two of the three different kinds of feeling tone; namely experiences that are accompanied by an unpleasant feeling tone and experiences that are accompanied by a pleasant feeling tone. When we are not aware of these feeling tones, they can easily evoke all kinds of inner reactions. When the tone is unpleasant, we may become angry, impatient, jealous or feel guilty. When the tone is pleasant, we may react with a desire for more, attachment or pride.

However, there are also a great many stimuli which do not register as clearly pleasant or unpleasant and where the feeling tone is more neutral. And if we are not aware of this, all kinds of reactivity can arise. Hedonists may then occupy themselves internally with the search for pleasant sensory stimuli or erotic fantasies. Adventurers become bored because it seems that nothing special is happening. The psychologist in us starts to doubt and become insecure: 'I haven't experienced sadness, strong emotions or inner patterns for half an hour. I have come to a standstill'. The hard worker becomes indifferent or anxious. A kind of rebelliousness can also develop; one participant put it all into words in the following poem that she later sent us:

Done with walking.
Done with sitting.
Done with lying down.
I'm going to stand on my head,
I haven't done that much yet.

All these kinds of reactions are very understandable. Acknowledging these forms of reactivity is valuable and ensures that inner freedom can arise again, which Buddhist psychology sometimes refers to as 'dismantling' reactivity that has already arisen. When we become more aware, we can intercept reactivity when it arises; it can sometimes even be prevented by simply noticing the pleasant, neutral or unpleasant feeling tone of an experience.

> Participant: *I have learned that there are many more neutral experiences than I thought. It was really new for me to look at neutral experiences and to discover that if you don't pay attention to them, boredom sets in and you can have all kinds of reactions to that, like enjoying yourself, having all kinds of thoughts, restlessness in your body ... I liked seeing how neutral, boredom and reactions were related. It helps me now to look at things in a more balanced way.*

The tracks of a tiger

The easiest feeling tones to recognise are the unpleasant ones. In the following metaphor, a tracker on a safari follows the footsteps of a tiger. First, the tiger walks on muddy ground, then it is easy to follow its tracks. This can be compared to unpleasant sensations, which are usually very obvious. When the tiger walks on sand, it is much more difficult. The prints of its paws will be less obvious or sometimes blown away by the wind. Most meditators, find it more difficult to notice pleasant feeling tones. Because of their pleasant atmosphere, the intoxicating effect is often stronger and we do not see them so clearly, as if sand is thrown into our eyes. The neutral feeling tone is like the tracks of a tiger walking over rocky ground; the tracker must now really make every effort to still be able to follow the tiger.

> Participant: *I have always suffered from feelings of emptiness. I used to work hard or look for pleasant things, so that I could get over it. But that didn't always work out. The explanation of the neutral feeling tone made me understand that ultimately there is nothing wrong with me and that the emptiness is just a neutral mood that I interpret negatively. Noticing this feeling now as just a feeling of emptiness or as a neutral feeling gives me much more peace and confidence.*

It is worth noting, however, that the feeling tone is rarely purely neutral and thus sits exactly between pleasant and unpleasant. Usually, it has a touch of unpleasantness or pleasantness, but so subtle that you can still call it neutral.

The rollercoaster of our moods

Our mood can swing from sky-high happiness to unfathomably deep sadness in an instant. Of course, there can be many reasons for this, such as hormonal irregularities or stressful experiences. Sometimes this can be so strong that it can be wise and compassionate to use medication, perhaps temporarily. In any case, becoming more familiar with and acknowledging neutral feelings as neutral feelings can provide a lot of peace and space.[1]

Strengthening spiritual abilities

In the time that I (Frits) first meditated for a longer period in Burma (now Myanmar) in 1985 in the Mahāsi Sasanā Yeiktha in Rangoon (now Yangon) I was fortunate that Sayadaw U Pandita (1993), who was then the head of this large meditation centre, gave Dhamma talks for non-Burmese meditators almost daily. A number of talks were about nine ways of strengthening the five spiritual faculties mentioned in the previous chapter, as they are described in the Visuddhimagga. For inspiration and as a reminder on this last full day of meditation, we thought it would be nice to briefly touch upon them.

1 Beholding with an inner attitude, whereby you do not have to push away experiences and also do not have to hold on to them, with the awareness that everything is ultimately impermanent.
2 Having a respectful attitude towards the practice. Making use of the time and the special opportunity to be in retreat.
3 Ensuring continuity of practice, not only in walking and sitting meditation but also in all daily activities.
4 Creating the most favourable conditions or *sappāya*. Very practical things to think about are the optimal arrangement of your meditation room or the hut where you are staying, the place where you sit in the meditation hall, the possibility of having regular inquiry meetings with the teacher(s) about the practice or to be guided in it. This is often referred to as 'good friendship', It means to

speak with wisdom when necessary and to be in silence when speaking is not necessary, not eating too much or too little, to make sure you are well adjusted to the weather conditions and to explore which practice position is most helpful at the moment – walking, sitting, standing or lying down.

5 Exploring how to achieve a state of good concentration.
6 Developing the seven factors of enlightenment or liberation: mindfulness, investigation of dhammas, dedication, joy, serenity, concentration and equanimity.[2]
7 Not worrying too much about your physical health during meditation.
8 Not being discouraged by physical discomfort and tuning in wisely to what is possible, without having to force it. A beautiful saying from the Zen tradition might fit in here: 'Meditation is falling down thirty times and getting up thirty-one times'.
9 Not stopping halfway but continuing the practice. This refers to the tendency to lose the motivation to continue the practice because of being fascinated by pleasant experiences and wanting to stay in this pleasantness, as was explained in the previous chapter. Here the determination that was addressed at the beginning of this chapter comes up again.

The invitation is therefore also on this last full day of retreat, to quietly continue the practice.

Walking meditation – *May you walk in beauty*

We do not usually give new advice about walking meditation on the last day, but invite you to continue walking and sitting quietly, sometimes with experiences of a pleasant feeling tone, other times with an unpleasant or a neutral feeling tone, granting all these experiences the right to exist. You can take along the Buddha's encouragement to go on 'without hesitating and without exerting oneself excessively'. May a relaxed dedication to mindfulness accompany you in the practice, even on this last full day of retreat, or as a blessing from the Native American culture goes: 'May you walk in beauty'.

Inquiry meetings – Looking back and to the future

We usually plan an inquiry meeting for everyone on the last full day, in which first of all we ask what the participants want to talk about. In addition, we pay more attention to evaluation regarding specific insights, struggles and open questions regarding the practice. In addition, we address the question of how to continue with the practice at home. It is often moving to hear all the discoveries and new perspectives.

Evening talk – Four expressions of kindness

May the blossoms of wisdom and compassion grow.
In the fertile soil of kindness.
Sprinkled with the fresh water of sympathetic joy.
In the cool shade of equanimity.

Starting with this poetic Tibetan saying, we would like to pay extra attention to what we believe is a very valuable model from Buddhist psychology. In it, four different relational qualities are named, which in addition to mindfulness and wisdom can support us in relating to ourselves and others. These four heart qualities are officially often called 'noble abidings' or *brahmavihāra*. In the compassion training mentioned in Chapter 5, we also call them 'four friends of life'; they are increasingly being embraced in contemporary positive psychology (Bohlmeijer & Hulsbergen, 2018). We are talking about kindness, compassion, joy and equanimity. Below we discuss these four friends of life one by one.

The fertile soil of kindness

In the Visuddhimagga, the characteristic of loving-kindness or benevolence (*mettā*) is the absence of malice. In an active sense, it includes the wish to promote the welfare of oneself and others. It provides a beneficial alternative when we are suffering from hatred and dissatisfaction and manifests as warmth, as helpfulness and as loveliness. A pitfall in practising the perfection of kindness is to get carried away with sentimentality.

There is a story in the scriptures about a number of monks who, during the Buddha's lifetime, were inspired to engage in intensive meditation in the forests of northern India. At that time it was customary to withdraw from daily life for a long period and so these monks sought a suitable place in the forest. However, they were rather noisy and did not take much care of the plants and trees. In the trees of that forest lived so-called *rukkhadevas*, tree spirits invisible to human beings who protected the trees. They became disturbed and decided to chase away the monks. At night, they would stand close to the monks and make strange threatening noises, or they created ghostly scenes by moving branches and plants at unexpected moments. The monks at first pretended that nothing was wrong, but they were quite frightened. Gradually, they started talking to each other and complaining about the noise and the hauntings at night. Not understanding who or what was frightening them, they decided to ask the Buddha for advice.

The Buddha immediately understood the situation and told the monks to be respectful to nature and the inhabitants of the forest by making less noise and not causing destruction. To show that the monks were well-meaning people and wanted friendship with the residents, he had the monks learn a text by heart about the value of loving-friendliness, with the advice to recite this teaching out loud regularly. When the monks practised the advice of the Buddha, the tree spirits understood that the monks had no evil intentions and they could continue to live together in harmony. This text, officially also called the Karaniya Mettā Sutta or the teaching on developing kindness, has become the basis for the practice of kindness meditation.

> Participant: *The story of loving-kindness and compassion for the forest spirits was very helpful. I have taken this to the spirits I meet regularly at night.*

Eleven benefits of kindness

Classic Buddhist scriptures list 11 benefits of *mettā*:

1 We can fall asleep well and easily.
2 We awaken peacefully.
3 We have pleasant dreams.
4 We make friends with ourselves and with others.
5 We are loved by animals and invisible beings.
6 We are protected by invisible celestial beings or devas.
7 Loving-kindness creates a protection against danger, such as poison, weapons, fire, fear or aggression.
8 Our appearance radiates more beauty.
9 We experience more inner peace.
10 We live and die without confusion.
11 Finally, according to the scriptures, we will be reborn into happy circumstances.

Explanation

It is remarkable that the first three valuable effects refer to sleeping and resting. Nowadays, many people struggle with complaints of fatigue and difficulty in falling asleep, sleeping through the night or getting enough sleep. The first three effects are related to our sleeping pattern, which according to Buddhist psychology can be improved by practising kindness.

According to points 4, 5, 6 and 7, we can gradually make friends with ourselves and with others, and kindness can also provide protection in dangerous circumstances. The practice of kindness also creates a peaceful mind and therefore has an effect on facial expression. The peaceful mind, in turn, makes for a more peaceful dying process and, according to Buddhism, a happier afterlife.

Protected by kindness

When I was working as a psychiatric nurse, I (Frits) was unexpectedly attacked by a big, strong man. To my own surprise, however, no anger or fear entered my mind at that moment, only genuine compassion for the pain and frustration of this confused man. When I simply said 'Gosh, you're angry. What has hurt you so?' he let go of me in bewilderment, burst into tears and told me a sad story about his frustration with some caregivers. While telling this, the man calmed down.

The rainbow of compassion

A second face of kindness is that of compassion, *karunā* in Pali. On the one hand, compassion implies a sensitivity to pain or suffering in ourselves and in others, and on the other hand, it implies a willingness to work to alleviate, remedy and, where possible, prevent such suffering. Compassion is the cure for cruelty and falsehood; it arises when kindness meets pain and suffering. Or, as a Tibetan saying goes, 'The rainbow of compassion appears when the rays of the sun touch the tears of pain and sorrow'.

Compassion manifests itself as warm, caring attention, as mercy, social involvement and selfless help. Empathy used to be considered a synonym for compassion. Nowadays, it is argued that while empathy is a very important ingredient of compassion, empathy alone, without wisdom and concern for well-being for others and ourselves, can easily lure us into the trap of pity and may in the cause burnout in the long run.

Scientific research on (self-)compassion

In *A Practical Guide to Mindfulness-Based Compassionate Living* (Van den Brink, Koster & Norton, 2018), we summarised a number of research findings. These show that (self-)compassion appears to be beneficial for our psychological and physical well-being. It correlates with

- A mitigating effect on the impact of negative events.
- A greater degree of personal initiative, a greater ability to cope with difficulties and taking responsibility for one's own actions.
- Less fear of failure and rejection.
- Greater self-respect, sympathy and understanding of one's own shortcomings.
- Better self-care and healthier eating habits.
- More emotional intelligence and healthier emotion regulation, by approaching emotions – even the painful ones – with kindness.
- More positive emotions, wisdom, happiness and optimism.
- More connectedness, with ourselves and with others.
- healthier functioning of our brain and neurobiological systems.

When we cultivate an accepting and acknowledging attitude towards what arises in us from moment to moment in insight meditation, there is kindness and compassion. There is a gentleness even when we acknowledge aversion. We naturally develop loving-kindness by doing this; this is how it comes to fruition in insight meditation.

The difference between acceptance and acknowledgement

Perhaps it is worthwhile to say something about the difference between acceptance and acknowledgement, using a true story. A participant in a meditation course whom we will call Bob left after the first inquiry meeting feeling very happy. He found the acknowledging attitude of insight meditation very healing and noted that he was always terribly strict with himself. Afterwards, he came to me and told me that the next week he would start meditating every day for a while with an attitude of 'everything is allowed to be'.

The next week he came in remarkably quietly and also remained aloof during the mindful sharing in the group. After the meeting, he made contact and confessed that something had not gone quite right that week. He had meditated with an accepting attitude and found this very revealing. He had recently moved in with a woman who had two daughters. The older one was going through puberty and rejected him. She challenged him regularly and he usually tried to remain patient. During the past week, she had become angry with him again, climbed out of the roof window and started dancing on the slightly sloping roof. Suddenly Bob had become very angry. Where he would otherwise have swallowed the anger, he now decided to accept and allow it completely. The result was that he raged against her and really started cursing. It had made an impression and the stepdaughter had gone inside immediately but she was so shocked that she did not want any contact with him at all.

This can happen when there is only acceptance and no wisdom. That is why we usually speak of acknowledgement or recognition rather than acceptance. In the case of acceptance, kindness can easily allow us to slip into resignation. This can then easily degenerate into a subtle form of fatalism. Besides, the word acceptance refers to something very big, while the kindness in insight meditation is much smaller: what is there in the moment is allowed to be there. We do not have to get rid of it, repress it, solve it or hold on to it; it is this subtle attitude that makes the practice of insight meditation so liberating.

The fresh water of sympathetic joy

Sympathetic joy (*muditā*) arises when there is something to celebrate, when the heart is glad because another heart is dancing. Sympathetic joy is not just a feeling of happiness. It shows itself as joyful sympathy with the prosperity and well-being of others and oneself and also manifests itself as gratitude. It is seen as a remedy for jealousy and stinginess and brings freshness to a relationship. Pitfalls in developing sympathetic joy are hypocrisy or feigned enthusiasm and an exaggerated cheerfulness, whereby the joy can morph into euphoria.

The cool shadow of equanimity

We can view equanimity as a stabilising force. It enables us to see people and situations clearly with balance and wisdom, and not to be blinded by attachment or aversion. In the Buddhist scriptures, you come across two terms that refer to this fourth friend of life. The word *upekkhā* literally means overview and refers to a meta-perspective through which the three shared worldly characteristics of impermanence, unsatisfactoriness and uncontrollability are viewed. The other term – *tatramajjhattatā* – means 'in the midst of it all' and refers to the inner balance that arises from equanimity. It is not cold and distant. It has an open, detached but generous attitude towards what are often called the eight 'worldly winds': success and failure; prosperity and adversity; praise and blame; joy and pain.

While loving-kindness, compassion and sympathetic joy have a clearly recognisable aspect of commitment, equanimity goes beyond them. This can be very liberating especially in relationships and in circumstances where we cannot or do not want to do anything further.

The four friends of life in cohesion

The four friends of life each cover a different area and can be developed in relation to yourself and in relating with others. We offer a metaphor for understanding this: a teacher has many pupils in their class. She wants all the pupils to learn and grow up well; this is typical of kindness. Some pupils have difficulties in the classroom or at home and here the attitude of compassion is most appropriate. There may also be some children who suddenly flourish or shine because of a previously hidden talent or because things are going better at home. Here the teacher can feel sympathetic joy. Finally, there may be some pupils who are difficult to support and whose learning style is often erratic. The feeling of equanimity is most appropriate in this case.

In a metaphor bhikkhu Anālayo (2015) compares kindness to the pleasant sunlight during daytime. When the sun goes down and it gets dark, we meet the darkness of difficulties with compassion. Sympathetic joy can be compared to the sparkling and refreshing effect of a sunrise, where the birds start to chirp happily. Equanimity may be compared to the light of the full moon, which is cooler than sunlight but brings light into the darkness, so that we can find our way again.[3]

Equanimity in joy and sorrow

Because equanimity is also mentioned as the (ninth) perfection, we want to highlight this quality or attitude. Equanimity and patience are sometimes called the father and mother of practice because they make for a supportive and balanced practice. Patience has already been described in Chapter 2; equanimity makes it easier for us to deal with life's ups and downs and to maintain inner balance in the face the 'one hundred thousand joys and one hundred thousand sorrows'. It is considered a medicine for everything that has a 'too much' in it, for example too much caring or involvement. A pitfall in developing equanimity is indifference, which has a consciousness-reducing and numbing character and closes rather than opens the heart. While many people in a retreat hear the word 'equanimity' for the first time, it is a quality widely described in Buddhist psychology. In total, ten types of equanimity are named. All these expressions of equanimity exhibit the quality of inner balance and calmness or 'coolness' in the capricious vicissitudes of life.

> Participant: *The difference between 'enduring' and 'acknowledge with mindfulness' is a gentle smile.*

Equanimity in mindfulness

According to Buddhist psychology, equanimity is by nature a constant companion of mindfulness. When we are mindful, an attitude of non-identification with what we are experiencing in the moment naturally arises. On Day 3, this was named as a form of wholesome neutrality. In this sense, you can compare equanimity with a satnav in the car. She will very calmly show us the way. If we take the right turn, she won't praise us; if we take the wrong turn, she won't scold us or call us an idiot. Even if we make a mistake several times in a row, she will calmly recommend, 'Make a U-turn'. Equanimity in practice has a similar friendly but also detached atmosphere. The only difference is that a satnav usually gives us a suggestion in advance, for example, 'Turn left after 150 metres', whereas mindfulness quietly only observes what is going on in the moment.[4]

> Participant: *I also caught a glimpse of equanimity and found it very special. That it doesn't matter whether I'm walking or sitting or cutting vegetables or going to the toilet. That the likes and dislikes that may be involved are as much an object of meditation as anything else that presents itself.*

To help participants feel the quality of equanimity in an experiential way, we sometimes offer a metaphor exercise inspired by a book by Nicholas Evans after the talk on the last evening (2020).

5

> *You can sit at ease, opening up your attention for the story. A teenage girl has one great love in her life: her horse. However, one day when she is riding in the snow, she is hit by a huge truck. Although the girl and her horse are seriously injured, they survive the accident. However, the horse is so traumatised that after the accident the girl can no longer make contact with it while the girl finds it extremely difficult to come to terms with what has happened to herself and the horse. In addition, it is doubtful whether she will ever be able to walk properly again.*

The girl's mother goes in search of help and healing for her handicapped daughter and the animal and discovers the existence of a horse whisperer, a man who has a special gift for working with horses. She travels with her daughter and the horse to the horse whisperer's remote ranch and explains the problem to him. He turns out to be a man of few words. He takes over the trailer and drives to a quiet, vast prairie. When he opens the trailer, the horse immediately jumps out and runs far away.

The horse whisperer then takes a very special approach. He makes no attempt to catch the animal, but stands or sits quietly somewhere on the grassy plain with a carefree attitude of: 'I can sit here with endless patience'. Every now and then, he softly whispers something friendly in the direction where the horse has run to, but otherwise he does nothing. At a certain point, the horse apparently becomes fascinated by the only other living creature in the vicinity and comes closer, step by step. Even when the horse has approached up to a few metres, the horse whisperer makes no attempt to catch it. Only when the animal gently makes contact with a shoulder, an arm or the hat of the man with its nose, does he give the horse a gentle pat or a stroke. At first, it is frightened and immediately backs away again. For the horse whisperer this is fine; he remains patiently present and whispers something in a kind way every now and then. But when the horse makes contact again, it allows the man to touch its head and stroke its neck. It calms down, gradually gains more confidence in the man and eventually the horse also allows the girl to make contact again. She is naturally overjoyed when it allows her again to go for a ride.

Perhaps this story is inspiring and you can imagine yourself as a horse whisperer. Anything you experience – thoughts, emotions, sounds or feelings – you may consider to be horses. You don't need to capture or push them away, but you can kindly greet them when they are in the foreground. You are there for them when they come to visit you. One moment you can gently greet a thought and give it a friendly pat, the next moment you can stroke a sound, thought or feeling without having to own it or hold it back or push it away. Sometimes there can be a whole herd of horses; you do not need to bring them under control, but you can perhaps calmly greet them as 'busyness'. And if sometimes there are no clear experiences, you can always 'let the mindfulness rest' in the stable and be aware of the breathing movements.

This metaphor contains two valuable perspectives. Firstly, there is the equanimous attitude of the horse whisperer, who opens up to the horse in a non-coercive, calm and grounded way. Then there is the perspective of the horse, which is initially frightened, hurt and distrustful and is difficult to approach. Sometimes we can also experience a hurt, shy, ashamed or capricious part of ourselves, a part that is full of pain, tension, trauma or hurt and that does not let itself be approached easily. Perhaps you can only learn to trust this part by adopting the patient, trusting, equanimous and

> space-giving attitude of a horse whisperer and giving this painful part all the space it needs. This part can then decide for itself when it wants to come closer and be whispered to, touched and reassured by your kind words and gestures. And when it feels the space to come, we can welcome and greet it with tenderness and understanding, without frightening it or forcing it.
>
> You can continue as long as you wish and sit like a horse whisperer for as long as you feel comfortable.

Participant: *An insightful moment happened while the metaphor of the horse whisperer was presented. I realised what the state of 'relaxed awareness' entails. A moment of insight that followed shortly after was when in the guided meditation it was said that awareness is a friend of everyone. I was able to let go of my implicit assumptions about how meditation should be, and for more than half a day I was able to hold the state of relaxed awareness without any effort. I realised that it is also possible to move through life in this relaxed way, instead of trying hard, and felt liberated by this.*

Kindness meditation – The last evening

After the evening talk on the last evening, we often offer space for a programme without a programme, as already introduced in Chapter 6. Everyone can then drink a cup of tea or coffee with each other in silence. I (Jetty) usually take care of an appropriate treat, so that the whole thing has an atmosphere of a 'silent evening party'. You are invited to continue practising according to your needs. For some this may mean going upstairs in silence, crawling under the covers and mindfully recovering or comforting yourself after a hard day. For others, at least in the summer months, this may mean going for a long walk and simply continuing the walking and sitting meditation for as long as is appropriate. In all cases, we invite you to continue in silence. A final night of meditation often proves to be very valuable and insightful. There will be no guided kindness meditation on the last evening, but we would like to end this seventh day with a poem. We choose here the poem *Frontiers* by Rachel Holstead, which seems appropriate for the story of the horse whisperer.

Frontiers

*On those difficult days, when a frontier looms,
decisions seem called for*

and the armies of your mind muster
and set off on a headlong gallop
towards the horizon,

they make so much noise
that the heart's soft voice
is drowned out,
and kick up so much dust
that compassion's anchor loses purchase.

The faster the armies gallop,
the farther away the horizon seems,
the bumpier the path
and the cloudier the dusty air

and we trip over innocent rocks
and trample innocent plants
and startle quietly grazing flocks,
causing them to scatter
and become embroiled in our turmoil.

But if we can persuade the horde
to slow a little
– that stopping a while will help
rather than hinder –
perhaps we can sit by the side of the track
and let the dust settle
and the noise die away.

And somehow, we find ourselves
where we need to be
– which is here –
and we can set anchor again.
And when, out of the silence,
the soft voice of our heart speaks,
it has all the answers we need.

Notes

1 Mark Williams and Danny Penman have developed an eight-week course for those who have already completed a mindfulness course and wish to explore the three feeling tones more specifically. It is described in their book *Deeper Mindfulness* (2023).

2 The seven factors of enlightenment or awakening or are named, among others, in the Satipatthāna Sutta. They are not explicitly addressed in this book because they have been integrated in other ways in this book.
3 See https://community.mindfulness-network.org/course/view.php?id=121 for a webinar titled *Four Friends for Life,* guided by Frits Koster and hosted by the Mindfulness Network UK.
4 See https://community.mindfulness-network.org/course/view.php?id=271 for a webinar titled *In the Cool Shade of Equanimity*, hosted by the Mindfulness Network UK.

Chapter 8

Fruits of the practice
Day 8 – Ethics and returning to daily life

On Day 8, we consider the various fruits of practice and the return home. We pay attention to ethics as the last perfection. We make suggestions for further practice in daily life and end the retreat.

> *Before enlightenment,*
> *I chopped wood and carried water.*
> *After enlightenment,*
> *I chopped wood and carried water.*
> — Zen saying

The last day of the retreat is focused on closing, farewells and return to daily life. At breakfast, we usually talk about some practical matters, such as how to leave the accommodation. If you have slowed down in your practice, we invite you to speed up without needing to rush. We also explore how a more comprehensive way of being aware can be present in the practice. To broaden your perspective, we also invite you to occasionally look around mindfully and greet other participants with a smile in silence. We ask you to stay in silence until the end of the morning, or if you would like to share your experiences with someone, to go outside for a walk together.

Fruits of the practice

We often offer a closing talk instead of the guided meditation in the morning, in which we pay attention to fruits of practice from a contemporary and an ancient Buddhist approach. These two approaches need not be mutually exclusive but can be complementary.

The neuroscientific perspective

The American researcher Richard Davidson, about whom we will say more later in this chapter, describes well-being as a skill or art, in which mindfulness plays an important role. Much of the research on how mindfulness works has found that the practice of mindfulness is associated with the valuable effects described below.

Attention regulation

Earlier in the retreat, we paid attention to focused attention and receptive attention; if you tend to focus mainly on what is not going well, it can be very expansive when you discover that you can also consciously focus your attention on what is going well. And if you have been feeling fatigued, it can be very liberating to discover that you do not always have to focus deeply on your work and that you can also be present or do something with less tension and a more receptive awareness.

Body awareness

In Chapter 2, the term interoception was mentioned as the ability to perceive one's own body from the inside, which appears to promote well-being. This also includes learning to relate to physical difficulties and limitations in a different way. Jon Kabat-Zinn expresses this very concisely as 'Pain is inevitable – suffering is optional'.

Emotion regulation

We could also see the practice as a training in emotion management and this promotes our resilience and therefore our well-being. We become less identified with the many emotions and moods that we experience that can whisk us off as buses might do, sometimes to places where we would rather not be. It is possible to cultivate an inner flexibility in working with this.

Shift in perspective

In the practice of mindfulness, we train a meta-perspective in ourselves, in which we are less automatically focused and fixated on the content of thoughts and can notice them as small flows of energy and information passing by. This subtle expression of equanimity is also called an attitude of non-identification or defusion and is realised with every moment of mindfulness. A shift in perspective also involves discovering a new and more helpful attitude or mindset in relation to any difficulties we experience. Finally, the term 'value clarification' fits well with this. By developing the ability to 'sit on the banks of our own lives', we more easily discover deeper values, which are often neglected in our hectic everyday lives.

Self-compassion and compassion to others

Research shows that by practising mindfulness we become more gentle and understanding towards ourselves, wise and compassionate self-care are developed implicitly.[1] Research shows that the practice of mindfulness also supports prosocial behaviour, such as showing kindness to others, comforting others, sharing,

> Participant: *When I am back at work, I get a lot of questions: how was your retreat, did you have a good time? Yes, it was good. I can best describe it as an emotional spring clean. I am calmer now, I feel more anchored in my body. And I have experienced again how important it is to take a lot of time to relax, to rest, to calm down. Then I also have real attention for my family – there is enough quality time every day. And if things get bogged down again, then I will opt again for the emotional spring clean of a week of silent retreat.*

The Buddhist perspective

'Why are you wearing shoes?' If you allow this question to sink in, you will come to the conclusion that humans once started wearing shoes to protect our feet. In a similar way, Buddhist psychology teaches us that mindfulness has a protective effect, as we become aware of how inner tendencies can grow and then overrun our lives like weeds in a flower garden. The protective effect of mindfulness is interceptive, disarming and preventive. It intercepts when we gently notice that a pressing desire, impatience, anxiety or confusion has arisen. This can disarm further strengthening of our conditioning and can allow us to see what is most helpful in the situation and how new suffering can be prevented.

This aspect of the practice is expressed in the fourth abode or field of awareness: *dhammānupassanā*. For this not only refers to 'awareness of phenomena', but also invites us down a path whereby we can intercept and prevent tendencies that cause distress through awareness and wise attunement or *yoniso manasikāra* and how we can cultivate qualities that enhance freedom. Bhikkhu Anālayo (2018) formulates this in the following reflection questions with which we can explore the fourth abiding for mindfulness

- How do the five forms of reactivity arise and how can we transcend them?
- How do the seven awakening factors arise and how can we promote them?

Inner freedom

In this context, the term *Nibbāna* is often mentioned in the Buddhist tradition. In Western languages, this is often appealingly translated as 'Enlightenment'. More carefully translated, this Pali word means 'not (or no longer) burning'. This relates to all kinds of reactivity that are latent in us and can easily restrict or sour our own lives, the lives of others or both. These tendencies are therefore often summarised as 'the three poisons': craving (*lobha*), hatred (*dosa*) and delusion (*moha*). When these three come into play, we need to handle them wisely if we want to avoid ruining our own, other people's lives or both. According to Buddhism, these tendencies are extinguished with the experience of Enlightenment.

Different stages of existential understanding

According to Buddhist psychology, Enlightenment does not happen suddenly and requires much more practice. A week's retreat is then usually considered a good start but not a complete journey. And the journey has many different stages. After a period of easy practice, the practice can lead you into a meditative landscape sometimes described as the 'dark night'. In this phase of the practice, fear, sadness, listlessness and repulsion or even disgust can be experienced, and all kinds of unpleasant physical sensations can suddenly appear. This is not an easy phase, we discussed it on Day 2 as the 'mat-rolling phase'.

When practitioners meet impermanence, unsatisfactoriness and uncontrollability on a deep experiential level it can feel destabilising, even in people who are otherwise psychologically healthy. It might be helpful to know that these phases can occur in the practice, that they are not a sign of 'not doing it right' and in fact, in Zen Buddhism, they are referred to as the 'more original face' in life.[3]

The rolling-up-the-mat phase

When I (Frits) first encountered the 'dark night' described above as a young man in Thailand on my first longer retreat, I was so shocked by it that I had to drop out. This was partly caused by translation problems with the teacher. Fortunately a very experienced Indian meditation monk took care of me in Bangkok. I will always be grateful to him for being there and supporting me.

The atmosphere can at some point return to a state of benign calm with continued practice. It becomes easy and effortless again; Sayadaw U Pandita from Myanmar sometimes spoke of meditative 'cruise control'. Then a specific form of equanimity arises, namely equanimity with regard to phenomena (*sankhārupekkhā*). This gets stronger as you continue with the practice and has the specific qualities of clear and relaxed presence, a natural wisdom in relating to 'unhelpful guests in the practice' and a grounded and composed inner attitude and balance in all experiences that come up.

Enlightenment with a big E

All these stages are impermanent and not 'mine' and in fact quite natural meditative maturation processes, with many meditators going back and forth between these stages.

If the conditions are favourable and if the five spiritual faculties or *indriya* – faith, dedication, mindfulness, momentary concentration and wisdom – develop well, then they are also called powers or *bala*. When these are well balanced, then, according to Buddhism, Enlightenment with a capital E (or Satori in Zen Buddhism) can be experienced as a liberating emptiness, which naturally extinguishes latent tendencies. One need not be a Buddhist for this; in many cultures, we can find examples of people who carry themselves with a very natural calmness and show little or no trace of addiction, jealousy, impatience and other inclinations where desire, hatred and delusion could easily arise.

Different perspectives are offered on the experience of Enlightenment. In early Buddhism it is described as an experience with a meditative path leading to it; in Zen Buddhism, it is also described as a state that we all already carry within us – Buddha-nature. The practice does not offer a path that leads somewhere, but rather provides a way to discover the deep inner freedom already present.

A well-known Buddhist teacher from the last century, Suzuki Roshi, author of the famous book *Zen Mind, Beginner's Mind* (1976), sometimes referred to Enlightenment as the Ultimate Disappointment. We think this is a very beautiful approach, because it no longer refers to disappointment as something negative but as a liberating emotion. After all, unrealistic, unhelpful expectations are extinguished with disappointment; we wake up from a dream which temporarily blinds us and are able to reconnect with the here and now. The well-known Swiss psychiatrist Carl Gustav Jung formulated this as follows: 'One does not become enlightened by imagining figures of light, but by making the darkness conscious'.

Enlightenment with a small e

There is also enlightenment with a small e. The danger of identifying with an ideal of perfect inner freedom can creep in. If, constrictive attachments, hatred, aversion, doubt, pride or other limiting habit patterns present themselves, then it is easy to become discouraged. Therefore it is good to realise that Enlightenment or freedom is also referred to with a small e; you realise it every moment you are aware. This is because the moment you notice and recognise something, there is no identification and no attachment to the object being observed. There is no aversion either, because the object of meditation is being noticed in recognition. Finally, there is no confusion or ignorance but rather a clear presence and knowing of what is occurring in the present. You dwell in an oasis; a cool place that protects you from the heat of craving, hatred and misunderstanding. Every possible meditation object can be used to come home to this oasis: the breathing movements, hearing, thinking, feeling and even anger, impatience, doubt, desire or fear. If, for example, impatience arises in the practice, just acknowledging it means you are no longer in that impatience. The impatience may still be there, but at the same time a subtle inner space has been created, so that you are less caught up in impatience. It makes the practice very accessible when we are not counting all the moments of inattention but are appreciating or even celebrating every moment of mindfulness. The Buddha put it as follows: 'Just like the ocean has one taste, namely the taste of salt, this teaching also has one taste, namely the taste of inner freedom'.

We can also experience Enlightenment with a small e when we spend a short or longer time in what Diana Winston (2019) describes as natural awareness:

- Your mind is fully and effortlessly aware and not distracted.
- Your mind feels like a wide open space, where all kinds of experiences come and go.
- You are aware, but not identified with the part of you that is aware.
- You feel calm and at peace.
- You are aware that you are observant and can easily dwell in that.
- Everything seems to happen automatically.
- You experience a sense of satisfaction that is not connected to external circumstances.
- You are just being – without an agenda – and this being creates a sense of timelessness and ease.

Participants experience these kinds of moments more often in the second half of a retreat. For one thing, they happen spontaneously, but for most of us it takes practice to experience them. Such experiences can be understood as little gems that strengthen our confidence, they can sometimes have a tremendously liberating effect. Some of our participants describe some of those fruits along the path of practice.

> Participant: *During a walking meditation, I suddenly felt very moved by the silence in the monastery, while I was aware that there were thirty people near me and it was dead quiet. That gave me a feeling of strength – I felt for a moment that everything coincided – with myself ... the others ... the surroundings ... nature.*

> Participant: *Walking, light-footed, and sinking into the snow with a pinkish blue-grey sky decorated with a group of flying geese, with horses in the field eating from their feeding rack, wishing myself 'May I be happy', I felt in my toes that I was happy. I was moved and touched with some tears finding their way down my face.*

Enlightenment with a small e can also carry over into everyday life. In one of the many evaluations we received, this is expressed as follows:

> Participant: *The main characteristic of this retreat is peace, a feeling of equanimity, self-confidence, warmth for and towards the outside world and physical relaxation. These effects continued for days after the retreat. I am curious about the*

> *long-term effects. The cigarettes have lost their attraction. I am still smoke-free, it is as if a switch has been turned on. All this made it easy for me to pick up the daily routine and deal with it effectively.*

Olympic meditators

We don't want to make exaggerated promises; after all, the effects of the practice show themselves in all kinds of different ways, often also in unforeseen ways, and this does not always coincide with more and more happiness and joy. Our Dutch colleague Johan Tinge puts this into words in the following statement: 'The advantage of becoming more mindful is that we start feeling more in body and mind. The disadvantage of becoming more mindful is that we start feeling more in body and mind'.

In the inquiry meetings, we regularly indicate that insight has two sides. One side is that becoming more mindful can be challenging and painful in the short term. Sometimes we are, perhaps unexpectedly, confronted by painful grief, an unconscious pattern or by confusion about how to proceed. Moreover, the existential insight that is deepened during the retreat may continue to have an effect for some time and need time to be integrated into our daily lives. In the long run, this appears to have an expansive effect, as a signpost to a freer life.

We are very happy that Daniel Goleman and Richard Davison published *Altered Traits* in 2017. Daniel Goleman is a well-known psychologist, author and journalist; Richard Davidson is believed to have been the first researcher into the workings and effects of meditation. Their book covers all sorts of discoveries from the many years of research Davidson and his team carried out. One of the remarkable discoveries is quite recent. When Davidson was sorting out all the research he had done over the previous decades, he suddenly came across an area he had not analysed before. For years he had been asking experienced meditators to come back every few years and take part in the same research. When he compared all the data from more experienced practitioners, he found that prolonged practice causes character traits to change. This does not appear to be unfavourable. He talks about so-called 'Olympic meditators', i.e. meditators who have meditated for at least 12,000 hours in their lives.

When we read this, we could calculate that we (Frits and Jetty) both fall into that category, even though we must confess that we have spent many of those hours asleep. Yet we both agree that we have gradually become softer and more patient in character and that is very inspiring.

Perhaps Rachel Holstead's poem *Change* embodies something of the liberating effect of the practice of meditation.

Change

> *The cloud lifts*
> *and the mountain is suddenly white,*
> *merging with grey-black sky and light.*

Everything changes
– bare branches suddenly adorned with blossom,
scarlet amaryllis outrageous in bloom
and now the sky
– lilac and lavender –
and, already, the snow melting and fading.

Let go of clinging
and join the dance.
Let soft body and supple mind
join the ongoing flow of life.

Each moment
– of glory or despair –
is just as it is,
as long as it is,
and it passes.

Be the flow, the movement,
the flicker of light on the hillside.
Be in every now, not just this now,
be the music and the dance.

Back to daily life

All men's miseries derive from not being able to sit quiet in a room alone.[4]
– Blaise Pascal, French mathematician, physicist
and philosopher (1623–1662)

On the last day, we will also spend time on the transition from being in retreat to integrating the practice into daily life. Here we want to give some advice and highlight a few things.

Taking time to return to daily life

We invite you to return to a 'normal' pace and practice what the Buddha called *sampajañña*: clear understanding. This involves a less detailed but calm presence in all actions; awareness and wise attunement play an important role here. If for example you need to drive home by car, do not drive too fast or on the other hand too slowly on the motorway.

Connecting with loved ones and colleagues

During the retreat, you were asked to go into silence as much as possible, as an aid to be able to sit more easily on the banks of the river of your own life. This is not recommended in daily life. It is then good to actively reconnect with others. Marie Mannschatz, a meditation teacher and colleague from Germany, has another good suggestion: when you get home, don't start talking about your own experiences right away, but first ask your partner, children or friends how they have been during the past week. While during the retreat you experienced one or more meditation teachers, after the retreat you can also consider your partner, the children, the 'difficult' colleague and other important people in your life as your meditation teachers. After all, they mirror you in many ways and can be seen as an infinite field for developing the ten perfections. Spiritual teacher Ram Dass, author of many books including the bestseller *Be Here Now* (1971) once stated: 'If you think you are enlightened, spend a week with your family'. Susan Gillis Chapman (2012), a Canadian meditation teacher, who has dedicated her life to deepening an understanding of communication, spirituality and relationships, speaks very beautifully in this about three attitudes: 'I-first', 'you-first' and 'we-together'. All three attitudes are of value, whereby we can generally focus more on the 'we-together' attitude.

Appreciating enjoyment

During the retreat, you have temporarily lived as a celibate monk or nun. You don't have to continue this at home and sexuality, romance and doing enjoyable things are highly recommended. You do not have to cling to the retreat lifestyle and can follow life values and needs in other ways, caring for yourself and others. Sometimes at the end of a retreat, the following question is asked: 'Do I have to be mindful all the time now? One participant formulated an answer for herself: 'Being a spectator of your own life? Is that preferable? Sometimes you want to lose yourself'. There are no rules, why not just light-heartedly explore how you can integrate the practice into daily life?

Practising ethics in relation to others

Ethical action or *sīla*, is a good thing to introduce here, it counts as a tenth fulfilment. It is described in Buddhist psychology as ethical virtue, moral discipline and protective life advice. In *Liberating Insight* (Koster, 2004) various aspects of ethics are described in detail, which can be briefly summarised in four parts:

Discipline

This does not refer to a military discipline or an 'obligation' discipline; in this context, it means creating time and space for what you consider important and beneficial in your life. It is sometimes expressed as the bridge between a goal we have in mind and its realisation.

Elementary ethics

This is the most basic ethical advice, by which you hold the intention to live as non-violently a life as possible and strive not to harm yourself, others and the practice. On Day 1 we mentioned the five pieces of advice for living during the retreat. For daily life, these five Buddhist guidelines can be expressed as follows:

- Respect for everything that lives.
- Not taking what does not belong to you.
- Not engaging in inappropriate or abusive sexual behaviour.[5]
- Not lying, gossiping or swearing.
- Not using alcohol and drugs to the extent that they cloud your mind and cause harm to yourself or others.

Beautifying ethics

Encourage the practice of the ten perfections and take to heart the intention of allowing generosity, ethics, simplification, wisdom, patience, dedication, determination, integrity, kindness and equanimity to flourish in your life as much as possible. It may also be helpful to build friendships with people who can inspire and support you on the path of meditation. Spiritual friendship (*kaliyāna mittatā*) is considered indispensable, to support each other in cultivating the wholesome and sometimes to bring each other back on track when the spiritual path has been lost. In the lockdown periods that restricted everyone during the Corona pandemic, for example, we saw how meditators started to meditate together at home via the internet and were able to support themselves and others in this. There is a saying that 'alone you go faster but together you go further'.

Venerable Ānanda, the attendant of the Buddha, once spoke the following to the Buddha[6]: 'This is the half of the holy life, Lord, namely having good friends, having good companions, having good confidants'. The Buddha replied as follows: 'Don't say that, Ānanda, don't say that! It is the whole holy life, that is, having good friends, having good companions, having good confidants. If a monk (read 'meditator' here) has a good friend, a good companion, a good confidant, then it is to be expected that he will develop and practice the Noble Eightfold Path'.[7]

Protecting the senses

This means dealing wisely with the many stimuli that come or can come to you through the six senses and through social media.

Mindfulness naturally plays an important role in all these perspectives. The Golden Rule we talked about on Day 1 is relevant to social interaction in daily life: not to treat others as you would rather not be treated yourself. Alternatively we can formulate this positively: to treat others as you would like to be treated yourself.

The courage of forgiveness

The above sounds good but in practice it is quite an art. We all slip up in this area from time to time. Usually, this does not happen on purpose but is the result of a lack of perspective, reacting from fatigue or tension, a temporary hijack of the consciousness by an instinctive reaction or simply because wisdom has temporarily 'gone on holiday' among other things.

Susan Gillis Chapman (2012) uses a traffic light model as a metaphor. When the light is green our communication flows, there are no bottlenecks. When the light turns orange there is ambiguity, caution and extra wisdom are then required. When the light turns red, we have somehow stalled or gone too far, and this happens to all of us from time to time. When the light turns red, a specific practice can be very valuable, namely forgiveness. We can practise this in three different ways. First of all, we can practise forgiving or reconciling ourselves when for example we have been disrespectful to others. Understanding this in retrospect, we then realise that nobody is perfect and that we have acted from powerlessness or fear which unfortunately translated into aggressive or disrespectful behaviour from a lack of wisdom.

Another area is asking for forgiveness, or to put it more simply, saying 'sorry'. We (Jetty and Frits) grew up with parents who did not readily offer their children an apology, even when it was obvious that they had failed. Both of us often found this very frustrating. The first sentence of Elton John's famous song *Sorry seems to be the hardest word*[8] expresses very concisely that this is not always easy. It takes courage to be vulnerable, but this can lead to improvement in a relationship or even a reconciliation. And if the other person is not open to this, then at least you can feel that you have tried to fix things.

There is another area in which forgiveness can be applied, and that is forgiving others when you feel you have been hurt, wronged or let down by someone else. This is not compulsory, but sometimes there can be room for softening when you realise that others, just like all of us, are not perfect either and cannot fully see how behaviour can affect the people around them. Sometimes there can be too little room for this, because it is about something that is still very fresh or because there has been serious hurt. In that case, you can at least forgive yourself that this is not possible, at least at this point. Sometimes reflecting on equanimity is more appropriate, for example: 'I cannot change others, but I can deal with myself in the wisest and most compassionate way possible'.[9]

Practice at home

The affairs of the world will go on forever. Do not delay the practice of meditation.
– Ancient Tibetan saying

If you find that the retreat has been of value, then it is good to explore how you can integrate the practice into your daily life, according to your own circumstances and needs. You will not lose the insight that has been gained, but it is quite normal that the clarity and concentration that has been built up during the retreat, will fade away in the busyness of daily life. All meditation teachers and contemporary research confirm that regular practice is of value, preferably daily. After all, we are a forgetful species; regular formal practice provides a supportive structure in daily life. This does not have to be done fanatically; a period of 30 minutes is fine. If 30 minutes is too long, then a quote from one of our meditation teachers is very appropriate: 'Every time is a good time to be in time'. Of course, there is no need to put yourself under pressure or beat yourself up if you don't manage it.

It can also be good to connect with others, via a live meditation group or an online platform. Meditating together and practising inquiry with teachers and other meditators now and then can be very supportive. In recent years, valuable training have also emerged in which mindfulness plays an important role, such as MBSR, MBCT or MBCL, Finding Peace in a Frantic World, Deeper Mindfulness, the Interpersonal Mindfulness Program (IMP), Insight Dialogue, Deepening Mindfulness & Mindful Communication (DMMC), the Mindfulness-Based Training in Forgiveness (MBTF) or another programme in which mindfulness plays an important role.

We recommend going on regular retreats rather than viewing it as a one-off experience. Many people, ourselves included, look for a suitable retreat every year to deepen our practice. Some teachers even recommend signing up for next year within a week of a retreat, or at least blocking time in the diary for next year's retreat. After all, dairies fill up quickly nowadays. Some participants like to participate a few times with the same retreat teachers, others are more inspired by signing up with new teachers. Both strategies are fine, trust your own wisdom and needs.

During the retreat, it was recommended not to read or at least to limit reading. In daily life, however, reading can be very valuable. That is why we offer a reading list at the end of this book with the titles referred to in the book. In addition, the internet offers wonderful opportunities, with an enormous wealth of information, audio files, lectures and/or online programmes.[10]

Dilemmas and problems

The American psychologist Ellen Langer (1998, 2014) defines mindfulness in a very accessible way as simply actively noticing what you experience. You don't always have to sit on a meditation cushion for this. She connects mindfulness with a higher sensitivity to the environment, openness to new information and ideas, and attention to different perspectives when solving problems. This description includes valuable suggestions about how to relate to dilemmas and problems, perhaps by first opening up to different angles, perspectives and (im)possibilities before dealing instinctively and impulsively with difficult mails, dilemmas or problems. This is where the old wisdom of 'counting to ten first' comes in handy, if you have a short temper.

Participant: *During the walking meditation I came across a group of chickens. Two of them were arguing. The other chickens did not pay any attention to the quarrelling pair, even the cockerel gave up by not intervening. At least, that is*

> *what I thought, because I felt a strong urge to do so. Then came the insight: why should I intervene? And how often do I feel this urge and act? I can also do nothing and watch it. After this profound moment of insight, the chickens, now no longer quarrelling, quietly walked on. It was resolved.*

Don't try persuading people to practise meditation

After a retreat, you can sometimes be very enthusiastic about how the practice has affected you. You can then be tempted to tell everyone around you about what you experienced and how good it could be for the other person to go on a retreat too. We don't recommend this. We have experienced ourselves that this is not helpful.

Conversion drive

After my first retreat in 1979, I (Frits) was wildly enthusiastic. I hardly knew what had happened to me but I had the feeling that I had met something very essential in my life. In those days I was doing 'community service' as an alternative to military service at a housing association in Groningen. The first days after my retreat, I started telling colleagues enthusiastically about the retreat and that it was much better than an ordinary beach holiday. Despite the fact that there were many people working in this organisation, it became increasingly quiet around me. I noticed that colleagues started avoiding me more and more. After some reflection, I realised that I was becoming a bit fanatical and remembered that I myself really hated it when people started telling me what I should and should not do.

A young American meditation practitioner once told Japanese Zen teacher Suzuki Roshi that she was very happy with the practice of meditation; she was convinced that it would also be very good for her partner. But the more she tried to get her partner to join her, the more they argued about it. Suzuki Roshi gave a very simple answer: 'Better not talk like a Buddha, just be a Buddha'.

With some people you may feel that they have a deeper interest in what you have been doing, then that is a good time to open up in more detail about what you have been doing this week. Others may not need to know the details. In the village where we live, when people ask us where we have been, we often reply along the lines of 'We have been on holiday for a week'. Then we don't have to talk about all kinds of things that might seem strange to the listeners. We can also let the practice be expressed in our actions and perhaps do not need to 'convert' everyone to meditation practice. And for those who are open to it, we talk more enthusiastically about the value of the practice.

Interpersonal mindfulness

We usually don't have meetings about the practice on the last day, but participants who still want to connect individually can put their name on a sign-up list for a short personal meeting. Also, a last night can sometimes stir up confusion or somehow be intensive for some so we always make space for this. Besides, we do give those who wish to the opportunity to do a short interpersonal exercise in pairs, so that you can get used to communicating with others again and explore how you can speak and listen with awareness. We use specific guidelines and principles from Insight Dialogue[11] and the Interpersonal Mindfulness Program (IMP).[12] We then offer you the opportunity to share, one by one, how you experienced the retreat and whether there is any additional challenge regarding your practice in your personal or work life. Afterwards sitting in a large circle, we will invite whoever wishes to share something, for example, a discovery, a 'thank you' to others, something funny. In the past participants have even spontaneously started singing, reciting a poem, telling an appropriate joke or doing a dance.

Kindness meditation – All beings

We end with kindness meditation, where you can first of all wish yourself well for the coming weeks. Then you can make a wish for one or more dear or important persons in your life. Then a wish for all meditators in this retreat group, then the employees of the retreat centre. Then a wish in relation to one or more groups, for example, all people who are ill, suffering from violence, all children, all animals or one or more other groups, and finally a wish for all beings, all people, animals, plants and trees, that kindness will flow out of you in all directions, to beings near and far to all beings.

Kindness is sometimes called boundless, because it can go beyond the ordinary boundaries of space and time. We are connected to all beings who are living now, who have already died, who are living and who will be born. Therefore you can send a wish to all beings: 'May all beings live together in happiness, peace, health and wisdom', not forgetting that you are also one of these beings!

We would like to leave you with a reminder from Jalal ad-Din Rumi:

Listen with ears of tolerance.
See through eyes of compassion.
Speak the language of love.

Notes

1 In the Mindfulness-Based Compassionate Living training, self-compassion and compassion to others are also developed in an explicit way. See www.mbcl-international.net for research on MBCL.
2 See https://link.springer.com/article/10.1007/s12671-023-02150-3 or www.researchgate.net/publication/371536429 for studies on the relationship between mindfulness and prosociality.

3 It is therefore important for retreat teachers to have a lot of retreat experience and to be well familiar with this more difficult phase in the practice.
4 *The Thoughts of Blaise Pascal* translated by C. Kegan Paul (1828–1902).
5 In this perspective, unwanted and violent intimacy are considered as harmful, but all kinds of consensual and loving forms of sexuality are of course not included in this.
6 From the Samyutta Nikāya or *The Connected Discourses* by the Buddha.
7 From Buddhist psychology, the noble eightfold path – as it is affectionately called by Buddhists – offers a number of practical suggestions and mentions eight practice suggestions:

- Right understanding.
- Right thinking.
- Right speech.
- Right action.
- Right livelihood.
- Right dedication.
- Right mindfulness.
- Right concentration.

The word 'right' here refers to balance and orientation towards inner freedom, it could be replaced by the word 'skilful' or 'wise'. The eight links of the eightfold path cover the last of four Noble Truths, which are endorsed in all Buddhist traditions as the core of the teachings of the Buddha:

- There is suffering.
- There is a cause for this suffering.
- Inner freedom is possible.
- There is a path that leads to inner freedom.

8 John, E. & Taupin, B. (1976). *Sorry Seems To Be the Hardest Word.*
9 Frits Koster and Joyce Cordus have developed a six-week Mindfulness-Based Training in Forgiveness (MBTF). In this training, the three different areas or flows of forgiveness and different ways in which we can develop it are explored. See www.traininginforgiveness.com.
10 See https://dharmaseed.org for a recommended online meditation platform.
11 Insight Dialogue was developed by Gregory Kramer (2007, 2020) as a method to meditate together and communicate mindfully.
12 See Chapter 3 in our book *Mindful Communication* (2023) for more information about the Interpersonal Mindfulness Program (IMP).

Chapter 9

A few last words of advice

Choosing a suitable retreat

Wherever you go, there you are.

—Jon Kabat-Zinn (2004)

I (Victoria) was worried when my brother announced he was going to run the London Marathon. At 57 he had never enjoyed athletic pursuits. However, I need not have been so concerned. He did lots of training, building up from shorter runs to full-length ones and seeking out expert advice on pacing, hydration and keeping glucose levels steady. It was a fulfilling moment for him when he crossed the finishing line, and a heartwarming one for our family, as he also raised a lot of money for a charity that means a lot to us.

We hope after reading the previous chapters you feel full of enthusiasm, not to run a marathon of course, but to undertake something that sounds simple but can be similarly challenging. Namely as the title of Jon Kabat-Zinn's book *Wherever You Go, There You Are* suggests, just being with your own mind without distraction for several days. Maybe you have already gained some practical training in meditation by taking a mindfulness course in person or online, and of course, we hope this book provides you with a wealth of helpful guidance. However, before you pack your meditation cushion and set off, here are few last words of advice and some checklists.

How do you find a suitable retreat?

You may already have attended a meditation programme with a teacher who also leads retreats. In that case, it may be quite easy to find something that fits your schedule and you will probably already be familiar with the type of practices you will be doing. However, if this is not the case, you will have to start looking for a suitable retreat, live or online.

Silent or not?

In this book, we have been describing a silent *vipassanā* retreat. This means that after the first few hours the group transitions into silence and apart from some individual or group inquiry meetings and a daily talk, most of the time is spent in silence. However, there are some retreats that are only partially in silence. You may have a daily schedule with activities such as mindful gardening, walking, yoga or Qi Gong when you can socialise with the group, but the programme might additionally include silent meditation sessions or a whole silent day.

If you however want to participate in the type of retreat we describe in the book, it is helpful to realise that whilst they may be similar in structure, they are not all exactly the same. There are more traditional Buddhist retreats and those that are secular and some in between. In addition, there are different schools and variants of Buddhism and the practices and style of retreat vary considerably. Some alternate sitting and walking meditation, some include chanting and various rituals such as repeating prayers or bowing to a statue of the Buddha, some offer a mindful silent walk each day or mindful movement in addition to sitting or walking. Sometimes the instructions may be a little different to the guidance offered in this book. Certain retreats can be quite challenging, with the first sitting starting as early as 4 a.m., and where only one or two meals a day are offered, and the guidance may not be given by the teacher in person but by videos.

The secular mindfulness retreats are structured roughly along the same lines of the more traditional retreats. They are offered by mindfulness teacher training institutes or organisations such as the Mindfulness Network UK or Breathworks, or the national or international mindfulness teacher professional associations. The retreat leaders however are usually experienced meditation teachers who are respected in both the Buddhist and secular mindfulness worlds such as Frits and Jetty.

Often the retreats will have a theme from Buddhism or from daily life. The retreat described in this book is based on the ten perfections. Other examples of themes are 'Meeting life with courage and compassion', 'Embracing uncertainty', 'Beginner's mind' and 'Living well with illness and pain'; the possibilities are endless. However, whether the theme is a more traditional one or not, the challenges that we address in this book will crop up: how to sit well, how to be in silence, how to be in the moment and work skilfully with your mind and how to cultivate wholesome attitudes.

A checklist for choosing a retreat

Here is a checklist with things to consider in choosing a retreat:

- Who is the main retreat teacher? If you don't know them personally, can you listen to their talks and guided meditations online[1] or read a book they have written to get an idea of how they teach.
- What is the retreat schedule? When does meditation start in the morning and when is 'lights out' at night? Is following the schedule mandatory or is it used as a friendly non-mandatory structure?
- How many meals are offered and how long are the meal breaks? Can the kitchen cater for specific dietary requirements with prior notice?
- What kind of practices are offered (sitting, walking, movement, chanting, rituals, other) and how long is each practice period?

- What kind of guidance is offered besides a daily lecture and guided meditations?
- In case of physical disabilities or chronic fatigue: is it possible to rest or to change posture in the meditation hall? Some retreatants will be reassured if they can practise sitting meditation in a reclining posture if necessary.

The venue

Sometimes retreats are held at dedicated retreat houses, sometimes at simple hotel or hostel-type training venues that cater for different groups, and sometimes at more comfortable hotels. Ask whether the centre hosts silent retreat groups and other groups at the same time, as it can be a distraction if not everyone in the centre is observing silence.

Sharing rooms

Dedicated retreat centres often only have limited number of single rooms, and these may be reserved for people who need privacy because of health issues. Some centres even have camping areas or dormitories and this can make it very low cost for participants to attend. Most venues offer shared rooms. Even if you haven't shared a room since your last school trip as a teenager, do consider it, as it can be a very useful part of the training. Being with others all the time can be surprisingly pleasant and supportive and it certainly helps keep you on the 'straight and narrow' as far as checking your phone is concerned.

> **On sharing a room**
>
> *I (Victoria) used to enjoy sharing a room before I developed serious health issues. Once I stayed in a beautiful, spacious room in a rambling old retreat centre near Hamburg with three other women. There was a comfortable bed in each corner and we had spent a very harmonious week together in a mutually supportive atmosphere. On the last day I went to the room after lunch to get a jacket when I noticed a beeping noise. I immediately launched into an angry inner narrative along the lines of 'someone has carelessly left their phone on'. I moved around the room, listening intently but could not identify where the high-pitched beeping was coming from. One of the other women entered the room, immediately realised what was going on and silently joined in the search. After a while we broke the silence and debated what to do. By chance one of us glanced up at the ceiling, which was at least four metres high, and recognised that the noise was coming from the smoke alarm. We burst out laughing and tried standing on the table to turn it off, but we were too short and could not reach it. We notified the management that the alarm was beeping loudly as its batteries were low, and we then went back into the silence.*

Even after I had cancer and developed ongoing health issues, I have occasionally shared a room with other women I had not previously met, whose care and compassion I felt very deeply, even though we hardly spoke. One of them turned out to have been an oncology nurse.

If you plan to share a room with people you don't know, get to the retreat centre early. It is normally possible to chat to the other participants for the first few hours. You can discuss and agree on who might prefer to sleep near the window and whether this is open or not at night. I am from Britain and am therefore immune to draughts. I live in Germany however, where draughts are commonly believed to pose a serious danger to health. We can use these situations to practise mindful communication and skilful negotiation.

Things to consider when sharing a room
- You will need to bring a dressing gown or robe.
- Especially if you are easily disturbed by sound, it will be very helpful to bring earplugs, so you can be compassionately accepting of snorers.
- Bring an eye mask if you are sensitive to light. For health and safety reasons communal areas are often lit all night and sometimes there are nightlights in shared rooms.
- It is best not to use shampoo or other products which are strongly perfumed.

What NOT to take on retreat

'What, you can't even take your knitting'? Sue, a very skilled knitter and one of my closest friends, was clearly horrified at my explanation of what being on silent retreat entails. Of course, crafts can be very valuable as a focus for quiet contemplation, and they can also help us cultivate love and compassion, as anyone who has knitted a jacket for a new baby knows. Despite this, we recommend not bringing any knitting on retreat, and the same goes for reading materials, even for books about meditation. Personally, I don't take a journal either or anything that might provide entertainment or distraction as I actually want to spend time with my own mind. If boredom makes an appearance, I am fully prepared to be with it. Our brains and minds are so over-stimulated, why not give them a rest? And in any case, as the teacher on one retreat I attended stated 'You will be surprised with what your mind brings up. If you can meet it with some humour, you might find it as entertaining as Netflix'.

Day long and shorter retreats

My brother did not start by running a marathon, but built up to the full 42 kilometres by doing shorter runs first. Similarly, meditation teachers or training centres will offer a day of mindfulness or a mini-retreat as a starting point. Indeed, a typical 8-week course such as MBSR or MBCT includes a silent day. You can get used to being in silence, alternating sitting and walking meditation and maybe working with difficulty if troubling thoughts or emotions come up. After doing a few silent days, you might like to participate in a silent weekend at an external venue and in time slowly build up to a longer retreat.

Traditionally *vipassanā* meditation retreats have often been 10 days. However, it is not always practical for meditators to take such a long time off from work, especially if there are also family or other commitments. A common length of time for a retreat these days is five to seven nights and most professional bodies of mindfulness teachers have a minimum requirement for their members to attend at least one six-day retreat each year.

Perhaps you are a 'no pain no gain' type of person and you want to jump in at the deep end? Before I accept participants into my MBSR programme, I like to get to know them personally. We meet for a walk in the park or a cup of coffee and have a chat. I always ask whether they have any previous meditation experience and if so, in what tradition. One man told me that he had been on a very strenuous 10-day silent retreat, getting up at 4 a.m. and subsisting on two and then after a few days one meal a day. I was curious and asked him how he found that. 'Well, I hated it to be honest, but I was really proud of myself as at least I stuck it out to the bitter end. Loads of the other people left early'. So I inquired further how he accomplished this extraordinary feat. He answered 'I gritted my teeth'. A little word of caution here: what do you intend to learn, practise and cultivate during the retreat? Gritting your teeth takes a lot of energy and your dentist might not be too happy with the result.

Work period

Some retreat centres keep costs low by asking retreatants to contribute to the running of the place by undertaking a daily work period. There is usually a list of jobs you can sign up for when you check in. I (Victoria) have enjoyed sweeping the yard, vacuum cleaning the stairs and yes, even scrubbing the toilets at various retreat centres. In addition, retreatants may be asked to set tables, clear away after meals, load/unload the dishwasher. You get the idea. One retreat centre I went to even offered 'feeding the chickens' but that is rare. 'Chopping vegetables for lunch' is on the list at some places and it is a popular slot. Retreatants have been known to arrive especially early to make sure they get assigned the most enjoyable task, or at least avoid getting landed with scrubbing the sanitary facilities. However, why not use this opportunity to practise acceptance, just taking what job comes your way and carrying it out with an open and generous heart?

The daily work period is an important opportunity to practise mindfulness in a daily task and it gives you an idea how to integrate the skills you learn on retreat into your life. When you get home, you may even find you can transform the drudgery of housework into an opportunity to cultivate relaxed and focussed awareness.

Most retreat centres provide everything you need for the work period, including gloves for potentially messy jobs. However, if you are allergic to certain types of protective glove, it might be helpful to bring a few pairs of your own.

Sadly, the retreat centre I most often go to, does not offer a work period. The staff do everything and look after everyone with great care. However, there is a list to sign up to for volunteers to wake everyone up in the morning and ring the gong between sessions. It can be quite a challenge to meditate and at the same time keep an eye on your watch during your 'shift', but is also a way of mindfully serving the community. At the end of the week, we practise generosity by making a collection for all the management, kitchen, gardening and cleaning staff who take care of us, and we also show consideration by removing the duvet covers and leaving the rooms tidy.

Paying for the retreat

Often there is one fee for the teaching part of the retreat but the costs of accommodation are separate. Therefore, you may need to make two bookings, first booking the teaching part and waiting for confirmation that you will be offered a place, before booking accommodation. Some retreats however offer the teaching on a donation or *dana* basis. There may be a small fee for the administration, but at the end of the retreat, there is a collection of donations for the teacher. It can be a challenge to work out what is an appropriate amount, sometimes guidance is provided. In my experience, you won't receive a receipt for the donation.

Receipts and confirmation

Some of us will need confirmation that we attended the retreat, especially members of a professional body who have committed to continuing professional development or regular retreat attendance. Some religious centres are unable or reluctant to provide this. There may be a creative solution, sometimes it will be possible to use the confirmation of the booking as proof. If you need any documentation for tax purposes, however, it may make sense to choose an organisation or centre that provides this.

Food allergies and intolerances

Although the food at retreat centres is usually wholesome and tasty, a silent retreat is not a gourmet or wellness holiday. Part of the exercise is to accept and be thankful for the food that comes your way, even if it might not be your favourite meal. Most centres offer vegetarian or vegan dishes and if they receive prior notice most centres can cater for participants who need to avoid lactose or gluten. I know from personal experience that more complicated allergies or food intolerances can be a challenge. On my last retreat, the kitchen provided me with boiled potatoes at lunchtime and I supplemented this with salads or plain vegetables from the buffet and a boiled egg. It was simple but perfectly adequate and it created minimal extra work for the kitchen.

Meditation-related adverse effects

For a while, meditation was thought to be and indeed promoted as something purely beneficial. This is strange as we all know that anything that has a positive effect has the potential to produce unwanted consequences. Sport is good for your health but it is possible to hurt yourself running.

> **Feeling sadness**
>
> *My friend Emma had just got back from her first short retreat having done an 8-week mindfulness course a few years before. It had been at a charming Georgian mansion house in spectacular countryside and the atmosphere in the group had been warm and the teachers good, but at times she had found the silence quite disturbing and when she got home, she felt very sad. Then she suddenly had a memory of how her mother had sometimes used silence or 'stonewalling' to punish her when she had been a little girl.*

If you experience difficulties on retreat don't assume you are simply 'not doing it right' or there is something wrong with you. In an emergency, someone from the leading team should be available, even during the night. Otherwise schedule a meeting with the retreat leader. If you experience adverse effects after getting home, contact the retreat organisation for support.

Willoughby Britton, contemplative researcher and Associate Professor of Psychiatry and Human Behaviour at Brown University Medical School was one of the first researchers to systematically investigate meditation-related difficulties or adverse effects. She is one of the founders of Cheetah House, an organisation which provides online help for those experiencing meditation-related distress.[2]

Safeguarding

In recent years, cases have come to light of people abusing their positions of responsibility in religious, sporting, media, educational and many other organisations. The first retreat I (Victoria) attended was led by a teacher who was under suspicion of having made inappropriate advances to a female retreatant and he had even been prohibited from teaching in some countries. Frits and Jetty have also come across this issue in the past. Luckily nowadays most organisations have taken this subject to heart and have put safeguarding procedures in place, so it is extremely unlikely you will experience or witness any improper behaviour. If you do, however, do not hesitate to report it.

Sleep

You may feel tired on retreat. You might feel resistance to the idea of lying down and taking a nap, but the meal breaks are usually long enough for you to get forty winks after eating. Why not just try going to sleep after 'lights out', even if it is earlier than your usual bedtime? This is an opportunity to enjoy being able to rest and sleep, something most of us don't get enough of in daily life.

What to take on retreat

We have done our best to prepare you for every aspect your retreat. You are almost ready to set off. Having written about what not to take on retreat, we would like to make a few suggestions about what to take. If you attend retreats on a regular basis, it might be an idea to make a checklist for your computer which you just need to download. Here are some things to consider:

Meditation cushion or bench and blankets

Most centres have cushions, chairs or benches, mats and blankets available. However many people like to take their own.

Medication

Retreat venues are often in rural areas, so you don't want to be wasting valuable meditation time locating a dispensing chemist and trying to procure medication you have forgotten. Don't forget prescription medication and maybe take a few items you occasionally need such as throat lozenges, antiseptic, insect bite cream or headache pills.

Toiletries

Shampoo, toothpaste and hygiene articles should be available if you forget. It is best to use perfume-free toiletries as strong perfume can be disturbing to others in the mediation hall. A small travel hairdryer may be useful as not all centres provide these.

Outdoor clothing

It can be invigorating and refreshing to do walking meditation outside in nature, even if it is cold, windy or raining. It is a good idea to take warm clothes and a rain poncho or an umbrella. If it is summer, you might need a sunhat or sun cream. Sturdy, waterproof boots that are easy to get on and off are also useful.

Sundry

A hot water bottle can be good for winter retreats. Earplugs and an eye mask are also helpful, even if you are not sharing a room. Outside areas are generally well lit at night for safety reasons and the curtains do not always keep the light out. Old houses can have thin walls and be a bit creaky and at one centre in Northern Germany, the local farmers are often active until midnight harvesting the maize with huge tractors, which can be very noisy. An old-fashioned travel alarm clock can be useful if you have one, although most centres wake retreatants with a gong. Flip-flops or beach sandals will be useful if you are using communal showers. A water bottle or thermos flask can also be very handy and it is important to take slippers or indoor shoes as many centres discourage the use of outdoor shoes inside the building.

An open mind, wisdom and compassion

Last but not least we may suggest that you bring an open mind, wisdom and compassion in relating to what you may encounter. In our experience, every retreat brings familiar themes and unexpected surprises. Sometimes a retreat can be experienced as tough and other times it can be surprisingly easy. In all cases, we have experienced all kinds of beneficial results. We really recommend going on a meditation retreat and may this book support you in this journey.

Notes

1 See www.dharmaseed.org.
2 See www.cheetahhouse.org for more information.

Chapter 10

Taking part in an online retreat
Dos and don'ts

We are like islands in the sea,
separate on the surface but connected in the deep.
— William James, American philosopher and psychologist (1842–1910)

In 2020, we started offering online retreats. The first few times were forced by the Corona epidemic – we simply had to cancel a lot of live retreats. Eventually, we also started offering online retreats as a new mode of offering retreats. We had to develop new abilities and skills but gradually found a way that seems to work well. In fact, online retreats may even be better for some people who cannot leave home, for example because of caring for a dog, struggling with a disability that makes it difficult to join an in-person retreat or simply for financial reasons as attendance at a residential retreat always incurs accommodation costs. That is why we continued offering online retreats, which can sometimes be very practical when an institution wishes to invite us but cannot find a suitable venue or wishes to offer a retreat internationally or even worldwide. I (Frits) guided an online retreat with participants in Japan and offering it online meant we could reduce the ecological footprint.

Some practical suggestions

Next to the advice in the introduction of this book, of this book, we usually require participants to have a good internet connection and to make it clear to friends, neighbours and family they will not be available during the retreat. Some people may be able to arrange to be at a holiday cottage or on a camping site. If you live with others in the same house or apartment, it would be good to practise and sleep in a separate room and to avoid social contact with others as much as possible. However, this will sometimes simply be unavoidable. In that case, we recommend that you be kind and mindful when there is contact with a family member or a partner.

We often plan a pre-interview with participants who don't have any online retreat experience, in which we can meet more personally and discuss possible difficulties in going on retreat and offer suggestions, for example on practical issues such as buying enough food in advance but also concerning how to support yourself during the online retreat.

A daily schedule for an online retreat

We use a similar schedule to the one described on page 9 and have an internet connection in the digital meditation room – in a pleasant corner of our house where we usually sit. In this way, meditators can always feel connected when they practise alone. We also ring the bell in changing from walking to sitting or from sitting to walking and suggest participants have a silent walk (or bicycle ride) outside once or twice a day. Another slight difference is that we schedule more time for dinner, so that participants also have time to mindfully prepare or cook their meal.

Joseph Roux, a French parish priest, poet, and philologist once said: 'Solitude vivifies; isolation kills'. We discovered that people following a retreat online can start to feel isolated. Therefore we started offering the inquiry meetings with the teacher(s) in little groups rather than individually. The feedback from retreatants was that the common humanity of meeting with fellow meditators and hearing and sharing with them about fruitful and difficult experiences is comforting and supporting. In addition, we usually try to offer a few words of guidance at the beginning of a new period of walking or sitting meditation more often than we would during an in-person retreat.

Some participants prefer a residential retreat, others prefer practising online. It is difficult to say which format might be better, we hope there will be some research in this field in the coming years. We recommend you trust yourself to explore and discover what is most suitable for you.

Bibliography

Anālayo, bh. (2003). *Satipatthāna. The direct path to realization.* Cambridge: Windhorse Publications.
Anālayo, bh. (2015). *Compassion and emptiness in early Buddhist meditation.* Cambridge: Windhorse Publications.
Anālayo, bh. (2018). *Satipatthāna meditation. A practice guide.* Cambridge: Windhorse Publications.
Andersen Stark, G. (2020). *Creating a life of integrity. In conversation with Joseph Goldstein.* Somerville, MA: Wisdom Publications.
Armstrong, G. (2017). *Emptiness. A practical guide for meditators.* Somerville, MA: Wisdom Publications.
Batchelor, M. (2007). *Let Go: A Buddhist guide to breaking free of habits.* Somerville, MA: Wisdom Publications.
Batchelor, M., & Batchelor, S. (2021). *Meditation for life.* Brattleboro, VT: Echo Point Books & Media, LLC.
Batchelor, S. (2020). *The art of solitude. A meditation on being alone with others in this world.* London: Yale University Press.
Beck, C. J., & Smith, S. (1995). *Nothing special. Living Zen.* New York: HarperCollins Publishers.
Bohlmeijer, E., & Hulsbergen, M. (2018). *Using positive psychology every day. Learning how to flourish.* London: Routledge.
Brach, T. (2004). *Radical acceptance. Embracing your life with the heart of a Buddha.* New York: Bantam.
Brahm, Ajahn (2005). *Who ordered this truckload of dung? Inspiring stories for welcoming life's difficulties.* Somerville, MA: Wisdom Publications.
Bregman, R. (2021). *Humankind. A hopeful history.* London: Bloomsbury Publishing.
van den Brink, E., & Koster, F. (2015). *Mindfulness-based compassionate living. A new training programme to deepen mindfulness with heartfulness.* London: Routledge.
van den Brink, E., Koster, F., & Norton, V. (2018). *A practical guide to mindfulness-based compassionate living. Living with heart.* London: Routledge.
Brown, B. (2007). *I thought it was just me (but it isn't). Making the journey from 'What will people think?' to 'I am enough'.* London: Penguin Publishing Group.
Buddhaghosa, bhad., & Ñanamoli, bh. (1976). *The path of purification (*part 1+2*). A classic textbook.* Boulder, CO: Shambhala Publications.
Burbea, R. (2015). *Seeing that frees. Meditations on emptiness and dependent arising.* Willenhall: Hermes Amāra Foundation.

Burch, V. (2008). *Living well with pain and illness. Using mindfulness to free yourself from suffering.* London: Piatkus.

Chah, A. (2001). *Being Dharma. The essence of the Buddha's teachings.* Boulder, CO: Shambhala Publications.

Crane, S. R., Karunavira, & Griffith, G. M. (Eds.). (2021). *Essential resources for mindfulness teachers.* London: Routledge.

Dews, A. (2018). *Still, in the city. Creating peace of mind in the midst of urban chaos.* New York: Skyhorse Publishing.

Evans, N. (2020). *The horse whisperer* (25th anniversary edition). New York: Delacorte Press.

Feldman, C. (2017). *Boundless heart. The Buddha's path of kindness, compassion, joy and equanimity.* Boulder, CO: Shambhala Publications.

Fredrickson, B. L. (2013). *Love 2.0. Creating happiness and health in moments of connection.* London: Penguin Publishing Group.

Gethin, R. M. L. (1992). *The Buddhist path to awakening. A study of the bodhi-pakkhiya dhamma.* Oxford: Oneworld Publications.

Gilbert, P. (2010). *The compassionate mind. A new approach to life's challenges.* London: Constable & Robinson Ltd.

Gillis Chapman, S. (2012). *The five keys to mindful communication. Using deep listening and mindful speech to strengthen relationships, heal conflicts, and accomplish your goals.* Boulder, CO: Shambhala Publications.

Gillis Chapman, S. (2024). *Which way is up? Finding heart in the hardest of times.* Boulder, CO: Shambhala Publications.

Goldstein, J. (2016). *Mindfulness. A practical guide to awakening.* Louisville, KY: Sounds True, Inc.

Goleman, D. (2014). *Focus. The hidden driver of excellence.* London: Bloomsbury Paperbacks.

Goleman, D., & Davidson, R. J. (2017). *Altered traits. Science reveals how meditation changes your mind, brain, and body.* New York: Avery Publishing Group.

Halifax, J. (2019). *Standing at the edge. Finding freedom where fear and courage meet.* New York: Flatiron Books.

Hanson, R., i.s.m. Mendius, R. (2009). *Buddha's brain. The practical neuroscience of happiness, love, and wisdom.* Oakland, CA: New Harbinger Publications.

Hanson, R. (2014). *Hardwiring happiness. The practical science of reshaping your brain - and your life.* London: Ebury Publishing.

Hanson, R. (2020). *Neurodharma. New science, ancient wisdom, and seven practices of the highest happiness.* New York: Harmony Books.

Heuvel Rijnders, J. van den (2017). *Terug naar de markt. Boeddhisme in het dagelijks leven.* Waarbeke: Asoka.

Jackson, M. (2023). *Uncertain. The wisdom and wonder of being unsure.* Lanham, MD: Prometheus Books.

Kabat-Zinn, J. (2004). *Wherever you go, there you are. Mindfulness meditation for everyday life.* London: Little, Brown Book Group.

Kabat-Zinn, J. (2013). *Full catastrophe living. Using the wisdom of your body and mind to face stress, pain, and illness.* London: Piatkus. First edition: 1990.

Keltner, D. (2023). *Awe. The transformative power of everyday wonder.* New York: Penguin Random House.

Kornfield, J. (2010). *Living Dharma. Teachings and meditation instructions from twelve Theravada Masters.* Boston: Shambhala Publications. N.B. This book was originally published in 1977 as *Living Buddhist Masters.*

Kornfield, J. (2008). *The wise heart. Buddhist psychology for the West.* London: Rider.

Koster, F. (2004). *Liberating insight. Introduction to Buddhist psychology and insight meditation.* Chiengmai: Silkworm Books.

Koster, F. (2015). *The web of Buddhist wisdom. An introduction to the psychology of the Abhidhamma.* Chiengmai: Silkworm Books.

Koster, F., Heynekamp, H. J., & Norton, V. (Eds.). (2023). *Mindful communication. Speaking and listening with wisdom and compassion.* London: Routledge.

Kramer, G. (2007). *Insight dialogue. The interpersonal path to freedom.* Boulder, CO: Shambhala Publications.

Kramer, G. (2020). *A whole-life path. A lay Buddhist's guide to crafting a Dhamma-infused life.* Seattle, WA: Insight Dialogue Community.

Langer, E. J. (1998). *The power of mindful learning.* Boston, MA: Da Capo Lifelong Books.

Langer, E. J. (2014). *Mindfulness* (25th anniversary edition). Boston, MA: Da Capo Lifelong Books.

Lokos, A. (2012). *Patience: The art of peaceful living.* Los Angeles, CA: TarcherPerigee.

Machado, A. (1983). *Times alone. Selected poems of Antonio Machado* (translated by Robert Bly). Middletown, CT: Wesleyan University Press.

Mannschatz, M. (2019). *Vollkommen unvollkommen. Zehn Qualitäten, die das Beste in uns zum Vorschein bringen.* München: O.W. Barth Verlag.

McGonigal, K. (2015). *The upside of stress. Why stress is good for you, and how to get good at it.* New York: Avery.

Neff, K. D., & Germer, C. K. (2018). *The mindful self-compassion workbook. A proven way to accept yourself, build inner strength, and thrive.* New York: Guilford Press.

Pandita, S. U., & Wheeler, K. (1993). *In this very life. The liberation teachings of the Buddha.* Somerville, MA: Wisdom Publications.

Porges, S. (2017). *The pocket guide to the Polyvagal Theory. The transformative power of feeling safe.* New York: W. W. Norton & Company.

Ram Dass (1971). *Be here now.* Victoria, ON: Crown Publications.

Reitz, M. (2018). *Speak up. Say what needs to be said and hear what needs to be heard.* Upper Saddle River, NJ: FT Publishing International.

Remen, R. N. (2006). *Kitchen table wisdom. Stories that heal.* New York: Penguin Random House.

Ricard, M. (2015). *The art of meditation.* London: Atlantic Books.

Rilke, R. M. (1929). *Briefe an einen jungen Dichter.* Berlin: Inselverlag

Salzberg, S. (1995). *Lovingkindness. The revolutionary art of* happiness. Boulder, CO: Shambhala Publications.

Salzberg, S. (1999). *A heart as wide as the world. Stories on the path of lovingkindness.* Boulder, CO: Shambhala Publications.

Schmidt, A. (2005). *Dipa Ma. The life and legacy of a Buddhist master.* New York: Bluebridge.

Schumann, H. W. (2024). *The historical Buddha. The times, life and teachings of the founder of Buddhism.* New Delhi: Motilal Banarsidass. First publication date 2003.

Siegel, D. J. (2010). *The mindful therapist. A clinician's guide to mindsight and neural integration.* New York: W. W. Norton & Company.

Siegel, D. J. (2011). *Mindsight. Transform Your brain with the new science of kindness.* London: Oneworld Publications.

Steindl-Rast, B. D. (1984). *Gratefulness, the heart of prayer. An approach to life in fullness.* Mahwah, NJ: Paulist Press.

Sumedho, A. (2010). *Don't take your life personally.* Totness, Devon: Buddhist Publishing Group.

Suzuki, S. (1976). *Zen mind, beginner's mind. Informal talks on zen meditation and practice.* Boulder, CO: Shambhala Publications.

Tejaniya, S. U. (2016a). *Don't look down on the defilements. They will laugh at you.* Malaysia: Auspicious Affinity.

Tejaniya, S. U. (2016b). *When awareness becomes natural. A guide to cultivating mindfulness in daily life.* Boulder, CO: Shambhala Publications.

Treleaven, D. A. (2018). *Trauma-sensitive mindfulness. Practices for safe and transformative healing.* New York: W.W. Norton & Company, Inc.

Williams, M., & Penman, D. (2023). *Deeper mindfulness. The new way to rediscover calm in a chaotic world.* London: Piatkus.

Winston, D. (2019). *The little book of being. Practices and guidance for uncovering your natural awareness.* Louisville, KY: Sounds True, Inc.

Audio and video downloads

The following MP3 files can be downloaded from https://www.routledge.com/Going-on-a-Meditation-Retreat-Embracing-Silence-to-Cultivate-Mindfulness-and-Compassion/Koster-Heynekamp-Norton/p/book/9781032856230 for personal and non-commercial use.

Audio 1. Kindness meditation - Yourself (Frits Koster)
Audio 2. Developing mindfulness - Sitting meditation (Frits Koster)
Audio 3. Kindness meditation - Self and others (Frits Koster)
Audio 4. Compassionate breathing with a difficulty (Frits Koster)
Audio 5. Sitting like a horse whisperer (Frits Koster)
Video 1. Posture advice (Jetty Heynekamp)

Index

Note: Page numbers followed by "n" refer to end notes.

access 10, 19, 56, 90, 100, 101, 134, 141
adhimokkha 110
aditthāna 116
adosa 15
allergies 150–151
alobha 61
Anālayo, bh. 47n2, 55, 124, 132
Ānanda, Ven. 139
anattā 76, 93
Andersen Stark, G. 81
anger 40, 43, 74, 78, 91, 94, 97, 105, 110, 121, 123, 134
anguttara 85, 98n4
anicca 68, 76
anxiety 18, 32, 41–43, 49, 115, 132
apilāpana 55
apilapati 55
apilapeti 55
appanā 100, 101
Asabha, A. 49, 55, 64, 65n4, 95, 107, 108
Asia 11, 35, 37, 59, 61
attachment 2, 40, 61, 63, 64, 74, 95, 110, 116, 123, 134
attention 2, 6, 10, 16, 17, 20, 25, 26n2, 37, 39, 40, 42, 43, 46, 48–55, 57, 61, 67, 73, 75, 76, 81, 82, 88, 89, 93, 95, 97, 99, 101, 105, 107, 109, 113, 117, 119, 120, 122, 125, 130–132, 134, 141
attitude 7, 10, 15, 16, 30, 35, 37, 42, 44, 51–52, 56, 57, 61, 62, 66, 67, 71, 74, 84, 86, 91, 92, 97, 104, 107, 108, 110, 112, 118, 122–126, 131, 133, 138, 146
attune 47n6, 78
attunement 36, 132, 137
Aurelius, M. 73, 80n4
avijjā 75
awe 74, 81, 87–88, 113

Bala 107, 134
Batchelor, M. i, xvii
Batchelor, S. xxi
Beck, J. 112
befriending 39, 70
benefactor 46, 47
benevolence 12, 120
bhavanā 14, 104
bingo 70–71
bodhisatta 12
Bohlmeijer, E. 120
bowing 21–23, 50, 146
Brach, T. 73, 74
brahmavihāra 120
Breathworks 146
Bregman, R. 72
van den Brink, E. 122
Britton, W. 151
Brown, B. 35
Buddha 3, 11–13, 19, 22, 30, 32, 34, 36, 41, 45, 46, 49, 57, 58, 60, 65, 68, 77, 85, 94, 95, 104, 105, 107, 111, 116, 119, 120, 134, 137, 139, 142, 146
Buddhaghosa, B. 54, 55
Buddhism 11, 14, 32, 35, 42, 50, 60, 74, 89, 90, 92, 101, 121, 133, 134, 146
Burma 118

Chah, A. 35
Chapman, S. G. 77, 138, 140
choiceless 69
cittānupassanā 57
cognition 94
commitment 35, 81–98, 104–106, 124, 149
compassionate breathing 81–98
concentration 33, 51, 53–55, 84, 86, 100–101, 103, 105–109, 119, 133, 140, 144n7

concomitant 94
constituents 94–96
contraindications xxi
Cordus, J. 144n9
Corona 28, 139, 154
Craving 55, 132, 134
Cross, J. of the 69
Cruijff, J. 72
curiosity 3, 65, 73, 81, 86–87

dāna 60, 61, 150
dedication 12, 35, 37, 81, 82, 84, 104–105, 119, 133, 139, 144
defilement 2
delusion 73, 77, 132, 134
depression 4, 76
Descartes, R. 57
desire 2, 27, 38–40, 43, 44, 51, 57, 61–64, 69, 82, 83, 88, 113, 116, 132, 134
determination 12, 104, 110, 115–116, 119, 139
detoxification 44
dhamma 75, 94
dhamma vicaya 75
dhammānupassanā 94, 132
dharma 47n5
dilemma 17, 75, 78, 79, 90, 91
Diogenes 70
Dipa Ma 81
disappointment 45, 74, 76–77, 91, 115, 134
discipline 12, 23, 138
discourse 30
dissatisfaction 40, 92, 106, 107, 112, 120
Davidson, R. 130, 136
ditthi 75
Dogen 96
Dosa 132
doubt 2, 16, 36, 37, 41, 43, 67, 108, 117, 125, 134
dukkha 36, 41, 42, 45, 46, 76
dullabha 13
dullness 41, 44, 52, 83, 84, 106, 111
dung 40–42

effort 12, 20, 24, 35, 44, 50, 51, 53, 55–57, 62, 69, 82–83, 85, 86, 90, 104, 107, 110, 117, 127, 133, 135
efforting 82
ego 65, 93
egolessness 93
Einstein, A. 96
emergence 69, 104
engagement 104

enlightenment 60, 119, 130, 132–136
equanimity 12, 85, 92, 115–129, 131, 133, 135, 139, 140
ethics 10–12, 130–144
Evans, N. 125

fabricated 57
faith 12–13, 104, 107, 133
fatigue 2–4, 16, 28, 30, 40, 42–44, 52, 83, 84, 92, 111, 121, 131, 140, 147
fear 2, 39, 41, 42, 59, 78, 82, 83, 91, 104–106, 110, 121, 122, 133, 134, 140
feeling 1, 2, 13, 15, 17–21, 24, 25, 27, 30, 32, 35, 37, 38, 41–46, 50, 52, 57, 63, 66–70, 72–74, 77, 78, 80, 82, 84–89, 91, 92, 94, 95, 105, 112, 113, 115–129, 131, 134–136, 142, 151
feeling tone 67, 87, 88, 94, 105, 113, 115–129
Feldman, C. 93
fitness 32
flexibility 33, 68, 95, 101, 106, 112, 131
flood 111
focussed 27, 149
forbearance 12, 43
forgiveness 139–141
Frankl, V. 67
Fredrickson, B. 79

generosity 12, 48–65, 90, 104, 132, 139, 150
Germer, C. K. 50
Gethin, R. 55
Gilbert, P. 101, 102
Goldstein, J. 11, 56, 63
Goleman, D. 136
gratitude 67, 99–114, 123
guilt 41, 45, 46, 77, 93, 105, 116

Haiku 103
Halifax, J. 82
Hanson, R. 58, 113
hatred 2, 55, 120, 132, 134
headbanging 84
heraclitus 66
Heuvel Rijnders, J. van den 35
Heynekamp, J. 80n6
Hippo, A. of 81
Holleboom, A. 68
Holstead, R. 6, 14, 25, 30, 79, 96, 127, 136
homesick 45–46
honesty 111

horizontal practice 42–43
horse whisperer 126, 127
Hulsbergen, M. 120
hypocrisy 123

IMP 43, 141, 143
impatience 17, 37, 38, 42–44, 63, 67, 83, 86, 132, 134
impermanence 35, 66–80, 124, 133
indriya 103, 107, 133
inquiry meeting 8, 27–47, 52–54, 70–72, 87, 90, 92, 95, 99, 103, 115, 118, 119, 123, 136, 145, 155
Insight Dialogue 141, 143
integrity 11, 58, 81, 99–114, 139
intention 10, 13–15, 18, 20, 21, 24, 29, 34, 50, 57, 70, 75, 78, 85, 88, 91, 97, 99–114, 116, 120, 138, 139
Interpersonal Mindfulness Program 43, 141, 143
Interview 33, 154
intolerances 43, 150–151
investigation 75, 119

James, W. 154
jealousy 78, 116, 123, 134
jhāna 101
Joy 14, 16–18, 33, 42, 44, 59, 60, 71, 94, 110, 114–116, 119, 120, 123–125, 136
Jumnien, A. 34, 47n5
Jung, C. G. 134

Kabat-Zinn, J. 58, 131, 145
karaniya 120
karunā 122
kāya 8
kāyānupassanā 30
Keltner, D. 113
khanika 54, 100
khanti 43
kilesa 2
King, M. L. 46
Kornfield, J. 49
Koster, F. 41, 116, 122, 138, 144n9
Kramer, G. 144n11
Kundalabhivamsa, U. 88
Kung Fu Panda 115
kusala 32

Langer, E. 79, 141
Lehrhaupt, L. ii, xvii

Lieberman, M. 67
lighthearted 54, 72, 81, 86, 108
lobha 132
Loesje 39
Lokos, A. 47
Longchenpa 1

Maex, E. 29, 73
Mahasi 17, 64, 118
Mahayāna 26n5
Manasikāra 36, 47n6, 78, 132
Mandela, M. 46
Mannschatz, M. 138
Masai 93
MBCL 90, 98n5, 141, 143n1
MBCT 4, 5n2, 98n5, 141, 148
MBSR 4, 5n2, 24, 58, 98n5, 141, 148, 149
MBTF 141, 144n9
McDonald, M. 80n5
McGonigal, K. 84
mettā 14, 15, 81, 120, 121
mettā bhavanā 14
mettavihari 7
Mindfulness-Based Cognitive Therapy 5n2
Mindfulness-Based Compassionate Living 90, 122, 143n1
Mindfulness-Based Stress Reduction 5n2, 58
Mindfulness-Based Training in Forgiveness 141, 144n9
Moggallāna, Ven. 85
Moha 132
Momentary 96, 100, 101, 133
de Montaigne, M. xxi
muditā 123
Myanmar 17, 37, 49, 55, 84, 88, 118, 133

ñāna 75
Ñanamoli, bh. 54, 55
natural 1, 3, 17, 31, 32, 37, 44, 52, 54, 57, 61, 62, 67, 69, 70, 74, 78, 83, 90, 95, 108–110, 114, 116, 122, 125, 126, 133–135, 139
Neff, K. 50
nekkhamma 99
neuroception 102
neuropsychology 31
nibbāna 132
nikanti 110
nikāya 85, 98n4, 114n4, 144n6
nīvarana 42
noble 8, 120, 139, 144n7
non-attachment 61, 74

non-claiming 74
non-clinging 18, 61, 74
non-grasping 74
non-identification 74, 80n5, 125, 131
non-judgmental 5n2, 68, 74, 84, 102
non-self 93–95, 98n7
Norton, V. 122

obhāsa 110
olympic 136
O'Neill, B. ii, xvii

paggāha 110
Pali 2, 5n2, 15, 54, 55, 68, 75, 76, 82, 104, 110, 116, 122, 132
pañcupādānakkhandā 95
Pandita, S. U. 55, 118, 133
paññā 67, 75
paradox 14, 15, 37, 46, 54, 60, 77, 90, 91, 97
paralysis 41
pāramī 11, 12
parinibbāna 68
Pascal, B. 137, 144n4
passaddhi 110
patience 12, 14, 22, 27–47, 49, 85, 90, 99, 104, 106, 124, 126, 139
Penman, D. 128n1
perspective 31, 35, 38, 42, 51, 54, 78, 87, 90, 94, 96, 107, 114n2, 119, 123, 126, 130–132, 134, 139–141, 144n5
pīti 110
Plautus, T. M. 27
Porges, S. 102
positivity 79, 81
posture 9, 10, 18–20, 22, 27–32, 38, 48, 50, 51, 56, 70, 85, 90, 99, 105, 147
posture advice 27–29
Potter, H. 50
prosocial behaviour 131
Proust, M. 114
purification 54, 113

RAIN 66, 73–74, 112
Ram Dass 138
reactivity 18, 27–47, 63, 105, 111, 117, 132
reality 4, 12, 46, 58, 75, 77, 93, 107
receptive 16, 20, 48–51, 86, 131
regulation 28, 101, 122, 131
Reitz, M. 63
relationality 58–59
Remen, R. N. 76
renunciation 12, 99

research 32, 63, 67, 68, 79, 84, 122, 130, 131, 136, 140, 143n1, 155
resilience 92, 131
resonance 53, 79, 81
restlessness 2, 3, 17, 37, 41–43, 45, 46, 86, 106, 110, 115, 117
Rilke, R. M. 47
Roshi, Jiun Hogen xv, xvii
Rukkhadeva 120
Rumi 37, 98, 143

sacca 111
saddhā 104, 110
saddheyya 104
Salzberg, S. 26n6
samādhi 54, 100, 101, 105
samatha 101
sammā 75
sammappadhāna 104
sampajañña 137
samyutta 114n4, 144n6
sankhāra 42, 80n3
sankhārupekkhā 133
sappāya 118
sati 2, 5n2
Satipatthāna 30, 47n2, 55, 129n2
sayadaw 17, 37, 51, 55, 64, 67, 77, 88, 100, 118, 133
schedule 10, 33, 40, 103, 145, 146, 151, 155
Schumann, H. W. 26n4
self 4, 15, 27, 65, 93, 95, 96, 110, 122
Seneca, L. A. 84
shame 35, 105
Siddhartha 11, 12, 99, 116
Siegel, D. 13, 60
sīla 138
silence 6–27, 37, 44, 48, 66, 68, 72, 76, 79, 89, 113, 119, 127, 128, 130, 135, 137, 145–147, 149, 151
simplification 12, 99–114, 139
sleepiness 34, 36, 83–85, 105
socks 43–44, 48
Somsak, A. 51, 55, 87
spontaneous 14, 15, 47, 50, 57, 61, 110, 135, 143
steadfastness 12, 110
steadiness 115–129
stinginess 123
suffering 3, 28, 36, 41, 42, 45, 46, 68, 77, 92, 97, 98, 105, 106, 110, 120, 122, 131, 132, 143, 144n7
sukha 110

Sumedho, A. 73
sutta 30, 68, 114n4, 120, 129n2
Suzuki Roshi 134, 142

tatramajjhattatā 124
Tejaniya, U. 37, 51, 55, 67, 77, 100
Thailand 59, 64, 65n4, 84, 133
Theresa, M. 46
Theravāda 5n2, 11, 54
Tibet 50, 66, 90, 120, 122, 140
tilakkhana 76
tonglen 81–98
trauma 126
trauma sensitive xxi
Treleaven, D. xxi
truth 12, 58, 99, 111, 112, 144n7
Twain, M. 102
Tzu, L. 1, 99

uncontrollability 35, 73–74, 76–79, 93, 124, 133
unfabricated 57
unsatisfactoriness 35, 41, 76, 124, 133
upacāra 100, 101
upakilesa 110
upatthāna 110
upekkhā 110, 123

vatthu 104
vedanā 116

vedanānupassanā 49
vertical practice 42
vimamsa 75
vipallāsa 77
viparināma 42
vipassanā 15–17, 19, 23, 28, 33, 38, 54, 55, 64, 65, 75, 94, 101, 103, 110, 145, 149
vīriya 82, 104, 106
vīriyupekkhā 37, 85
visuddhi 113
visuddhimagga 54, 55, 104, 118, 120
viveka 8
vulnerability 10, 41, 76

weariness 41
Williams, M. 128n1
Winston, D. 135
wisdom 2, 3, 12, 22, 26n5, 29, 32, 36, 44, 46, 58, 66–80, 87, 94, 97, 101, 107–109, 111, 116, 119, 120, 122, 123, 133, 139–141, 143, 153
worry 8, 38, 41, 54, 76, 78, 91, 119

yang 48, 50, 51, 88
yin 48, 50, 51
yoniso 36, 47n6, 78, 132

Zen 57, 74, 119, 130, 133, 134, 142

'This is a wonderful book. It shows how from a safe and caring silent space and time, mindfulness and compassion are uncovered and radiate, which you can then take out into the world. *Going on a Meditation Retreat* is full of practical details which will prepare you for a silent retreat but also tell you how it is to be there. The book contains inspiring testimonies and the teachings are relevant and applicable to our modern times.'
> **Martine Batchelor** *teaches meditation retreats worldwide and is the author of* Meditation for Life *(2007) and* Let Go: A Buddhist Guide to Breaking Free of Habits *(2021). See www.martinebatchelor.org*

'In this beautifully written and practical book, Buddhist teacher Frits Koster skilfully leads his readers through the ups and downs of the inner journey that occurs in a silent meditation retreat. The narrative is encouraging, the gentle voice of an experienced leader who offers examples from participants about the kinds of challenges and breakthroughs that can occur when we turn inward to meet ourselves in an environment that promotes mindfulness and self-reflection. I am grateful to the authors for this excellent book and highly recommend it for anyone interested in going deeper with their spiritual path.'
> **Susan Gillis Chapman** *is a retired family therapist, Dharma-teacher, author of* The Five Keys to Mindful Communication *(2012) and* Which Way Is Up? *(2024) and founder of Green Zone Communication. See www.susangillischapman.com*

'For people who are going on a mindfulness retreat and are unsure what to expect, this is a wonderful overview. It guides readers in a detailed step by step, day by day programme, outlining the process and functions of the different practices. Written by highly experienced meditators and retreat guides it offers a wealth of insights into possible ways to relate to our minds. This book captures the essence of the experience of a retreat in ways that are unique and profound. This is a major addition to the literature on meditation and the experience of retreats.'
> **Prof. Paul Gilbert**, *OBE, author of, among others,* Compassion Focused Therapy *(2010), co-author (with Choden) of* Mindful Compassion *(2015) and co-editor (with Gregoris Simos) of* Compassion Focused Therapy: Clinical Practice and Applications *(2022)*

'This lovely warm book is a wise and gentle guide for any kind of meditation retreat. From their own ups and downs on retreat, the authors give many practical suggestions for how to get the most of it. They offer both contemplative and therapeutic perspectives on how to manage challenging experiences, and how to open into the wonderful depths of our own being. Highly recommended.'
> **Rick Hanson**, *PhD, Senior Fellow of UC Berkeley's Greater Good Science Center, author of* Buddha's Brain *(2009),* Hardwiring Happiness *(2014) and* Neurodharma *(2020). See www.rickhanson.com*

'In this book the reader will find the enormous richness of Frits and Jetty's multifaceted, non-dogmatic approach to leading a retreat. It is full of practical advice and inspiring examples. It is a must for the beginner as well as for the experienced practitioner, who wants to take steps on the path of mindfulness, compassion and wisdom.'
> **Joost van den Heuvel Rijnders** *is a* vipassanā *meditation teacher and author of several books in Dutch language. He is the co-founder of the Dutch online meditation platform 30NOW. See www.joost-meditatie.nl*

'This is a wonderful book, and one I would heartily recommend to anyone. It is not only excellent for first-timers, but equally supportive to those who have been on retreat already. With careful attention to what would be most helpful, a great deal of experience and an inviting and considerate tone, the authors draw on both their personal meditation experience and their decades of leading retreats to create an eminently practical and inspiring guide. I am very happy such a book exists, and I will recommend it not only to students in our various training programmes but also for my own students.'

Linda Lehrhaupt, *PhD, is the Director of the Institute for Mindfulness-Based Approaches, see www.institute-for-mindfulness.org. She is also a Roshi in the White Plum Lineage and a guiding teacher for Zen-Herz Sangha, an international community of Zen practitioners based in Germany*

'*Going on a Meditation Retreat* is an absolute must for anyone interested in the adventure of going on retreat. The authors take you along as spiritual friends who openly and honestly share about what the experience of being on retreat can be like: both for beginners and for those who have been on retreats many times before. This inspiring book is blessed with the richness of personal experiences, the deep knowledge of Buddhist psychology and the special relationship between Jetty and Frits. Reading this book feels like a retreat, and it makes me really eager to go on retreat again!'

Bart van Melik *is a meditation and Insight Dialogue teacher. He is a co-author of* Still, in the City *(edited by Angela Dews, 2018) and the guiding teacher at the Community Meditation Center in NYC. See www.bartvanmelik.com*

'This book is a true gem; the authors describe retreat experience with great clarity, humour and kindness. Their account is packed with practical wisdom from their years of experience in sitting and leading silent retreats and their depth of familiarity with contemplative teachings. The presence of participants' voices adds richness and brings the challenges, delights and benefits of retreat to life. This book offers invaluable support for all those who are new to retreat and may be wondering what to expect and provides fresh views and new insights for experienced practitioners. It is a generous gift and I highly recommend it.'

Bridgette O'Neill, *D. Clin. Psych., Senior Lecturer at the Centre for Mindfulness Research and Practice, Bangor University and Retreat Leader with the Mindfulness Network, author of* Developing your personal practice *(Chapter 20) in* Essential Resources for Mindfulness Teachers *(2021)*

'This book is a very welcome and helpful guide to everyone who is interested or experienced in going on a silent retreat. It provides very clear information about the structure and content of retreats, complemented by more personal experiences of both the authors and their participants. I warmly recommend it and hope it might enable more people to seek stillness in our busy lives. This might not only contribute to our own healing, but hopefully also to the healing of our world as a whole.'

Anne Speckens, *Professor of psychiatry and founder and Director of the Radboudumc Expertise Centre for Mindfulness in Nijmegen, the Netherlands. She trained as a meditation and retreat teacher at Bodhi College. See www.radboudumc.nl/expertisecentra/mindfulness*

For Product Safety Concerns and Information please contact our EU
representative GPSR@taylorandfrancis.com
Taylor & Francis Verlag GmbH, Kaufingerstraße 24, 80331 München, Germany